Reviving

Hinduism

Prakasarao Velagapudi, PhD

President and Co-Founder,

Global Hindu Heritage Foundation

Rare Books

RARE PUBLICATIONS
CHENNAI

Reviving

Hinduism

(Collection of Articles)

Prakasarao Velagapudi, PhD

President and Co-Founder,

Global Hindu Heritage Foundation

First Published : 2017
Pages : 358
ISBN : 978-93-83826-33-9

Cover Courtesy: **Shri. Som Gangadhar**

Published by

Rare Books

RARE PUBLICATIONS
Marketing Office:
No.23, Periyar Road,
T. Nagar, Chennai – 600 017.

E-Mail : info@rarebooksonweb.com
Website : www.rarebooksonweb.com
Printed in India at Mani Offest, Chennai

CONTENTS

INTRODUCTION

'It is already becoming clear that a chapter which had a Western beginning will have to have an Indian ending if it is not to end in self-destruction of the human race. At this supremely dangerous moment in human history, the only way of salvation is the ancient Hindu way. Here we have the attitude and spirit that can make it possible for the human race to grow together as a single family. So now we turn to India.

This spiritual gift, that makes a man human, is still alive in Indian souls. One can go on giving the world Indian examples of such souls. Nothing else can do so much to help man-kind to save itself from destruction..., that in the 21st century "India will conquer her conquerors." Arnold Toynbee (A British Historian, 1889-1975)

Over the years, Hindus have slowly forgotten the amazing treasures that are hidden in the land of Bharath. The resilience of Hindu mind; suppleness of its soul; suppleness of Hindu character; gracefulness of Hindu cultures; equanimity of Hindu moral compass; gracefulness of Hindu traditions; the inner strength of Hindu scriptures; sacredness of rivers, mountains, animals and trees; the genuineness of the simple living and high thinking; the astounding principles of ahimsa — belief in nonviolence, grandeur of the principle of Vasudaika Kutumbam; the potency of spiritual life and glory that **was and is Bharath**; and all-embracing live and let live principles are the gems that are essential for the survival of Hinduism and human race itself.

The richness of Bharath was clouded by ignorance, her glory seared with communalism, enveloped with the fog of secularism. The Hindu pride was tarnished with greed and smeared with Macaulyism. The future of Bharath looks bleak, depressing and miserable. Bharath Mata is attacked from all quarters. She is not even spared by vocal Hindu secularists, liberals and communists. Media has created havoc by denouncing the Hindus, Saints and Hindu organizations and leaders. Beneath every Hindu, there is the presence of divinity, dharma, spirituality and ahimsa. Somehow, he has forsaken the ancient richness and allowed it to be smeared with greed, name, fame, power, position, wealth and recognition that only satiate the present not the future. Divine intervention can only reverse the trend and malaise.

Hinduism is being attacked by selected Hindus as well as the two Abrahamic religions. **Patience, tolerance and ahimsa made Hinduism a defenseless religion in the world.** It has become a soft target with no retaliation or any plan to protect itself from enemies both within and without. Unlike other two major religions, Hinduism does not preach for expansion, does not believe in terrorism and does not practice deceptive techniques to convert people; nor do they believe in the expansion through conversion techniques. Their emphasis is on the development of the individual, self-improvement and enlightenment.

Muslims and Christians have ruled India for more than ten centuries. They have ruled India with iron fist by converting scores of Hindus, killing millions for refusing to be converted, destroying thousands of Hindu Temples, breaking the images of Hindu Gods, building mosques on the ruins of Hindu Temples, rampaging villages, and kidnapping the women. They have openly, inhumanely and blatantly applied all means to dominate, suffocate, suppress and convert the gullible, hapless Hindus into their religions. Their assaults and atrocities have broken the will of Hindus who kept silent to avoid further destruction and demise. In the process, they became disoriented, ignorant and lost self-pride.

It is time to revive the Hindu culture, traditions, ethos and values and enshrine them in the heart of every Hindu and every human being in order to avoid the impending catastrophe. We must impress upon the rich philosophical underpinnings that are the basis for human survival. Efforts must be made to wake up Hindu society from the doldrums of apathy, indifference, silence, negligence and selfishness. Close attention must also be made to the spiritual advice of all saintly people who have been the torch bearers of preserving and propagating Hindu dharma for millennia. RSS Chief Mohan Bhagavat stated that we have the responsibility of reviving Hindu culture. "In our country, there is a tradition of believing saints' teachings as truth.

Saints, with their 'Tapsya' (austere devotion) used to unite Hindu Samaj and create awakening." The RSS Chief also stated that, "for social awakening whatever the saint Samaj does any work, that always bring very positive results." (The Times of India, February 24, 2015).

Chief Justice Gajendragadkar explained in 1966 that, "Unlike other religions in the world, the Hindu religion does not claim any one prophet. It does not worship any one God. It does not subscribe to any one dogma. It does not believe in any one philosophical concept. It does not follow any one set of religious rites or performances. In fact, it does not satisfy the traditional feature of a religion or creed. It is a way of life and nothing more." If Hinduism is not a religion, Hindutva is much less than that. It cannot be construed as anti to any religion. It does not fit into the definition of religion.

The first chapter is about "Hindu Identity – Panacea for Social Ills and Human Extinction" deals with the richness of Hinduism and its universal appeal to bring peace, harmony and togetherness. In order to enjoy the spirit of Hinduism, we have to make an effort to identify with our faith. To identify with timeless wisdom of Sanatana Dharma, we need to learn about the three pillars, breadth of scientific knowledge, depth of the literature, uniqueness of Sanskrit, vibrations of chanting mantras, energy embedded in Hindu Temples, power of worship services, benefits of yoga and meditation and other subject matters.

The second Chapter calls for declaring India a Hindu Rashtra to protect the universal principles that give unlimited freedom, allow explorative mind, tolerate differences and accommodate diversity of beliefs without any agenda to destroy other cultures. Declaration of Hindu Rashtra cannot be against any other faith. Hindus have never conquered any other country to establish the hegemony of their faith. As Indian Supreme Court observed, Hindutva is a way of life, it is not a religion the way other religions are defined. Dharma is the central theme of Hinduism that calls for promotion and preservation of unity and harmony among material and non-material world without creating conflict and chaos.

IX

The third chapter deals with a number of suggestions to revise the School curriculum: to present the factual history of India, study the national heroes who have sacrificed their lives for us the enjoy the freedom, teach the universal values found in Ramayana and Mahabharata, explain the stupendous knowledge fond in Bhagavad Gita, pass on the Panchatantra stories to exercise proper judgement and enlightenment, know the experiences and the power of great saints of Bharath, the sacredness of Gomata (mother cow), practice of yoga and meditation for purification of mind and soul, and know the atrocities committed on Hindus by other faiths.

The fourth chapter demands the government to make Bhagavad Gita mandatory for all students in India. The school curriculum until 2014 was revised to denigrate Hindu way of life, demean it as Hindu fundamentalism, negate the entire history of Hindu India, bolster the image and contribution of Muslim leaders and insult the scriptures. Since Independence, the ruling party deliberately tarnished the image of Hinduism calling it as representing "saffron terrorism." Bhagavad Gita deserves to be part of the curriculum once we realize the greatness of its message as seen in the statement of Henry David Thoreau who said, "One sentence of the Gita, is worth the State of Massachusetts many times over." This chapter highlights the contribution of Bhagavad Gita for humanity.

The fifth chapter deals with the merits of memorizing Bhagavad Gita by children and its universal message. More than 50 children, ages 5 thru 13, memorized and chanted in front of Sri Ganapathy Sachchidananda Swamiji at Karya Siddhi Hanuman Temple in 2016 abiding by the command of their Sadguru. This chapter discusses the grasping and memory power of children as compared to adults, how their brain functions compared to the adults, the benefits of memorizing, scientific nature and structure of Sanskrit language, the power of OM, merits of chanting Sanskrit mantras, and the innumerable lessons in leading one's life as offered by Bhagavad Gita to the students.

The sixth chapter describes the need for reviving the Gurukula concept where the transmission of knowledge is passed on to the Sishyas by Guru. There is a long tradition of Guru-sishya relationship explained in greater detail in all the scriptures. Topics discussed in the chapter include the definition of a guru, the characteristics of a guru, the difference between Guru and Sadguru, importance and the need for guru in one's life, the belief that Guru is even greater than God, significance of worshipping Padukas, and the benefits of associating with spiritual personalities.

The seventh and eighth chapters highlight the importance of mother who is described as the most selfless person and as the embodiment of sacrifice and protection. Scriptures are replete with the respect showered on the role of mother. Ramayana, Mahabharata, Manu Smriti, Vedas and other scriptures have gone to the extent of declaring that deities reside in places where women are respected. Bhishma even admired mother in an exceptional way: "There is no shelter like the mother. There is no refuge like the mother." Many Sadgurus praised the sacrifices of mothers in raising and protecting their children. Swami Vivekananda aptly describes the nature of mothers as thus: "Women as mother is marvelous, unselfish, all suffering and ever forgiving."

Chapter nine on dharma and dereliction of dharma starts with the definition of dharma as duty, righteousness, obligations, and justice that promotes harmony and common good in the society. It is the dharma of all Hindus to preserve and protect the universal values which are the bedrock of Hindu way of life. Many Hindu leaders and organizations are failing in their responsibility to defend the atrocities committed against Hindu Temples, insults hurled against Hindu Gods and Goddesses, and abuses tossed against Hinduism. Hindus should remember the Islamic onslaught that killed millions of Hindus and Goa inquisition by Christians who made the Hindu blood flow from the "Big House" by using such techniques as torture by rope, fire, and water. If Hindus do not take appropriate steps to protect their religion, the history will repeat itself to witness biggest Hindu holocaust.

Chapter ten and eleven discuss the sacredness of Cow as revealed in the scriptures that have extolled its virtues. Cows were treated as mother and hailed as auspicious. It is said that in every part of cow's body a particular god or goddess resides. For example, Brahma resides in her head, sun and moon in her eyes, Saraswati on her tongue, Lakshmi in her cow dung, Parvati in her urine etc. Rig Veda, Yajur Veda, Sama Veda and Atharvana Veda have commended the cow and suggested that she should not be killed. Although Article 48 of Indian Constitution requires the state to implement prohibition of the slaughter of cows and calves, the central government failed to take appropriate action to close the illegal slaughter houses. Cow slaughter mafia is very active with years of central governments tacit support and making India as the highest exporter of beef. In fact, government even subsidizes the export of beef to the foreign countries. Several recommendations were made to protect cows from being killed and close slaughter houses.

Chapter twelve on Ramayana enunciates the immortal values that are passed on across the globe for millennia. Hinduism has developed the eternal universal principles that cut across all the ages which are reflected in Ramayana. Each character in Ramayana is unique, and has exemplified the highest morals for all of humanity with no physical boundaries and no time limitations. Lord Rama, as an ideal son, obeyed the commands of his father without ever questioning his judgment; as ideal enemy, asked his brother to learn the life's lessons from Ravana and also asked Vibhishana to do the funeral services; and as an ideal brother, taught Lakshman that righteousness is the best of all qualities. Similarly, Hanuman's devotion and selfless service are the virtues for all of us to practice. Sita as an ideal wife followed her husband to the forest willingly to experience the hardships.

Chapter thirteen deals with the transcendentalists' admiration for Bhagavad Gita. Ralph Waldo Emerson, David Henry Thoreau and Walt Whitman were the three stalwarts who paved the way to trek and experience the Hindu spirituality and sowed the seeds to make the American soil fertile to reap the fruits of yoga crop. Emerson, who was the first American to read Bhagavad Gita, said that, "it was as if an empire spoke to us, nothing small or unworthy, but large, serene, consistent, the voice of an old intelligence which in another age and climate ...." Thoreau said every single word was elevating and "One sentence of the Gita, is worth the State of Massachusetts many times over." Walt Whitman was the one who practiced yoga, experienced the peace of mind and even insisted that during his meditation the senses are lost to experience the trance – to mean Kundalini.

Chapters fourteen and fifteen expose the hypocritical statements made over the years supporting the minorities and demeaning the majority population. Killing of one Muslim and a rationalist writer prompted these intolerant intellectuals to criticize the Modi government while they remain silent when Hindus were killed by minority religions. In 2015 five Hindus were killed by Muslim mob, Hindu leader, Karthick Methia was killed, and many Hindu houses were burned. None of these so-called liberals failed to even recognize the brutality of the minorities. Similarly, when President Obama made statement following his visit to India that "India will succeed so long as it is not splintered along lines of religious faith, splintered along any lines and it is unified as one nation." His statement equates the tolerant Hinduism to the centuries of Islamic and Christian atrocities. History has documented countless deaths, destruction of Hindu Temples, deceptive conversions, and rampage of villages with no reaction from these liberals and secularists. Buddhists, Jews, Parsis, Jains and other non-proselytization religions lived with no discrimination since they do not force their religion upon the Hindus. It is the Christians and Muslims who splintered along the religious lines to condemn the Hindus to hell.

Chapter sixteen describes the nature of spirituality, the benefits of spiritual living and its contribution to human survival. Religion has killed millions of people across the globe to establish their domination over the countries of other faiths. Religion divides and spirituality unites. Religion brings untold misery while spirituality fetches happiness and peace of mind. Spirituality brings out the godlike qualities such as love, compassion, forgiveness, gratitude, kindness, Ananda (bliss), and truth in the humanity. Several Hindu scriptures conveyed the essential nature of spirituality and how it will serve as a key to human survival. Evidence was documented to show how yoga and meditation are revolutionizing the concept of connecting the individual soul to Super Soul to experience the freedom from fear, misery, stress, hostility and enmity.

Chapter seventeen details the deceptive practices Christians have adopted for centuries to convert people in different countries into Christian nations. In India they are more aggressive, belligerent and violent in destroying the ancient civilization by converting gullible Hindus into their fold. Even John Pope Paul II asked his followers to plant the cross firmly in the vast Indian soil. Several verses from the Bible are listed about the deceptive practices to follow, breakdown of the sacred stones to pieces, and condemn followers of other faiths to hell. Hindus should realize that all religions are not the same. Hinduism cherishes the ideal of peaceful coexistence while other religions are bent on destroying other faiths. No Hindu can afford to forget the atrocities committed on Hindus in Goa. Hindus should not allow the history, that witnessed the bloodbath of their forefathers to repeat itself.

The last chapter deals with the efforts of Muslim leaders to annihilate Hindus, suffocate the country, throttle the freedom of speech, and replace the democracy with Islamic totalitarianism. Until Independence, majority of Muslim leaders had argued that they need to have a separate home land and vehemently advocated the division of India into two countries: Pakistan for Muslims and India for Hindus. That did not materialized at the time. Now the Muslim population is increasing day by day and they want to fulfill their dream of fulfilling the "unfinished business" of converting India into a Muslim country. Unfortunately, Islam is incompatible with democracy, freedom, women rights, and secularism. The article argues that it is time to implement the two-nation theory by sending Muslims to Pakistan, however difficult that may be. Knowing the difficulty of implementing **two nation theory**, Hindus should consider advocating introduction of **benign dictatorship** for a period of time to stop the Hindu holocaust.

ACKNOWLEDGMENTS

These articles have been written over the last eight years. I want to acknowledge the able and admirable contribution of my wife, **Nandini**, in revising and editing these articles. Her continued support in our efforts to challenge the Endowment Act for the last ten years is acknowledged. My sincere appreciation to **Sandeep Mamidenna, Pavan Neti and Laxmi,** who helped in editing these articles. Assistance of **Pratap Velagapudi** regarding computers and data management is recognized.

Dr. Subramanian Swamy is a great source of inspiration to carry out the mission of GHHF to challenge the Endowment Act. His constant and continued guidance is a source of inspiration for all of us. I am grateful to Dr. Swamy for writing the Foreword for the book.

Sri Paripoornananda Swamiji is one of the Hindu activist who has been portraying the Hinduism as per the scriptures and defending dharmic and universal believes by challenging the critics who have been misinterpreting the true nature of Hinduism and demeaning our worship practices. We appreciate his willingness to write FOREWORD to the book.

Dr. Ghazal Srinivas, the Brand Ambassador of GHHF, is conducting various programs in India through his various contacts. He is also managing the SaveTemples office in Hyderabad and monitoring the government activities. We are very appreciative of his passionate assistance.

I want to express my deep appreciation for **Shri. Som Gangadhar** who has designed the cover page. It is stunning, fantastic and loaded with ideas of revival of Hinduism in his drawing. I have known him for several years and have seen thousands of his pictures. More I see his pictures, more appreciation burst forth from my mind.

I have come to know **Sri S. Ranganaathan**, of RARE Publications recently. I have found him to be professional, polite, pleasant and patient in all my dealings, I want to acknowledge and thank him for his timely effort in publishing the book.

I want to express my gratitude to all the individuals who served as **The Board of Directors of GHHF** for their support, encouragement and contribution. Their indispensable assurance and passion to free Hindu Temples from the government control is contagious.

Similarly, the Executive Committee members and many others in Dallas area have been active participants in organizing numerous activities over the last eight years. Too many members and volunteers to name them individually. Their continued participation, encouragement and commitment to the cause is greatly appreciated. The credit goes to all these members and other volunteers for organizing several successful programs.

Jai Hind.

FOREWORD -DR.SUBRAMANIAN SWAMY

I have known Prakash Rao for years. He is a devout Hindu who is actively involved in building a magnificent Hanuman Temple near Dallas, Texas in USA. He has sponsored conference in India and other countries for the liberation of temples from government's clutches in India. Hinduism may a long history but this century it will emerge as the salvation of the world

Remember the assessment of the impending human predicament and the possible solution by the eminent historian Arnold J Toynbee:

> **"It is already becoming clear that a chapter, which had a Western beginning, will have to have an Indian ending if it is not to end in self-destruction of the human race. At this supremely dangerous moment in human history, the only way of salvation is the ancient Hindu way .... So now we turn to India. This spiritual gift, that makes a man human, is still alive in Indian souls. Go on giving the world Indian examples of it. Nothing else can do so much to help mankind to save itself from destruction."**

In a judgment, the Indian Supreme Court ruled that…

> **"No precise meaning can be ascribed to the terms 'Hindu', 'Hindutva' and 'Hinduism'; and no meaning in the abstract can confine it to the narrow limits of religion alone, excluding the content of Indian culture and heritage."**

The Supreme Court also ruled that…

> **"Ordinarily, Hindutva is understood as a way of life or a state of mind and is not to be equated with or understood as religious Hindu fundamentalism. A Hindu may embrace a non-Hindu religion without ceasing to be a Hindu and since the Hindu is disposed to think synthetically and to regard other forms of worship, strange gods and divergent doctrines as inadequate rather than wrong or objectionable, he tends to**

believe that the highest divine powers complement each other for the well-being of the world and mankind."

As author of *"Hindus under Siege"* [Haranand Publishers, New Delhi], I argued in 2007 that every country must have an identity of it's own. Accordingly *"Hindutva hence, is our innate nature, while Hindustan is our territorial body, but Hindu Rashtra is our republican soul. Hindu panth [religion] is however a theology of faith. Even if an Indian has a different faith from a Hindu, he or she can still be possessed of Hindutva. Since India was 100 percent Hindu a millennium ago, the only way any significant group could have a different faith in today's India is if they were converted from Hindu faith, or are of those whose ancestors were Hindus".*

Prakash Rao thus advocates: "Be a Proud Hindu, be a practicing Hindu, be a disciplined Hindu, be a protector of Hindus edifice, and be a promoter of Hindu way of Life. Jai Hind".

We Hindus should be happy that he is publishing 18 of his articles written over the years for expounding his thesis. I strongly recommend we read these and debate amongst ourselves.

New Delhi, India

May 24, 2017   **Subramanian Swamy**

FOREWORD - SWAMI PARIPOORNANANDA

Most of the NRIs that I came across in the USA are patriotic. They love motherland. They think of Bhaarat, they spread good words about Bhaarat, and they strive to pass on our culture through generations even on western soil.

Yet, only some NRIs feel concern for protection of Hindu Dharma, and a few among them have deep commitment for the same. Velagapudi Prakasa Rao, president and co-founder of Global Hindu Heritage Foundation, is one of those NRIs who is committed to the cause of Hindu Dharma.

This book, 'Reviving Hinduism', speaks the efforts he put in understanding the power of Hindu dharma as a panacea to many conflicts and cultural wars that the world is engulfed in today.

While saying that Bhagavad Gita could address all kinds of problems arising out of human emotions or lack spiritual wisdom, he mentioned that Seton Hall University in New Jersey made 'study of Bhagavad Gita' mandatory in its curriculum

While referring to the power of Yoga, he quoted the experience of America's first vibrant yoga practitioner, Henry David Thoreau (1817-1862) as "rapt in reverie .... in undisturbed solitude and stillness".

He didn't ignore the perils of proselytization, with reference to Christianity, and cautioned that Apostle Paul openly admitted deception was necessary to convert people from other religion to Christianity.

Allowing idol worship in churches, contrary to Bible philosophy, is one of such methods, he said quoting Father Joseph Menengis. He dwelt on Bhagavad Gita, Guru-Shishya parampara, treasure of Hindu epics like Ramayana, onslaught of Islam and Christianity on Hinduism need to protect our indigenous cows and the time immemorial temple culture, and so on.

Velagapudi Prakasa Rao's literary work, 'Reviving Hinduism', reflects his urge for protection of Hindu dharma.
Aum Namo Naarayanaaya …

Swami Paripoornananda

FOREWORD - DR GHAZAL SRINIVAS

The holy sage of Sanathana Dharma I know is Prof. Velagapudi Prakash Rao. Our meeting and bonding occurred with the common goal of service to Sanatana Dharma. I was lost in my world of Ghazal songs but it was Prof. Velagapudi Prakash Rao who brought my attention towards Schools of Veda which were becoming extinct, temples which were in ruins, cows which were being sent to slaughter houses. Even at the age of 78, he is a noble soul desperate to do something for Sanatana Dharma. He cannot tolerate injustice to Dharma. In my five years of journey with him, his only anguish has been protection of Sanatana Dharma. Whenever something wrong happens to Dharma, he is the first to react, respond. He has churned out several essays digging out historical facts and enlightened many on the issues. The Anthology of his essays is like a Tsunami. It doesn't matter how big anyone is, if they mock Dharma, he would either call them directly or email them appropriately. These are examples of his courage and pious dedication. It is mandatory you and everyone read every essay in this book. His desire is to see not devotees but soldiers for Sanatana Dharma.

His daily life revolves around protection of temples, cows, Sanathana Dharma. I take this as my fortune and blessing to be the brand ambassador for Save Temples Organization and Global Hindu Heritage Foundation established by Prof. Prakash Rao and other Dharmic minded people. Working with him and reading his essays is a gift for me. Those who read these articles will have abundant awareness, anguish, and initiation towards Sanatana Dharma. After reading this book, one is bound to march toward the protection of Hindu Dharma. This is the key essence of this anthology. This great work can drive lakhs of people towards his goal of preserving and protecting Hindu Dharma. I am deeply grateful to Prof. Velagapudi

Prakash Rao and board members of the Global Hindu Heritage Foundation for giving me the opportunity to write the foreword.

Save Temples To Save Yourself!

Dr Ghazal Srinivas,

Brand Ambassador

Global Hindu Heritage Foundation & SaveTemples.Org

HINDU IDENTITY
PANACEA FOR SOCIAL ILLS & HUMAN EXTINCTION

(Condensed version of this message was presented at Bala Datta Annual Function held on May 8, 2011 at Karya Siddhi Hanuman Temple, Frisco, TX)

> *"There is only one India! It is the only country that has a monopoly of grand and imposing specialties. When another country has a remarkable thing, it cannot have it all to itself --- some other country has a duplicate. But India – That is different. ITS MARVELS ARE ITS OWN; THE PATENTS CANNOT BE INFRINGED; IMMITATIONS ARE NOT POSSIBLE. And think of the size of them, the majesty of them, and the weird and outlandish character of most of them! …. the one land that all men desire to see, and having seen once, by even a glimpse for all the shows of all the rest of the globe combined, even now, after a lapse of a year, the delirium of those days in Bombay has not left me and I hope it never will."* **Mark Twain**

It is indeed a pleasure to see so many parents and children attend the annual Bala Datta Function to celebrate the glory and grandeur of our ancient yet modern religion, traditional yet scientific, and customary yet meaningful.

At the outset let me say that Hinduism is not a 'religion,' It is a way of life. The word Hinduism has only few hundred years of history. We should identify Hinduism in terms of 'Dharma,' 'Vedanta Philosophy,' Vedic culture, or 'Sanatana Dharma, and the Perennial Philosophy (as termed by Aldous Huxley) that has thousands of history. According to Whitman, "Hindu traditions promote living with integrity, causing no harm, and progressing further on a spiritual path by living according to dharma, stage of life appropriate guidelines" (Whitman, 2007, p: 608).

DO WE NEED TO IDENTIFY WITH OUR FAITH? (HINDUISM OR SANATANA DHARMA)

We all identify with something. We have our own identification. By mentioning your name, we come to know about your identity with respect to your name, your status, your family heritage, your family, your history, your job, and your affiliations with your friends etc.

Similarly, our identification with our religion is equally important. You have been born into it, you have been raised in that atmosphere, you have been shaped by it, you have been molded by it, and you have developed a set of values, ethics, and moral compass. Many people who grew up in this country identify themselves as Irish Americans, Jewish Americans, Polish Americans, Arab Americans, Greek Americans, Mexican Americans, African Americans, etc.

There is nothing wrong in identifying yourself as Hindu Americans. We should be proud of being a Hindu whether you live in USA, India or some other country. Why do we say that we have to be proud of being a Hindu? Because we never conquered a country, we never caused untold misery to anybody, we never massacred any nation in the name of religion, we never looted the treasury of other country, we never plundered the religious institutions of the other faiths, we never wanted to plant the cross on another's soil with deception and destruction, we never build our temples on the ruins of other religious institutions following the demolition of other institutions, and we never depleted the natural resources of other nations. In fact, we openly welcomed them with open arms never realizing that they will stab you in open daylight. We always respected others to practice their religion without realizing that their only and sole mission is to convert us into their religion, dominate us with deception and terror, conspire to destroy and root out our Hindu way of life from the face of this earth.

But Hinduism represents different kinds of values, beliefs, attitudes, mores, rituals, traditions, and practices which are different from other religions. These are the values that promote harmony, universal brotherhood, peaceful coexistence and the philosophy of 'live let live.' We believe that ahimsa, inclusiveness, and sanctity of life, are

24

an integral part of our religion. We are pluralistic, non-interfering, contemplative and spark of the divine.

In order to feel proud of being a Hindu, first we should know our hoary history of our way of life, the past glory of Vedic and Puranic culture and also the gloominess of the past 10 centuries of foreign rule that defaced our pride, robbed our confidence and stripped our knowledge from our scriptures and succeeded in doubting our own dharmic values. Now it is time to reckon with the history. If we fail to learn the lessons of the past atrocities inflicted on our forefathers, and us we will make the same mistake our ancestors made. Read about Goa Inquisition, Hindu Kush Mountains, Destruction of 2000 Hindu Temples, killing of millions of people etc., to find out what happened to us. Never again we should make similar mistakes.

Many of us are not knowledgeable about our religion–scriptures, our worship services, our mantras etc. That should not be an excuse for all of us to criticize, bash and trash our religion. We as parents should never say that I do not know to our children. Our ignorance or lack knowledge should not push our children to look for alternatives outside. There is not a single thing under the sun that has not been explained, explored, discussed, dissected, analyzed and scrutinized by our rishis in our scriptures. Let our ignorance be target for exploitation by other religions. Let us not sacrifice our children for exploitation by others. Let us take a firm stand to learn and impart our faith to our children.

Let us also advocate that freedom of religion and expression is not freedom to convert people to other faiths based on incentives, allurements, bribes, exploitation, ignorance and manipulation.

Hinduism is known for accommodation of different views – in fact in our own family we see one member worshipping Lord Hanuman, another Shiva, another Devi, and yet another Ayyappa Swami.

HOW DO WE DEVELOP HINDU IDENTITY?

We must be cognizant of the pressure other religions exert on our children and ourselves. We can only withstand that pressure with adequate knowledge about our religion. Let us all commit ourselves to learn some fundamentals of our faith and be refused to be exploited by other religions. Our strength is our knowledge in our scriptures. Let us remember the words of Bhartrihari written in Neeti Shatakam: *"Knowledge is a special beauty of man. It is a hidden treasure. It gives one happiness, enjoyment and fame. It is the teacher of great teachers. It is one's relative when he is in a strange place. It is the God divine. It is knowledge that is to be worshipped not money. One who is bereft of knowledge is a beast."*

1 Learn about three pillars of Hindu religion that set us apart from the other religions – karma philosophy, reincarnation and concept of gurutattva. These pillars were established more than several thousand years ago. They are as relevant today as they were millenniums ago.

2 Learn about our scriptures – Vedas, Upanishad, Puranas, Dharma Sastras, Itihasas (Ramayana and Mahabharata), Tantras etc. Start with reading the Puranas and slowly move to Upanishads and Vedas. The more you read, the more you want to read. Appreciation of the richness of our culture and depth of knowledge will overwhelm you.

3 Learn about the scientific nature of our religion. Everything that is written and everything that is practiced has scientific explanation. There is never conflict between our religion and science. In fact, we welcome scientific research about our beliefs and practices.

4 Let us learn about the width and depth of the subject matters that were described in our scriptures – mathematics, astronomy, physics, chemistry, geology, medicine, dentistry, music, metallurgy, philosophy, human anatomy, etc.

5 Mantras are the cornerstones of our worship both at home and in the temples. Mere chanting or listening will pierce through your body and heart. They give peace of mind and happiness. Hundreds of universities in USA and other countries have done research on the efficacy of these mantras. Sanskrit is *deva bhasha* and let us learn to communicate in that language to yield better and faster results.

6 Many of us keep saying that we do not know what they are chanting. Of course, if we know the meaning we will appreciate

more and our experiences will be different. Please know that even without knowing the meaning these Mantras, chanting and listening of Mantras will affect every part and particle of our body, and our chakras. Their effect on the mind and body are well documented. Research is well documented on this topic.

7 Let us all learn to visit the Temples as often as possible. This is a Gods abode. You feel the vibrations and you feel the energy. The atmosphere is different. Let us maintain silence when we enter the Temple, meditate few minutes closing our eyes, and experience the connectivity between you and the divine. Only in silence, you receive something in.

8 Let us all learn about the significance of the temple and shodashopachara puja. All sixteen steps are meaningful and significant to approach the Divine. Let us use all our god given angas (parts of our body) to serve God in the Temple. They are all His? What better way to use them?

9 Let us take pride in our religion. Pride comes with knowledge. The more we know about our faith, the more we relish, the more we cherish, the more we admire, the more we appreciate and the more willing to share the glory.

10 Let us not let other faiths define who we are and what our religion is all about. Let us not allow anyone to falsify our religion, hijack our faith, distort our worship practices, and misrepresent out scriptures.

11 Let us engage in practicing yoga and meditation – they are the stress busters, peace promoters, mind stabilizers, health boosters, body builders and energy stimulators. Let us build Peace Palaces, not Terror cells, quota quarters and exploitative citadels.

12 Let us make sure that we all stand for *mutual respect* from all other faiths. Let us not keep saying that Hinduism is **tolerant**. When we say that we are tolerant, we are telling other religions that we will tolerate all your atrocities, all your exploitations, all your deceptions, all your distortions of our scriptures, all your brutal attacks on our places of worship, all your mass killing of our brothers, sisters and forefathers. Let us STOP saying that we are TOLERANT.

13 Let us be assertive, confident and forward looking Hindus to make an imprint on the shores of each and every country we live in. We need to be the ambassadors of our faith. Never miss an opportunity to talk about our depth, richness, glory, grandeur, genius, beauty, and brilliance of our rishis, who have written all these scripture with unmatched intelligence and foresight. Let us go to different schools, different associations and different people with curiosity to talk about it.

14 Let us also be reminded that all religions are NOT the same. Even a cursory reading of the scriptures of other religions would tell you that they want to dominate the world and destroy anything that would not fit their goal. We, Hindus, are all inclusive, while others are exclusive. They say if you do not believe in what I believe in, you are doomed. The do not subscribe to our philosophy of "Live, Let Live."

15 Finally, let us all resolve ourselves that we will learn about our religion, we will take pride in our scriptures, we will impart our knowledge to our children, we will practice it, we will preserve it and finally PROTECT our way of living that is freedom. Make sure that the extremists and jealous gods do not blow our house away.

If we want to save the world from self-destruction and human annihilation, Hindus have a monumental task ahead of them. Once you know what Hinduism stands for, you can be a harbinger of peace on earth.

Remember the assessment of the impending human predicament and the possible solution by Arnold J Toynbee:

It is already becoming clear that a chapter, which had a Western beginning, will have to have an Indian ending if it is not to end in self-destruction of the human race. At this supremely dangerous moment in human history, the only way of salvation is the ancient Hindu way .... So now we turn to India. This spiritual gift, that makes a man human, is still alive in Indian souls. Go on giving the world Indian examples of it. Nothing else can do so much to help mankind to save itself from destruction.

Be a Proud Hindu, be a practicing Hindu, be a disciplined Hindu, be a protector of Hindus edifice, and be a promoter of Hindu way of Life. Jai Hind

DECLARE INDIA AS HINDU RASHTRA - HINDUS MUST GET UNITED TO PROTECT THEIR FREEDOM

(This is an expanded version of the ideas presented in Tenali meeting on February 7, 2014)

Hinduism is not just a faith. It is the union of reason and intuition that can't be defined but is only to be experienced. Dr. S. Radhakrishnan.

We briefly traced the history of GHHF as to when and how GHHF was started, the kind of activities undertaken over the last eight years, and some of the milestones of the movement. We informed the gathering that the Andhra Pradesh government passed Hindu Charitable and Endowment Act whereby all the Hindu Temples making 50,000 rupees or more are brought under the government control with full control on the management of the funds donated by the devotees, supervision of the endowed lands of the Hindu Temples, conduct of all religious activities, overseeing the protection of jewelry, administering Hindu Temples and recruiting the employees to manage the operations of the Temples. The government has abused and looted the funds, diverted the funds to other religions, allowed Temple lands to be encroached with no recourses, neglected to oversee the preservation of jewelry and the integrity of Temples structures, allowed the Hindu Temples to be dilapidated, closed their eyes as the Rajagopurams and other structures are collapsed, and permitted Labor Unions to be formed allowing them to fully exploit the Temple resources and blackmail the administration.

GHHF has taken several steps to make Hindus aware of the plight of Hindu Temples and the potential danger to Hinduism due to the hateful attitude of the government toward Hindus in order to appease the minorities. The government takes advantage of tolerance, non-violence, broadmindedness and ignorance of Hindus to pass any laws that undermine the underlying unity of Hindus. Blinded by their party affiliation, Hindu politicians never even consider the future of their country. Their only obsession is to please the party bosses in order to satisfy their thirst for power and pockets. Many Hindu politicians would never even question as to why only Hindu Temples are taken over by the government but not the churches and mosques. Why only Hindu Temple lands are used to start government programs such as Indiramma project to distribute the lands to the poor?

Three main points were discussed as to their implications for the survival of Hinduism and the fate of India.

HINDU RASHTRA.

India should declare itself to be a **Hindu Rashtra** giving special recognition and also accepting the preeminence of Hindu culture based on rich scriptures such as Vedas, Upanishad, Puranas, Darshans, Ramayana, Mahabharata and others. Principles such as "universal brotherhood," "all humanity is one family," "may all be happy and healthy," "may there be peace among living and nonliving entities," inclusive philosophy, and "live let live ideology" should form the rock-solid foundation for Bharath. Any religion that advocates exclusive philosophy, condemns others to hell for not accepting their religion, seeks special privileges based on religion and destroys the places of worship of other religions should be subjected to sever punishment.

All Hindus irrespective of their party affiliation and philosophical outlook should realize that there are 58 countries for Muslims to call them as their homelands; hundreds of countries in Europe, North America, South America, Australia, and other countries for Christians to call them as their countries; and Jewish people have Israel as their own country. It is only Hindus, with 1.2 billion populations across the globe, have no country to call it as their own country with their cultural background. The sooner we declare India as Hindu Rashtra, the better it would be for Hindus and every other religious group. Liberals, media, communists, Muslims, Christians and many other nations would make loud noises, criticize vehemently, denounce us as fundamentalists, condemn us as anti-Muslim and anti-Christian, and deprecate us as being undemocratic. The same people would not criticize, condemn, deprecate or criticize Muslims who depleted Hindus in Pakistan and brutalized Hindus in Bangladesh. The same people would not say even one word against Saudi Arabia for not allowing even a picture of Hindu God. They would not even open their mouth when Mullahs issue Fatwa to kill people who criticize Islam.

Our failure to declare India, as Hindu Rashtra, would land us into the jaws of Islamic exclusive philosophy. It would become an Islamic Country in the next two-three decades as the Muslims increase their population with multiple wives and rampaging the country with terror, torture and killings. They will slowly deplete Hindu population from India the way the Muslims have done in Pakistan and are doing in Bangladesh. Muslims have been advocating the breakup of India into three Islamic Countries – Mughalisthan, Dalitisthan and Dravidisthan.

One of the great poets, Bhushan, underscores the significance of the success of Shivaji over Mughals by saying, *"You kept alive Hindutva and pride of Hindus. Smiritis, Puranas, Vedas and Dharma on earth remained alive oh! Great son of Shahi, Shivraj, in virtue of your might and intellect."*

In a judgment, the Indian Supreme Court ruled that…

"No precise meaning can be ascribed to the terms 'Hindu', 'Hindutva' and 'Hinduism'; and no meaning in the abstract can confine it to the narrow limits of religion alone, excluding the content of Indian culture and heritage."

The Supreme Court also ruled that…

"Ordinarily, Hindutva is understood as a way of life or a state of mind and is not to be equated with or understood as religious Hindu fundamentalism. A Hindu may embrace a non-Hindu religion without ceasing to be a Hindu and since the Hindu is disposed to think synthetically and to regard other forms of worship, strange gods and divergent doctrines as inadequate rather than wrong or objectionable, he tends to believe that the highest divine powers complement each other for the well-being of the world and mankind."

Hindutva is commonly identified with the guiding ideology of the Sangh Parivar, a family of Hindu Nationalist organizations, and of the Rashtriya Swayamsevak Sangh in particular. In general, Hindutva represent the well-being of Hinduism, Sikhism, Buddhism, Jainism and all other religions prominent in India along with Zoroastrianism and Judaism.

Jonah Blank, an American journalist, who traced the Lord Rama's footsteps from Ayodhya to Sri Lanka, writes: *"India's land may be ruled by aliens from time to time, but never her mind, never her soul...In the end, it is always India that does the digesting."*

Veer Savarakar said, "If you wish, O Hindus, to prosper as a great and glorious Hindu nation under the sun, and you well have a claim on it, that State must be established under the Hindu Flag. This dream would be realized during this or the coming generation. If it is not realized, I may be styled as a daydreamer, but if it comes true, I would stand forth as its prophet. I am bequeathing this legacy to you".

Seshadri Chary, the editor of The Organiser, stated "the concept of Hindu Rashtra is absolutely different from what is known as a theocratic state, like, say, Pakistan or a Vatican. Hindutva is not a religious dogma. One should understand the distinction between rashtra (nation) and rajya (state). Hindu Rashtra is a geo-cultural concept."

Vishweshar Bhat, editor of *Kannada Prabha*, said "Being pro-Hindu does not mean you are anti-Muslim. It is a misconception that people have. Hindutva preaches love for the nation and not just love for Hindus."

Dr. Subramanian Swamy, the author of *"Hindus under Siege"*, argues that every country must have an identity of it's own. According to Dr. Swamy *"Hindutva hence, is our innate nature, while Hindustan is our territorial body, but Hindu Rashtra is our republican soul. Hindu panth [religion] is however a theology of faith. Even if an Indian has a different faith from a Hindu, he or she can still be possessed of Hindutva. Since India was 100 percent Hindu a millennium ago, the only way any* *significant group could have a different faith in today's India is if they were converted from Hindu faith, or are of those whose ancestors were Hindus. "*

Babu Suseelan strongly advocates the reasons for declaring India as Hindu Rashtra as follows: *"Hindus call our way of life as Santhan Dharma. Hindu Dharma promotes freedom, democracy, pluralism, and respect nature and wholeness of all living and non- living entities. Our great Rishis have developed different thought systems and means to achieve equanimity, patience, health, forgiveness, control of mind, purity of thought and action, peace, progress, development of the intellect, knowledge and transcendental living."*

Even the Member of Parliament (Congress Party}, **Shashi Tharoor**, is able to differentiate between Hinduism and Hindutva. "Hindutva has nothing to do with Hinduism as a faith or a religion, but rather **as a badge of cultural identity and an instrument of political mobilisation,**". He further stated that "Hinduism is a religion without fundamentals – no founder or prophet, no organised Church, no compulsory beliefs or rites of worship, no single sacred book…What we see today as Hindutva is part of an attempt to 'semitise' the faith – to make Hinduism more like the 'better-organized' religions like Christianity and Islam, the better to resist their encroachments."

Yogi Adityanath, the Chief Minister of UP, said that no one should have a problem in accepting a Hindu nation if such a move helped people live a better life and brought joy to them. "Hindu Rashtra ki awadharna kahin galat nahi hai … desh ki full bench ki Supreme Court ne iss par apna aadesh jaari kiya hai yeh. Hindutva koi mat, koi majhab ya upasana vidhi nahi hai. (There is nothing wrong in the Hindu Rashtra concept. The Supreme Court has defined Hinduism as a way of life.)."

"For far too long we have been pseudo-seculars who frowned upon anything that is Hindu. What's wrong in the CM's statement? He said that he would follow the path of peace and progress. Hinduism has always stood for peace," state BJP general secretary **Vijay Bahadur Pathak** said.

HINDUTVA/ HINDU RASHTRA – WHAT IT STANDS FOR

- Unlimited freedom is allowed to the individuals to excel in their talents to contribute to the society. Hindus never used their freedom to stifle or choke the life style of the other faiths.

- Dharma is central Hindu philosophy that bring harmony, peace and love to the humanity without imposing any restrictions to the survival of cosmos.

- Vasudaiva Kutumbam – the whole family is one family. It refers to the inclusiveness. It means the whole world has to live by some rules where everybody is treated as a member of the family, enabling to live in peace and harmony.

- Ahimsa – meaning not to cause pain to others. By this approach, all enmity, animosity and hatred cease. If one practices ahimsa in thought, speech and action, societies live in peace.

- Never believed in conversion. Conversion by allurement, deception and adharma (unrighteousness) is considered to destroy the culture and promote hatred toward other faiths.

- Never condemned other faiths to hell or called the followers of other faiths as sinners.

- Hindus will not be abused, insulted, demeaned, and humiliated in the hands of Christians, Muslims, media and so-called liberal.

- Polytheism was essentially tolerant, each group worshiping its own god or gods, offering no objection to the worship of others.

- Never invaded any country to dominate religiously.

- No fatwas are issued to curtail the freedom of others. Severe punishment should be enforced to anybody who issues fatwa directed at killing.

- Emphasizes the self-improvement, self-assessment and self-realization

- Practices tolerance, patience and understanding

- Believes that Yoga and Meditation improves the well-being of the humanity and help reduce the stress.

- Hindu Rashtra will not condemn anybody to either hell or inferno.

⅄ Promote spirituality, the backbone of our nation. It encourages compassion, allows one to enjoy life without being intimidated, encourages one to fulfill goals, and permits you to develop self-esteem.

⅄ Respect, revere and preserve Mother Earth

⅄ Respect and Worship Cow

⅄ Bestow good health, happiness, peace of mind, auspiciousness and no suffering to all.

⅄ Respect and preserve the ecological system that enables the humanity to exist with the nature. Preservation of earth, mountains, rivers, animals, trees and birds should be the motto to be passed on to the next generation.

⅄ Uniform Civil Code should be passed to eliminate the artificial barriers created by the earlier governments for the sake of vote bank politics. Everybody should enjoy the same privileges instead of denying the opportunities for the talented, skilled and innovators. Mediocracy should not rule the meritocracy.

⅄ Cow must be declared as a national animal for its contribution to humanity for providing urine, cow dung, milk, yogurt and ghee. No other animal can be compared with cow in this respect.

ALTERNATIVE TO HINDU STATE

People and organizations from Christianity and Islam along with so-called intellectuals, media and a number of political parties are pouncing on the idea of Hindu Rashtra. If these people succeed in their efforts to deny India to declare India as a Hindu Rashtra, one of the alternatives is to make India into an Islamic State. We can vividly see the life style of these 53 Muslim countries. In that Allah based country, freedom is curtailed, deny other religions to practice their faith, impose Jizya tax, demolish Hindu Temples, kidnap and convert Hindu girls into Islam, conduct genital mutilation, kill all those who refuse to be converted, divorce the wives with triple tallaq, enforce sharia law, issue Fatwa to either harm or kill, and the list goes on. Muslims have been talking about breaking up India into three Muslim countries by illegal infiltration from Bangladesh. Hindus have seen enough destruction of more than 2000 Hindu Temples including Rama Temple in Ayodhya, Krishna Janmasthala in Mathura and Vishwanath Temple in Kasi. Many Muslim leaders say that the conversion of India into an Islamic State is remaining as "unfinished business" to be fulfilled.

OPPOSITION TO THE CONCEPT OF HINDU RASHTRA

Every time we hear somebody talk about Hindutva or Hindu Rashtra, the opposition parties and both domestic and foreign media assemble like bees to bite the Hindu leaders. With their giddy minds following the election of Modi as Prime Minister, they become even more forceful in criticizing the concept of Hindu Rashtra. Shocked, shaken and stunned with the announcement of Yogi Adityanath as Chief Minister of Utter Pradesh, they have been trying to rouse the sentiments of Muslims and Christians by saying that the minorities should behave themselves. New York Times (March 18, 2017) bemoaned and bewailed by saying BJP "appointed a firebrand Hindu cleric to lead the country's most populous state, a turning point for a government that has, until now, steered clear of openly embracing far-right Hindu causes." It admitted that this announcement came as a shock to many political observers. One of the so-called observer even stated that "Mr. Modi "is unveiling a vision of benign majoritarianism." Another expert lamented that the selection of Yogi Adityanath is "a regressive choice and a lost opportunity for prime minister."

Maria Wirth wondered why Hindu Nation alone is chosen for criticism. There are many Muslim countries that deny basic human rights. Why do these journalists dare say something about the abuses of human rights, denial of freedom to express, demonization of Muslim women, practice of genital mutilation and refusal of worship by the followers of other faiths? Media would not comment on Western nations when they are called Christian nations and the middle east when they openly declare as Muslim nations by changing the Constitutions. The author says that the goal all Hindus is self-realization to mean connecting individual consciousness to cosmic consciousness. "From this follows that 'good' Hindus are those rare human beings whose dharma makes them regard all others as brothers and sisters. Their dharma makes them further respect nature and not harm unnecessarily any living being."

Hindu MLAs and MPs, and Hindu businessmen are mortgaging the country for their selfish acquisition of money, fame and name. If we look at how many thousands of acres of Hindu Temple lands are sold by the government without the approval of the original donors, we will all be surprised. It is Hindu politicians, Hindu businessmen and Hindu donors to the political party who have bought the temple lands, encroached the temple lands, and approved the transfer of lands to the government and they never ever discussed the transfer of either Church lands or Mosque properties. In fact, Churches are India is believed to be the largest landowner next only to the government. Minority appeasement and vote bank politics are creating havoc in the society and generating terror in the hearts of majority of the Hindus.

It is sad to find out how grateful some of the politicians are for fulfilling their political wish. To pay back for their political favors, they even announced to recognize Sonia Gandhi, who is a Christian, by constructing a Temple, although Christianity abhors image worship. In fact, one of the TTD chairmen openly announced that he would be grateful all his life to Sonia Gandhi for selecting him for the post. This kind of slavish mentality is ruining the country and destroying the Hindu principles of freethinking, intelligence, freedom, independence and liberty. All these politicians are becoming bonded slaves to the party to mortgage the motherland.

It is worth remembering KS Sudarshan, former Chief of RSS, who has explained in one of his speeches the salient features of the Hindu Rashtra as perceived by the RSS, "One of the cornerstones of the cultural foundation of the ancient mansion of Hindu Rashtra is 'unity in diversity'." He went on to add, "In Bharat, keeping with the genius of Hindu Rashtra, only that state set-up would be best which is democratic and secular...Favoring of one creed, or its propagation at state expense has been totally contrary to principles of Hindu polity."

Those opposing Hindu Rashtra have always tried to paint a completely misleading picture. They have successfully raise fears among Muslims and Christians by implying that would be second class citizens in a

Hindu nation. They even generate the impression that the Hindu majority will subjugate minorities in a Hindu nation. Sudarshan countered their argument by stating that "The Hindu state has never been theocratic, there being never any institution like the Pope of Rome and the caliph in Turkey. Therefore, to assert that the Hindu Rashtra whose glory lies in its liberal values of life was anti-secular is only to betray one's gross ignorance."

Minhaz Merchant also believed that many secularists and the media has been interpreting the concept of Hinduism as denying the rights of minority religions and impose Hinduness without ever understanding the underlying unity that has been the kernel for thousands of years. They forced themselves to believe in secularism without ever defining. Minority reservations, minority appeasement, mediocracy and bashing Hinduism have been their fodder since Independence in 1947. The author stated, "The problem with Hindu Rashtra is not its underlying concept of national unity within religious diversity which has been India's civilisational ethos for 5,000 years but the way the word Hindu is misinterpreted. A Hindu Rashtra does not mean, and certainly should not mean, a Hindu-centric Rashtra where Muslims, Christians, Parsis and Jews are treated as second-class citizens. It simply means an all-encompassing civilisational unity that transcends religion." (dnaindia, April 13, 2017)

Engage in Open dialogue

There is no real dialogue or open discussion taking place in the media about the role of Muslims in fomenting hatred toward Hindus, about the appeasement policies, reservation of educational seats, rampant terrorist activities, abuse of Hindu Temples and Deities, loud speakers blasting at high decibels, widespread use of houses as Churches in residential colonies and villages, failure of Police Department to file FIRs, the rampant abuse of Atrocities Act, and astronomical abuse of Dowry Act and so on.

TV stations routinely ask the interviewers not to talk about other religions, their atrocities, their abuses, their outspoken hatred toward Hindus and their outright zeal to convert India into an Islamic country. No TV station will take the risk of Muslim rampage. Law and order in India is tilted toward the minority appeasement. In fact, one TV executive even confessed that he agreed to apologize to Muslims by scrolling on the screen for one month for showing Muslims reading the Quran. Their threat would have been too costly to take a moral stand.

Many media outlets, journalists and the two major religions have criticized the concept and even threatened people. In 2012, three journalists – Vishweshara Bhat, Pratap Simha and Vijay Sankeshwar – were on the target list for being close to pro-Hindu groups. Assassination plot by eighteen youth was busted by police in Bengaluru.

Next one decade is crucial for the survival of Hindus in India. If the Hindus do not get united, shed their greed, challenge the laws that are undermining the very fabric of Hindutva, remove their shackles of political affiliations, question the appeasement policies, enforce uniform civil code, stop the deceptive conversion practices, control the population explosion, they will be ransacked, rampaged, terrorized and plundered. For Hindus, there would not be any place go, any place to hide, any place to run and any place to seek asylum. Let us be the true inheritors of the richest culture handed down by our ancient rishis for us to enjoy the freedom, democracy, pluralism, independence, and liberty. Hindus must wake up before they are wiped out and shoulder the responsibility of preserving their ancient Sanatana dharma.

The Hindus have always kept their religion and politics separate. They never imposed their religion upon other religious people. They never invaded any other country to convert people of other religions to their religion. Hindus always welcomed all other religions, hosted them, sheltered them and protected them. They never killed them, tortured them, looted them, raped them, plundered them, and converted them. Let us remember the words of the former President of India, Dr. A P J Abdul Kalam: *"In 3000 years of our history, people from all over the world have come and invaded us, captured our lands, conquered our minds. From Alexander onwards, The Greeks, the Turks, the Moguls, the Portuguese, the British, the French, the Dutch, all of them came and looted us, took over what was ours. Yet we have not done this to any other nation.*

We have not conquered anyone. We have not grabbed their land, their culture, their history and Tried to enforce our way of life on them. Why? Because we respect the freedom of others." That is enough justification to declare India as Hindu Rashtra.

REVISE SCHOOL CURRICULUM
ACROSS BHARAT.

Let us remember the words of Bhartihari written in Neeti Shatakam:

"Knowledge is a special beauty of man. It is a hidden treasure. It gives one happiness, enjoyment and brings fame. It is the teacher of great teachers. It is one's relative when he is in a strange place. It is the God divine. It is knowledge that is to be worshipped not money. One who is bereft of knowledge is a beast."

Global Hindu Heritage Foundation (GHHF) is very happy to know that you are working tirelessly to revamp the school curriculum from Class I and all the way up to college education to reflect the true nature of the cultural heritage of Bharath. You should make every effort to incorporate the rich cultural heritage dating back to thousands of years, morals that were the pinnacle of the country, and the scriptures that have addressed all issues that you can find under the sun.

Emphasis should be made to assure that values, morals, and character development from age five and up should be at the core of our educational system. This kind of value system would instill confidence, trust, conviction, and faith in the universal principles, and develop self-awareness and determination to succeed. It should mold, shape, and chisel the personality of the students. Mutual respect, equality, freedom, ahimsa, peaceful coexistence, and justice culled from our ancient scriptures should be the hallmark of our youth for years to come to enable them to appreciate the greatness, glory, grandeur, and grandness of the majesty of our culture.

Till recently, most of the books written by "Marxists, Muslims and Western historians" are so slanted, abusive, hateful, repulsive and intolerable to the true history of India, derogatory to the national freedom fighters, demonizing to Sanatana dharma, negligent of the contributions of great emperors to establish Hindutva, and boastful of the Muslim aggressors as contributors to the Indian culture. Dr. Subramanian Swamy was calling for burning of the writings by Nehruvian historians. We feel that it is time to fire all these left-wing historians who have stabbed the Mother India for many decades and employ those scholars who appreciate the richness of the Sanatana Dharma into National Council of Educational Research and Training (NCERT), Indian Certificate of Secondary Education (ICSE), National Censor Board and other agencies. It is time to reclaim what is lost, revamp the whole school curriculum, and rewrite the history debunking the leftwing Nehruvian historians.

Following are the topics that should be included in the curriculum depending on the level of education:

BHAGAVAD GITA.

Mere chanting of few verses is enough to awaken the consciousness of the individual and maintain the balance between the body, mind and soul. In fact, it improves the brain capacity to absorb the knowledge; teach the individual the responsibility of their dharma; emphasize the importance of bhakti, Jnana, karma and raja yoga; equip an individual to be fearless and give the needed strength to face the problems at hand; encourage him to think and uphold the dharma to protect human existence; and so on. No age is bar to learn and chant Bhagavad Gita. As young as three year olds can chant the divine song. Its message is unmatched, unparalleled and unrivalled.

Ralph Waldo Emerson writes, *"I owed a magnificent day to the Bhagavad-Gita. It was the first of books; it was as if an empire spoke to us, nothing small or unworthy, but large, serene, consistent, the voice of an old intelligence which in another age and climate had pondered and thus disposed of the same questions which exercise us."*

RAMAYANA

Rama's name is on the lips of every Hindu. He taught us to be a perfect son, a perfect brother, perfect husband, a perfect enemy, and a perfect king. He taught us how to live according to dharma in the face of un-surmountable hurdles.

Lord Rama, who is known for his compassion, gentleness, kindness, righteousness, non-hatred, and integrity, has served as role model for all of us to follow for millennia. His respect for father and obedience to his command was unparalleled that all humanity should emulate. Guru-Sishya relationship was emboldened in Ramayana for all of us follow, cherish and nurture, especially in the modern society.

Sita, Lakshmana, Bharatha, Dasaratha, Jataayu, Vali, Vibhishana, and Lord Hanuman have shaped the mind, body and soul of Bharath for many millennia. Every character teaches us how to live a dharmic life and how to establish Ramarajya where justice is rendered without consideration for name and fame. **Ramayana has taught us the richness of valor, dharma, loyalty, mutual respect, bhakti, spirituality, wisdom and Jnana to be followed in daily life to uplift the spirit of human life. The message of Ramayana spread all over Asia and even today its popularity is unabated in countries like Cambodia, Java, Laos, Malaysia, Philippines, Sumatra, Thailand, Mauritius, Bali and other countries.**

MAHABHARATA.

Mahabharata is one of the greatest epics and every single character teaches us the richness of our culture and traditions, morals and ethics that surpass the time. Numerous are the characters and numerous are the lessons one can learn from Mahabharata. **Yudhishtira** taught us how to follow dharma in face of numerous difficulties also the weakness of (gambling) that can bring down the kingdom; **Bhishma** taught us how to fulfill the wishes of his father and sacrificed his life as well as keeping his word for the rest of life and maintain celibacy; **King Santanu** taught us danger of yielding to sensate pleasure and the weakness toward other sex; **Karna** taught us the consequences of blind loyalty and passion for power as well as the generous nature of dana (gift); **Dhritarashtra** taught us how blind love for children can cause untold misery and destruction for the humanity, also how passion for children can smog the moral and impartial judgment; **Draupadi** taught us how even a small weakness resulted in a giggle lead to war of destruction and also taught us how to behave with the husbands;

and other characters such as **Pandu, Veda Vyasa, Kunti, Dushyasana, Shikhandi, Satyavati** and others were equally important in teaching us the morals and code of conduct.

Finally, the teaching of Bhagavad Gita by Lord Krishna to Arjuna about the responsibility of a Kshatriya and in general about Swadharma is unmatched in humanity in recognizing the importance of Stithipragna.

Puranic Stories and Morals

In Naimisharanya, the assembled sages worshipped the learned **Romaharshana** and said, "Please tell us the stories of the Puranas. Who created the universe, who is its preserver and who will destroy it? Please instruct us in all these mysteries." There are **18 main Puranas and18 Upapuranas** that describe the various aspects of cosmology and are considered as the storehouse of stories that is enriched with morals and traditions; manifestations of (Dashavataras) **Vishnu** incarnations, and the paths of karma, bhakti and Jnana yogas. **In fact, they even described the origin of the universe, life cycles, trials, tribulations and richness of human life, respect for living and nonliving elements and scientific nature of the universe.** They talk about the worship services, numerous Samskaras, formation of earth, and mathematical expressions of the universe. They give us the experiences of people through their stories, symbols and rituals. Every community has its own reality, but underneath all these realities there is an underlying theme governing the basic principles and morals that guide the human life.

Panchatantra Stories

Panchatantra is a collection stories that teach us how to behave in a particular situation; how to solve the problems one faces; whom to trust and not to trust; how to keep your word against all odds; how to use your intellect instead of arms; how to avoid distrust among friends; how one should not deny the shelter to a needy person; how one should work toward accumulation of wealth and how to protect it; and how one should share their wealth and with whom.

It is worth remembering the words of **Arthur W Ryder**: "The Panchatantra contains the most widely known stories in the world. If it is further declared that the Panchatantra is the best collection of stories in the world, the assertion could hardly be disproved, and would probably command the assent of those possessing the knowledge for a judgment."

President Obama acknowledges the simple yet moral principle that guided the Bharat for many millennia in a speech delivered to Indian Parliament on November 2010. He said: It's a simple lesson contained in that collection of stories which has guided Indians for centuries — the Panchatantra. And it's the spirit of the inscription seen by all who enter this great hall: "That one is mine and the other a stranger is the concept of little minds. But to the large-hearted, the world itself is their family."

NATIONAL HEROES

We should teach about the national heroes who fought for the independence of India from British. The previous governments tarnished their reputation. They were called extremists, militants and even terrorists. **Balagangadhar Tilak, Lala Lajpat Rai, Bipin Chandra Pal, Subhash Chandra Bose, Veer Savarkar, Bhagat Singh, Raj Guru, Sukhdev, Chandrasekhar Azhad, Vasudev Balwant Phadke, Chapekar brothers** and many more sacrificed their life to guarantee freedom for the future generations. It is time to teach about their heroism, their love for Bharath, their struggles with British rulers, their imprisonment, their hangings and/or suffering. Their martyrdom is unparalleled and unmatched. They cheerfully sacrificed their life for the sake of the people of Bharat to enjoy their unbridled freedom with dignity and pride.

SCIENTIFIC ACHIEVEMENTS

It is time to create pride among our youth about our scientific achievements. It was the Yogic seers who invented many mathematical calculations such as **Zero, Decimals, Phi, Geometry, Algebra, computer language and more. Aryabhatta was the champion of Astronomy and Mathematics, Bhaskaracharya was the genius** of Algebra, Acharya Kanad was the founder of Atomic Theory, Nagarjuna was the wizard of Chemical Science, Acharya Charaka was the father of Medicine, Acharya Sushruta was the champion of Plastic Surgery, Varahamihira was the eminent Astronomer and Astrologist, Patanjali was the father of Yoga Sutras, Acharya Bharadwaja was the pioneer of Aviation Technology, Acharya Kapila was the father of cosmology, and many more.

GREAT SAINTS OF INDIA

School books should include the history, message and glory of great saints of India such as **Adi Sankara, Madhvacharya, Ramanujacharya, Meerabai, Kabir, Tukaram, Eknath, Gnaneswar, Namdev, Bhagawan Nityananda, Satya Saibaba, Sri Pada Vallabha, Narasimha Swamy, Samarth Ramdas, Veda Vyasa, Valmiki, Sri Aurobindo, Muktananda, Gorakhnath, Sri Prabhupada, Chinmayananda, Ramana Maharishi, Ramakrishna Paramahamsa, Swami Vivekananda** and host of others. They have kept alive the richness of our culture in spite of the attempts to destroy the ancient civilization.

The saints have played significant role in the preservation and propagation of the ideas and philosophies that were necessary to bring unity and much needed reforms, bring the appropriate changes in the society. Considering the Mughal domination of India, the saints veered and helped bhaktas toward Bhakti Marga, the path of devotion, instead of encouraging them to conduct Temples pujas, especially in North India.

HINDU TEMPLES - HISTORY AND RELEVANCE

It is time to know the power, energy, and vibrations present in Hindu Temples. They are the places of worship where devotees worship their chosen Gods at different times, day in and day out. Devotees go to the Hindu Temples to experience the infinite divine power through their individual prayers as well as collective worship. Hindu Temples have been built over more than twenty centuries providing opportunity to practice their social, religious and cultural milieu. Each Temple is dedicated to one of the manifestations of infinite power of the unfathomable divinity of the Almighty. Every Temple will have a sanctum sanctorum with a presiding Deity who represents the power and energy of GOD. Hindus believe that God is ever powerful, all pervasive, everywhere and that everything is in God.

The Hindu Temples have served as centers of learning and knowledge; foci for social gatherings; institutes for art, dance and music; hubs for upholding the dharmic values; nucleus for peace and nonviolence; lighthouses for philosophy and spirituality, cornerstones for worship services; promoters of age old, time tested universal values; institutes for yoga and meditation; holy places for conducting different festivals and rituals; and nexus for expressing devotion through music, singing and chanting; and centers for social services.

GOMATA

Cow is revered, respected and honored and is regarded as a holy mother. Cow's milk is light and easily digestible for a child. Its products such as milk, ghee, urine, cow dung and curd, are considered sacred and has many medicinal values that improve the health of the humans and purifies the climate. Cow is considered as Kamadhenu (wish fulfilling Deity). Lord Krishna worshipped cows, used to play flute that attracted the cows which assembled around him.

All the scriptures such as Vedas, Upanishads, Puranas, Mahabharata, Manusmriti, and others extoll the virtues of the cow. All the Gods reside in her and killing her is considered the most heinous crime. It is often said "jivantu avadghnyah ta me vishasya dushanih" meaning that let cows live without slaughter for their whole life-they remove poison and toxins. Many sages, many Hindu Temples and numerous Ashrams maintained Goshalas (cow shelters) for centuries recognizing the numerous benefits that accrue from the cows.

YOGA, MEDITATION, AND SURYANAMASKAR

Yoga classes, meditation and Surya, Namaskar exercises must be introduced at all levels of classes in the school system to ward off stress and disease. Patanjali Yoga Sutras has played vital role in integrating the body, mind and soul. The eight limbs of Yoga according to Patanjali are:

Yama focuses on internal purification or moral code
Niyama focuses on external purity or personal discipline
Asana deals with the performance of various postures of Yoga
Pranayama is breath control
Pratyahara result in withdrawal of sense organs
Dharana is concentration
Dhyana is meditation
Samadhi is the final state of spiritual absorption

Voluminous literature is available to show the mental and physical health benefits of yoga and meditation. Not only survey studies have provided ample evidence to prove the benefits of these exercises but, neuro-imaging and genomics technology that measure physiological changes in the brain and body in greater detail also have shown similar results. "There is a true biological effect," said Denninger, Director of research at the Benson-Henry Institute for Mind Body Medicine at Massachusetts General Hospital, one of Harvard Medical School's teaching hospitals. "The kinds of things that happen when you meditate do have effects throughout the body, not just in the brain."

Nobel Prize winner Elizabeth Blackburn, University of California at Los Angeles, found that 12 minutes of daily yoga and meditation for eight weeks increased telomerase activity by 43 percent, suggesting an improvement in stress-induced aging. Similarly, Sophia Dunn of King's College, London, also stated that "Yoga and meditation are tools for enabling us to swim in difficult waters."

HINDU HOLOCAUST

It is high time that all the students learn the unadulterated, unbiased, impartial, balanced and true history of India. Last ten centuries of atrocities, murders, terrorism, rape, slavery and genocide inflicted on Hindus must be taught in the schools. We have a moral responsibility to learn from the past; lest we commit the same mistakes and make our future generation the sacrificial lambs in the hands of Muslims and Christians.

Let us remember the words of former President of India, Dr. Abdul Kalam: "In 3000 years of our history, people from all over the world have come and invaded us, captured our lands, conquered our minds. From Alexander onwards, the Greeks, the Portuguese, the Mughals, the British, the French, the Dutch, all of them came and looted us, took over what was ours. Yet we have not done this to any other nation. We have not conquered anyone. We have not grabbed their land, their culture, their history and tried to enforce our way of life on them. Why? Because, we respect the freedom of others."

India welcomed all the religions with open hands only to be stabbed by Muslims and Christians. According to Koenaard Elst, Muslims have massacred as many as 80 million Hindus between the years 1000 and 1525. "Hindu Kush" mountain is the testimony to that cruel and barbaric slaughter of Hindus. Hindu Kush means slaughter of Hindus. Millions of Hindus, who refused to be converted to Islam, were taken to the top of this mountain and killed only to see the blood flow from the mountain to the streets below. One of the Afghan historians, Kondamir, had written that as many as 1,500,000 Hindus were killed by Muslims in one of their invasions in the heart of the city of Afghanistan. Students should be aware of this darkest period in the history where Hindus were subjected to long monotonous vicious, brutal, heartless and inhuman rape, torture and slaughter. Let us not make our Hindus the beasts without the knowledge of their history as Bhartrihari mentioned.

OTHER TOPICS:

Students should also be given realistic picture of nearly ten centuries of brutal regimes that inflicted untold misery to the citizens of Bharath. How many Temples were rampage, how many Murthies were broken to pieces, how the remnants of Hindu Gods statues were used to build the Mosques, how many women were subjected rapes, how many Hindus were massacred at Hindu Kush mountains in Afghanistan, how many Temples were converted to Mosques, how many Christians are converting the Hindus with deception and allurement, how minority appeasement is affecting the quality education. All such similar issues should be addresses. Vast literature dealing with "Islamic onslaught" and "Goa Inquisition" should also be included to know the history of denial of fundamental rights to Hindus.

Also, school text books should also include as to how Krishna Janma Sthala was destroyed, how Ayodhya was converted to Babri Masjid, how Kashi Vishwanath Temple was destroyed and a Mosque built in front of the Temple, and how more than 2000 Temples were converted to Mosques.

George Santayana, a Spanish-born American author of the late nineteenth and early twentieth centuries, said that, *"Those who forget the past are condemned to repeat it."* Let us not repeat the mistakes, let us not forget our forefathers, let us not overlook our rich cultural heritage and let us not be the cause to sacrifice the lives of our children and grandchildren.

(NOTE: *This is a modified version of a letter submitted to Honorable Smriti Irani in the first week of September 2014 by Prakasarao Velagapudi and Ghazal Srinivas*).

BHAGAVAD GITA SHOULD BE MANDATORY IN SCHOOLS

"Read the Gita and other good works on Vedanta. That is all you need. The present system of education is all wrong. The mind is crammed with facts before it knows how to think. Control of the mind should be taught first." **Swami Vivekananda**

Global Hindu Heritage Foundation (GHHF) appreciates and congratulates Supreme Court Justice A K Dave for expressing his views to introduce Bhagavad Gita and Mahabharata in Class I to revive the rich cultural heritage that Bharat has been known for centuries. It is high time that the present government embark on revising the curriculum from Class I thru university that is currently highly slanted, openly anti Hindu, clearly pro minority religions and undoubtedly adharmic. All organizations that are stabbing the very fabric of Hindutva principles must be removed from their present positions and replaced them with people who are knowledgeable about the rich cultural heritage, guru-sishya sampradaya, importance of morals from all our scriptures like Ramayana, Mahabharata, Bhagavad Gita, Puranas, Upanishad, Yoga and others. Justice Dave, as well as BJP and other concerned leaders should stand firm to defend dharma. It is the need of the hour. As RSS leader Mohan Bhagwat had stated, "As long as dharma exists in India, the world will continue to respect this country. But once dharma is gone, no force on earth can stop the country from crumbling."

GHHF is ready to stand by the introduction of Hindu scriptures into the educational curriculum at all levels, will support all measures that can be adopted to negate the present curriculum and rewrite history to reflect the eternal contribution of Sanatana Dharma to humanity. We have to stand up to nourish and nurture the roots that will invigorate the much-neglected cultural heritage of India, so that the present adharmic curriculum can be rooted out from the educational system. As the former President observed, India is the only country that has not conquered other countries for the expansion of their faith. Bharath has not spoken her last word, it's contribution will me immeasurable in the next few decades. It is the responsibility of every Hindu to take the ownership of their religion, support it, tender it, practice it, preserve it and protect it from within and without. As **Anne Besant** observed, "If Hindus do not maintain Hinduism, who shall save it? If India's own children do not cling to her faith, who shall guard it. India alone can save India and India and Hinduism are one."

On August 3, the Supreme Court Justice made history in giving a lecture on "Contemporary Issues and Challenges of Human Rights in the Era of Globalization' during the inaugural ceremony of a workshop by saying, "Somebody who is very secular... so-called secular will not agree... Had I been the dictator of India, I would have introduced the Gita and the Mahabharata in class 1. That is the way you learn how to live life."

The SC judge stressed the importance of preserving the rich cultural heritage and also urged people to go back to tradition to solve modern problems. "Our old tradition such as 'Guru-Sishya parampara' is lost. If it had been there, we would not have all these problems (violence, conflicts and terrorism) in our country. Now we see terrorism in other countries." On the requirement of being good to form a just society, he said, "If I am good, if every person of my country is good, my administrator is bound to be good. If everybody in a democratic country is good, then they would naturally elect somebody who is very good. And that person will never think of damaging anybody else." Dave also said that to curb terrorism and violence, children at the young age should be introduced to religious books like Mahabharata and Bhagwat Gita.

BJP WELCOMES THE JUDGE'S VIEWS

BJP leader **Nalin Kohli** welcomed Dave's statements, emphasizing that one should not look at it through the prism of religion. "There is nothing wrong with Mahabharata, Gita, or Ramayana. We should learn from them, and not view his statement as something against secularism."

CONGRESS DISAGREES

Congress Party spokesperson, **Rashid Alvi** said, "Logics are missing in AR Dave's statement. Class I students don't even know how to read." National Congress Party spokesperson, **Majid Memon**, strongly condemned the views by saying "I cannot understand how a learned Supreme Court Judge can talk like this, or for that matter any other powerful politician say something derogatory. Dave's remarks the constitution of our country."

On Alvi's comment that Class I students don't even know how to read; the question is what else do these children do in class? Did they not come to read, learn and write? The children at the age of 5-6 learn faster, grasp quicker, and memorize easily. In fact, this is the right age to learn how to chant the Bhagavad Gita. These spokespeople may be surprised to know that there are 3 year olds who can chant quite a number of verses from the Bhagavad Gita. Anyone can search Google and find child prodigies chanting Bhagavad Gita.

COMMUNIST PARTY SPOKESPERSON

Sitaram Yechury, the Communist Party of India Marxist (CPI-M) leader stated that Judge Dave's suggestion that Mahabharata and Bhagavad Gita be introduced in class level 1, is completely wrong. He said "that means that you give religious education in schools and that too regarding one religion. It's given in our constitution that each religion has equal rights. So, if you talk about one religion this is going against the judgment of his own. Being a sitting judge he should not have said that."

The **Polit Bureau of CPI-M** announced that the views expressed by the Supreme Court Judge Justice A R Dave that Gita and Mahabharata should be taught in schools, was termed as "improper and unwarranted." "What Justice Dave has advocated is religious instruction in all schools from Class I. Compulsory religious instruction in government schools violates the basic secular principle enshrined in the Constitution".

First of all, the Gita is not a religious book the way the Bible and the Quran are described. No one finds any statements which suggest that Hindus should go covert other religion's followers into their faith, or that they should kill other religious people if they refuse to be converted, ask their faithful to destroy the idols/symbols of other religions, or to condemn others to hell for refusing to be converted, calling others as born sinners, or say that their God's WORD is infallible and cannot be questioned, or be opposed to the principles of secular concept since they believe in in vasudaika kutumbam ideology.

Secondly, CPI-M should know that **Income Tax Appellate Tribunal** in Nagapur declared on November 9 2012, that Hinduism is not a religion. It said, "The word "Hindu" has not been defined in any of the texts nor in judgment made law… Therefore, it cannot be said that Hindu is a separate community or a separate religion. Technically Hindu is neither a religion nor a community. Therefore, expenses incurred for worshipping of Lord Shiva, Hanuman, Goddess Durga and for maintenance of temple cannot be regarded to be for religious purpose."

Thirdly, if Hinduism is not considered a religion, then why do these parties classify Christianity and Islam as minority religions and give special reservations and privileges.

Fourthly, If India is a secular country, why do you identify certain communities as Christians and Muslims and give privileges based on religion. Don't you expect the government to be color blind or religion blind so that nobody will be identified by either religion or community?

It is unfortunate these politicians have no civility or knowledge to make such false statement for their self-glory and lime light. They should be exposed of their ignorance and lack of knowledge.

JUDGE KATJU'S OUTRAGE

Markandey Katju criticized A R Dave's suggestion by saying that "In a country of such diversity as ours, nothing of this kind should be compelled or imposed, as this is against our country's secular feature and Constitution and will do great harm." He goes on to say that he is against making Gita and Mahabharata compulsory in schools.

Rebuttal to Katju, Former Supreme Court Judge and Chairman of Press Council of India: On November 14, 2011 Justice Katju delivered a speech at Jawaharlal Nehru University himself praising the Sanskrit language. He stated that Sanskrit was the most scientific language and has nothing to do with religion. Acknowledging that Sanskrit was called "devavani" (language of God), he said that it was the language of people with an enquiring mind, who enquired about everything, and therefore there is a whole range of subjects which have been discussed in Sanskrit.

"As I was saying, Sanskrit was the language of people with enquiring minds, of people who enquired into every aspect of life. Therefore it is the language of not only Hindus or North India but it is in that sense the language of everybody who has a rational approach, because the emphasis in Sanskrit is on reason. There is emotion also in it, but the emphasis is on reason."

"People think that Sanskrit is a language of chanting mantras in temples or in religious ceremonies. However, that is only 5% of Sanskrit literature. 95% of Sanskrit literature has nothing to do with religion. It deals with a whole range of subjects like philosophy, law, science (including mathematics, medicine and astronomy) grammar, phonetics and literature." <kgfindia.com)/ http://timesofindia.indiatimes.com/india/ Markandey-Katju-What-is-India/articleshow/10994212.cms

Once you read what he said in 2009, then you wonder why would he have any objection to Dave's belief since 95 % of Sanskrit literature has nothing to do with religion but only with philosophy, law, mathematics, medicine, astronomy, grammar, phonetics and literature? Since the Bhagavad Gita is written in Sanskrit, how can 95% of the book can be against secular. When did scientific literature become non-secular or religious? Why can't children and the youth have the scientific knowledge and inquiring mind to explore a whole range of subjects for their development and for the development of Bharath? Is Judge Katju opposed to the Bhagavad Gita and Mahabharata because it broadens the knowledge and empowers the students to equip themselves to excel in the scientific field? Since the Bhagavad Gita is filled with scientific knowledge why can't it be made mandatory for students? How do we reconcile the fact that the present curriculum of mathematics, physics, astronomy, medicine, and law can be mandatory for the students, but not the Bhagavad Gita? Would Judge Katju say that the Bible and the Quran have similar percentage of scientific knowledge to be made compulsory? Since Justice Katju himself acknowledges the meaning of Sanskrit as "prepared, pure, refined or perfect" when did these noble adjectives become non-secular? Is he saying that Muslims and Christians should not be allowed to be prepared, pure, refined or perfect?

Pro-RSS, VHP, BJP and Hindu Activists

Many spokespersons who are interested in the philosophy of "vasudaika kutumbam" welcomed Judge Dave's belief in preserving the rich heritage of Bharat, upholding the moral fiber of the ancient literature, maintaining the guru-sishya sampradayas, and promulgating unity among different sections who want to live in peace, harmony and happiness.

P. Parameswaran, Director of Bharatiya Vichara Kendra noted that Bhagavad Gita is not a religious book, but a spiritual and philosophical classic that should be declared as the notional book. "It's influence is beyond time and space. It is a treasure house of knowledge for any fertile mind and it's influence is eternal. Mahatma Gandhi figuratively called Gita his Mother and he said whenever he felt confusion and sorrow, he had taken refuge in Gita. Gita has influenced decisively our freedom struggle," He even observed that the original copy of the Indian Constitution had the picture of "Gitopadesha". Then he queried, "The book approved by the constitution, if taught, how does it become unconstitutional?"

The Vishwa Hindu Parishad (VHP) has demanded that the Bhagavad Gita be included in school curricula without delay. VHP spokesperson Vinod Bansal said a resolution at the Parishad headquarters demanding that the Mahabharata in its entirety, or at least the Bhagavad Gita, should form part of the school curricula at the State and Central levels as the solutions to all contemporary social and moral problems can be found in the study of these epics. VHP vice-president Ram Krishna Srivastava said, "If our children had been brought up in the traditions of invaluable epics such as the Mahabharata and the Bhagwad Gita, India would have never had to face the kind of problems we are facing today."

BHAGAVAD GITA'S INFLUENCE

The Bhagavad Gita, Mahabharata, Ramayana, Upanishad and Puranas have influenced the greatest minds all across the globe for many centuries that include mathematicians, astronomers, physicist, Chemists, political leaders, scientists, artists and philosophers of diverse backgrounds. Many Nobel laureates admired our scriptures as they provided spark and life into their research

The Bhagavad Gita would equip the youth and children to cope with challenges they face in life, trials and tribulations they encounter on a daily basis, problems they meet in the modern world, frustrations they may be bumped into the competitive world of work, adjustments they have to make in the family life, ancient wisdom they may use to differentiate between the dharmic and adharmic values, and stress they may face in their hectic, hurried and materialistic world. Bhagavad Gita would teach the highest morals that promote peace and harmony.

WHAT DID NOBEL LAUREATES SAY ABOUT BHAGAVAD GITA?

"Bhagavad Gita is one of the most beautiful and profound texts of world literature." **Octavio Paz**, Nobel laureate

Eugene Wigner, winner of the Prize for Physics in 1963, said "In particular it acquainted me some with the Bhagavad Gita. I learned that the basic philosophical ideas of this on 'existence' are virtually identical with those which quantum mechanics lead me to."

"The curiosity of the Bhagavad-Gita is its absolutely admirable adumbration of life's acumen which enables aesthetics to bloom into religion." **Herman Hesse** (1877-1962), recipient of the Nobel Prize in 1946.

Albert Einstein expressed his admiration by saying, "When I read the Bhagavad-Gita and reflect about how God created this universe everything else seems so superfluous."

OTHERS ON BHAGAVAD GITA

"I owed a magnificent day to the Bhagavad-Gita. It was the first of books; it was as if an empire spoke to us, nothing small or unworthy, but large, serene, consistent, the voice of an old intelligence, which in another age and climate, had pondered and thus disposed of the same questions that exercise us." — Ralph Waldo Emerson, American philosopher and poet

"When doubts haunt me, when disappointments stare me in the face and I see not one ray of hope on the horizon, I turn to Bhagavad-Gita and find a verse to comfort me; and I immediately begin to smile in the midst of overwhelming sorrow. Those who meditate on the Gita will derive fresh joy and new meanings from it every day." Mahatma Gandhi.

BHAGAVAD GITA AND BUSINESSMEN

The Bhagavad Gita has become one of the top books that has impacted top executives in India and Abroad. In 2006, **BusinessWeek** published an article with title "How Bhagavad Gita has charmed US corporates" describing how many top executives of different corporations attended the seminars to learn about the Indian philosophy in order to balance the business ideas of amassing wealth with the desire to live with inner happiness. It says, "Big business is embracing Indian philosophy. Suddenly, phrases from ancient Hindu Texts such as Bhagavad Gita are popping up in management tomes and on websites of consultants." Almost all the major Business schools in USA have at least ten percent faculty members are of Indian descent. In fact, Dean of Kellogg School says, "When senior executives come to Kellogg, Wharton, Harvard or Dartmouth's Tuck, they are exposed to Indian values that are reflected in the way we think and articulate." They are learning to expand their horizon with Indian values, embrace more holistic approach in life and getting motivated a broader outlook than just money.

In 2013, **Debashi Chatterjee** felt that Bhagavad Gita would bring back the honesty and integrity so lacking in modern society. "Bhagavad Gita's time has come. It is not a religious manual in as much as a manual of practice... It tells you how to regain your equanimity in a war-like situation." The importance of learning the intrinsic nature of the human mind to focus with determination, Gita's perennial philosophy is needed for every dimension of human life including business management. Senior Analyst of Deutsche Bank says, "The Gita is even taught in a course called Leadership, Inspiration, Dilemma and Action and is very relevant to modern managerial dilemmas."

Bhagavad Gita also became a management mantra that found it's way into the curriculum of **Indian Institute of Management** (IIM) in Indore. Ten different sessions on Bhagavad Gita took the students through the discourses on Raja Yoga and Karma Yoga. The students were imparted many lessons on "how to develop and channelize their spiritual and mental energies to achieve excellence in the field of business management." The aim of this program was to make students not only good managers, but also responsible corporate citizen.

In USA, the study of the Bhagavad Gita became a mandatory at **Seton Hall University** in New Jersey from 2008. The university wanted to be different and transformed as they started developing a new university wide curriculum.

MAHABHARATA

By accident **Nhilde Davidson** came into contact with the Mahabharata serial and was hooked on. He was fascinated and enthralled by the complexity and the human drama in the great epic. He admired the philosophical depth and psychological profundity of the story that touched the very soul of the student of Mahabharata. He said *"I never considered taking the Mahabharata off the shelf ... Use this epic tale as an inspiration to solve your problems. The story is your armor and also your weapon . . . Be heir to Light, to Justice and to Truth. Turn the Kurukshetra of your heart into Holy Ground -- That is Salvation!"*

SCHOOL CURRICULUM – WHAT CAN BHAGAVAD GITA TEACH?

The Bhagavad Gita's message universal and eternal. It is a book for all ages. It is addressed to each and every human individual, irrespective of one's religion, to help solve the difficult vexing and puzzling issues one faces in daily living whether it is at work or home. It transcends race, religion, boundaries, time and space. **Swami Sivananda** says that Bhagavad Gita is a *"divine wisdom addressed to mankind for all times, in order to help human beings face and solve the ever-present problems of* *birth and death, of pain, suffering, fear, bondage, love and hate. It enables man to liberate himself from all limiting factors and reach a state of perfect balance, inner stability and mental peace, complete freedom from grief, fear and anxiety... This is the experience of everyone in this world, the drama of the ascent of man from a state of utter dejection, sorrow and total breakdown and hopelessness to a state of perfect understanding, clarity, renewed strength and triumph."*

For too long, Hindus have been insulted and denigrated. Their nobility is disrespected. Tolerance was considered weakness. Their disunity was taken advantage to the fullest. Their national heroes like Bhagat Singh, Rajguru, Sukhdev, Chandershekar Azad, Kartar Singh Sarabha, Veer Savarkar and many more who donated their last drop of blood for Indian struggle were maligned in the textbooks as terrorists. But pity and shame on Indians who have forgotten these heroes. If we as Indians cannot respect our martyrs we have no right to say that we are Indians. Hindu Temples were damaged and destroyed, but we remain indifferent. Our scriptures were insulted, but we remain silent. Our people were raped, and massacred, but we failed to learn any lessons from it. They hurt our sentiments by calling us Saffron terrorists, but we have not responded. Our people welcomed different religions with open arm only to be stabbed, but we have neglected our responsibility to protect our Bharat Mata. It is time to wake up. It is time to bring changes. It is time to be proud of being a Hindu. It is time to protect the humanity from being sacrificed to the terror. It is the dharma of every Hindu to shoulder the responsibility to safeguard the Mother.

GURU SISHYA SAMPRADAYA

From ancient times onwards, the Guru-Sishya relationship existed in Bharat where mentoring of a student by a spiritual teacher is undertaken. Selfless transmission by genuine, dedicated and committed teachers passing on the information to a student who is expected to receive the knowledge with commitment, faith, devotion, respect and sincerity. The tradition of dialogue, discussion, debate, questioning, dissecting and deciphering is the hallmark of exchange of opinion. No WORD is taken for granted. Tradition of un-questioning the scriptures is unheard of this tradition. It is this kind of questioning that encouraged the freedom that is essential for the intellectual growth and survival of humanity. Just imagine how much valuable, eternal, immortal and everlasting message was rendered by Lord Krishna to Arjuna who asked a simple question about his confusion and dilemma about waging a war that might kill all his relatives and gurus?

REMOVE THE CONFUSION AND INDECISION.

In Gita, Lord Krishna delivers the message in order to remove the confusion and sorrow that engulfed Arjuna, who asks the question: "With a heart contaminated by the taint of helplessness, with a mind confounded as to my duty, I ask you to tell me what is assuredly good for me. I am your disciple. Instruct me who have thrown myself on your indulgence."

BALANCING

Samatvaṁ yoga ucyate(Gita 2.48): Equilibrium, evenness, harmony, adjustment, adaptability, unity, the blending of the subject and the object in harmony is Yoga. In everything that we do, we must be able to balance various facets of life. Balance must be maintained in our daily life with regard to work, family, leisure, friends, opportunities, children and other pursuits. Decisions must be made based on the priorities as to what we consider as important in life based on dharmic values without expectation of rewards or fruits. Let us remember the words of Lord Krishna:

"Fixed in yoga, do thy work, O Winner of wealth (Arjuna), abandoning attachment, with an even mind in success and failure, for evenness of mind is called yoga"(2:48)

NISKAMA KARMA

Bhagavad Gita is the source of for one's ethics with regard to the discharge of one's duty without expectations on the fruits of this action. Performing duty without motivation, thinking, deliberating and calculating about its outcomes tends to purify one's mind and see the value of desire less action. These concepts are vividly described in the following verses:

To action alone hast thou a right and never at all to its fruits; let not the fruits of action be thy motive; neither let there be in thee any attachment to inaction. (2:47).

The Gita advocates action, relentless action regardless of the rewards. It preaches the mantra of karma yoga and defines it as dexterity in action; 'yagahe karmasu kaushalam' gives new dignity to work.

STITHIPRAGNA

In life, many decisions are made with vagaries of mind. The Mind is always changing, not stable. Decisions made without having an agitated mindset yields better results. Lord Krishna says that one should be able to make decision effortlessly, naturally and calmly based on the pros and cons of the situation with no attachments. One must do sadhana to reach that state known as Stithipragna. It is the stage where one will be able effective control on Mind and the Indiriyas (sense organs). Just like a driver of Charioteer can control the horses, mind should be able to control all the sense organs. To achieve this stage, one must be trained by a living guru and practice control mind under his guidance. Stithipragna is always alert, wakeful, efficient, attentive and careful. In this stage whatever we do, it is done with the full control of mind and control of all Indiriyas based on wisdom not based on whims and fancies. Decisions must be made without attachment, fear and anger. A steady mind is a prerequisite for making rational decisions.

MUCH MORE TO LEARN

The sessions conducted at IIM in Indore will serve as guiding principles that can be introduced at different levels in the educational system subject to the level of knowledge. Ten modules developed by **Swami Samarpananda** of Ramakrishna Mission are appropriate for proper discussion to be included in the curriculum: (1) Harnessing mental energy (2) Values in leadership and administration (3) Philosophy of life and its importance (4) Acquiring excellence (5) Managing stress, (6) Duty, (7) Karma Yoga, (8) Dynamics of work (9) Self-Upliftment (10) The goal supreme and looking back.

HINDUISM REPRESENTS HUMANISM

For many liberals, so called secularists, media, Congress spokesperson, Communist Party Polit Bureau, Macaulay's children and other minority religious representatives the words like Hindu, Hindutva, Hindustan, Hinduism, Hindu Rashtra immediately drive them to a panic level because of their selfish personal interest, their exclusive religious belief, their vote bank formula and their greed for unlimited wealth. They have so much to lose. So, they have to oppose and paint these words as anti-minority.

Hinduism is more of a humanistic way of life that embraces the dignity of an individual rather than looking through the glass of religion. They want to deny the rights and privileges of Hindus for the sake of the 20 percent people from other religions. It is time to meet the needs of the majority population rather than succumb to fraction of the people whose intention is to disintegrate the country by building barriers along religious and caste lines. What is wrong with teaching the humanistic values as espoused in Sanatana dharma? Dharma is humanism which means rationality, righteousness, responsibility, justice, compassion, peace, tolerance, truthfulness, service, caring, charity, respect, dialogue, freedom, forgiveness and compassion. These humanistic values do not promote violence, hatred, terror, illegal conversion, denigration, and animosity toward other people? These universal values do not call others as kafirs, pagans, or sinners? Do they condemn certain religions to hell and burn them in eternal fire? Let everyone shine, progress and evolve without ever discussing the religion. Let universal humanistic values spread the earth. Do these liberals digest the idea of equality, freedom, humanism and independence? Let us transmit these eternal humanistic values from Bhagavad Gita, Mahabharata, Ramayana and scriptures to our next generations. Let us support the efforts to revise the curriculum to reflect the ethical compass of Bharat.

As Albert Einstein said, everything else is so superfluous compared to Bhagavad Gita. Let us enrich the humans to be good citizens by teaching Bhagavad Gita and other scriptures.

BHAGAVAD GITA
IMPORTANCE AND SIGNIFICANCE

MERITS OF MEMORIZING BY CHILDREN AND ITS UNIVERSAL MESSAGE

"I owed a magnificent day to the Bhagavad-Gita. It was the first of books; it was as if an empire spoke to us, nothing small or unworthy, but large, serene, consistent, the voice of an old intelligence, which in another age and climate, had pondered and thus disposed of the same questions that exercise us." - **Ralph Waldo Emerson, American philosopher and poet**

"Sanskrit …. is extremely elaborate, almost artificial, and is capable of describing multiple levels of meditation, states of consciousness and psychic, spiritual and even intellectual processes. As for vocabulary, its richness is considerable and highly diversified. Sanskrit has for centuries lent itself admirably to the diverse rules of prosody and versification. Thus, we can see why poetry has played such a preponderant role in all of Indian culture and Sanskrit literature." - **Georges Ifrah, French historian of Mathematics**

In August 2015, **Sadguru Sri Ganapathy Sachchidananda Swamiji** commanded the Children and youth, who were sitting in a newly inaugurated Karya Siddhi Hanuman Temple in Frisco, Texas USA to memorize the entire Bhagavad Gita that contains 700 verses and chant them by the time He comes the next year. Many children with so much enthusiasm, gusto and determination agreed by saying "Yes, Appaji," "Yes, Tataji," and "Yes, Swamiji." With that announcement history was in the making. Sri Swamiji asked Srikanth Challa to take the responsibility. The arduous, laborious, grueling and the very difficult task of memorizing the Bhagavad Gita verse by verse started. Parents and children went through the hard task of adjusting their time, foregoing holidays, working around their school schedules, sacrificing their leisure time, and postponing their travels to make sure that the children will attend the Gita classes on a regular basis. They all realized that it would be hard to catch up with the memorization even if they miss one class. Parents and children spent countless number of hours memorizing to make sure that they will be ready to chant all 700 verses by the time Sri Swamiji arrived in July 2016.

History was made on July 17, 2016 with 43 children ages 6 thru 14 sitting for about four hours chanting all 700 verses of Bhagavad Gita with Sri Swamiji sitting next to them admiring and appreciating the discipline, dedication and devotion of the children. More than 4000 people along with special invited guests for this historical event listened with awe, amazement, excitement and astonishment. The sounds, rhythm, energy, and vibrations created by chanting touched the audience, infused them with vigor, infiltrated their body, touched their hearts and penetrated their soul. By the time they completed chanting, a number of people shed tears in appreciating the commitment, dedication and discipline of the children. Some of them have seen even Sri Swamiji wiping His tears. Many of them became speechless and left numbed cherishing the unprecedented historical event. Sri Swamiji's power and blessings permeated the majestic Temple and cleansed the hearts of the people and purified the atmosphere.

WHY MEMORIZE?

Why did Sri Swamiji say that the children should memorize and chant? Are there any benefits of chanting that may help children as they grow up? Memorization of information based on repetition is as old as human history. It served the purpose of preserving cultures and helped develop individual personalities. In every society, we find children learning the alphabet of their mother tongue and other languages. Similarly, if we look at all school going children, they will be learning multiplication tables and spelling words. As they move up thru middle and high schools, they will be memorizing a number of mathematical formulas, algorithms, chemical numbers, poetry and historical dates. At the high school level, the elements and their chemical numbers must be memorized by rote. Many times, teachers use rote learning without even realizing they do so.

In the early stages of civilization before writing on palm leaves started, the vast reserves of material were passed on orally from one generation to another. It has become an end itself. The information acquired by rote learning cannot be stripped from the learner, it is always with him, and travels along with him allowing him to tap into this knowledge at will. At an early age, they may not know the meaning of the scriptures they learnt by heart, but they will slowly absorb, digest and dissect the meaning of the scriptures they memorized. **Vyaas Houston** says, "Learning in his tradition is a yajna, an act of offering rather than possessing. Tapping into an unlimited memory is a constant and wondrous process of discovery that is without doubt unique to every individual."

Memorization will allow us to absorb the information that can be stored and retrieved at one's will. Memorization will help you to learn the elusive phrases at early age that defy one to learn after certain age; permit you to hammer every word for precise pronunciation; make you twist your tongue for proper clarity and crispness; and save so much time that could have been wasted by repeatedly looking for the same information, and infuse confidence in knowing that he can retrieve the information from the memory bank.

As we memorize and chant the slokas, they keep reverberating in our mind, instilling energy, minimizing the evil tendencies and accumulating the dharmic virtues. One would enjoy repeating the mantras for all the pleasure and happiness it brings. One can chant these mantras at any time of the day - before getting out from the bed, while cooking, eating, going to school, before the exam time, before going to bed and so on to avert any potential problems. They will help us stop worrying and focus on the essence of the mantras directed toward the specific deity. It becomes addictive and one will not be able to stop it.

According to **Brad Leithauser**, "The best argument for verse memorization may be that it provides us with knowledge of a qualitatively and physiologically different variety: you take the poem inside you, into your brain chemistry if not your blood, and you know it at a deeper, bodily level than if you simply read it off a screen."

Catherine Robson puts the point succinctly: "If we do not learn by heart, the heart does not feel the rhythms of poetry as echoes or variations of its own insistent beat."

Mahatma Gandhi says it is important to understand the meaning of mantra and the purpose of chanting a mantra. "There is a definite advantage in memorizing these scriptures. It will stay with us all the time even when our faculties may get impaired. It will prove to be a guiding light during moments of despair and distress. One cannot imagine of any other source more reliable than Gita during such disasters."

WHY CHILDREN?

Why did Sri Swamiji encourage children to learn Bhagavad Gita? Do they learn faster and better than adults? Do they absorb and digest better than adults? Do they retain more information than adults?

According to science, a brain contains about 100 billion brain cells called neurons. This number remains the same irrespective of the age and would not actually change very much at all from birth to death. Then the question is how do the children learn faster and remember better than adults. The main difference between children and adults is found in the number of connections among the neurons. As we grow, the connectivity to each of the neurons changes a lot. The number of connections change as we learn new things and have different experiences.

There is a common adage that children's brain can absorb and soak up information like a sponge. Is there any scientific evidence to prove it? Scientists reveal that there is a fundamental difference in the learning processes between children and adults known as *synaptogenesis* and synapse elimination or pruning, respectively.

Children have more neurons start establishing more and more connections with other neurons as they start learning. Every sound they hear, every sensation the experience, every movement they make, and every stimulation they are prodded to are all stored in the brain. These neural connections cause the brain to learn anything and everything as the brain is developing at a faster rate with very little effort. This learning process is known as synaptogenesis.

Among adults, the learning process is different. Brain starts to discriminate and try to specialize the areas that need to be stored. At this stage, brain collects lot of useful as well as useless information by spending more energy. Instead of overloading the energy, adults use their brain to eliminate the pathways/ neural connections to reduce the overload. An effort will be made as to what is useful and relevant based on special interest and start eliminating or pruning the information instead of storing everything that comes to the brain. This process is called synapse elimination or pruning.

Most of the experts who are concerned about children's brain and their education believe that children have the higher ability to connect their neurons with other neurons compared to adults. As a result, they can learn much more easily than adult can do. Thus, it is advised that it is better for the parent or teacher to expose their children to lots of different stimulations and experiences to allow more and more connections to be formed as often as possible. Some experts also proved that the foreign words are easier to remember in a childhood age than in adult age. Secondly, research also showed that joy, energy and innocence peak between the ages of six and nine years, before children start worrying about how they look, what their friends think and how well they do at school. The Galaxy Research poll of Australian parents found that children are bestowed with boundless energy and enthusiasm, have retained a sense of awe and wonder with the world and remain uninhibited in their behavior at this age. It is the best time for children to learn about many things such as foreign languages or any new material.

According to **Alison Gopnik**, children's "brains are more active and more flexible, with more connections per brain cell, than the brains of adult human beings, the researchers have discovered. By age three, the child's brain is actually twice as active as an adult's. It has some 15,000 synapses or connections per neuron, many more than in the adult brain." The more you stimulate their brain, the more connections to neurons are established. With more connections, they will think better, learn faster, and draw logical conclusions.

Harold Chugani of Children's Hospital of Michigan conducted research to find out the process of learning among children by using PET scans to examine the brain structures and concluded that the brains that were metabolizing the most glucose were the most active. The brain continues to consume glucose at this feverish pitch through age 10 and then slows down until age 16, when it levels off at adult values. He also observed that the child's brain burns much more glucose than an adult's brain because it must maintain trillions of connections between neurons, more than twice as many as are ultimately retained.

Researchers also reveal that "If we teach our children early enough, it will affect the organization or 'wiring,' of their brains." It will stay with them whatever they learn during their formative years even if they discontinue the process. Chugani says, "Once a child has learned an instrument, he or she can stop playing, then pick up the instrument 20 years later and do much better than an adult just starting out." **Martha Pierson**, a neurobiologist at Baylor College of Medicine, argues that "Children need a flood of information, a banquet, a feast." Early education, she adds, "shapes the basic architecture of the computer (brain). If you are exposed to enough things, you'll develop a processor that can handle the flood of data that life throws at you later."

Some people argue that children are better learners. It is believed that the kids are less afraid to take risks having less responsibilities and less vulnerability for mistakes. A child's environment is a big motivational factor in their learning. They are at school studying many different subjects all day, playing different sports, and taking part in different extra-curricular activities. This child environment contrasts with adults who are usually focused on one subject area and are less open to different learning opportunities in their lives.

It is believed that children are more creative, spontaneous and energetic than adults, making them better learners. Adults may be less inclined to be corrected and feel like they have learnt what they need to know in comparison to a learning toddler.

"The human brain is a storehouse of feelings, thought processes and experiences. It receives, stores, processes, generates, visualizes and sets in motion a chain of thoughts, which then gets converted into action. Though an abstract entity, the mind holds the key to superior intelligence and memory. The brain, which is the repository of all thoughts of the past and the present can be trained, honed and motivated to realised its full potential and become a window of the future. The mantras of the Vedas are the secret but powerful agents to improve the mind as the vibrations caused in the brain by the Vedic mantras provide the mind with the most conducive environment for growth."

SANSKRIT: ITS UNIQUE FEATURES

Sanskrit was considered as "Dev Bhasha", " Devavani "or the language of the Gods by ancient Indians. The word samskrit, meaning "refined," "complete", "perfect," "definitive," or "purified," is the antonym of prakriti, meaning "natural," or "vulgar." It is made up of the primordial sounds, and is developed systematically to include the natural progressions of sounds as captured by the human mind. Our ancient rishis were able to capture the natural sounds of panchabhutas such as wind blowing, raining, hissing, roaring, ocean waves, thunder, fire, silence, and birds chirping and translate them into oral language and finally into written language.

"Vedic Sanskrit literature developed first in an oral form, and was first set down in writing after centuries of oral transmission. The gap between the composition of and the written recording of the literature makes dating difficult, but most of what survives can be assigned either to the Vedic or Classical period. Although the art of oral transmission in a pre-literate society required exact memorization, scholars cannot confidently say how close what was finally recorded in the third century B.C. is to the original composition." (http://colfa.utsa.edu/drinka/pie/lang_sanskrit.htm)

71

Sanskrit is probably the oldest recorded language in the world. Sanskrit is the most important medium in lending the continuity to Indian civilization for centuries. Sanskrit is a highly adjustable language and has a huge vocabulary with which to render even the most abstract of philosophical, psychological, and scientific concepts. Sanskrit was the language used by ancient Indians in the wide variety of fields such as astronomy, medicine, mathematics, literature, chemistry, algebra, kavya, drama, politics, spiritual, religious scriptures and others. **Swami Vivekananda** says, *"This Sanskrit language is so intricate, the Sanskrit of the Vedas is so ancient, and the Sanskrit philology so perfect, that any amount of discussion can be carried on for ages in regard to the meaning of one word."*

There is also a story to indicate that Sanskrit was first introduced by Brahma to the Sages of the celestial abodes and it is still the language of the celestial abode, so it is also called the **Dev Vani.**

The phonology (the speech sound) and morphology (the science of word formation) of the Sanskrit language is unique and entirely different from all languages of the world. The main feature of Sanskrit is that it contains 16 vowels and 36 consonants. The sounds of these 52 alphabets are fixed and precise since the very beginning. They withstood the time and were never changed, altered, modified, or improved. From times immemorial, the words created by combining the alphabets of the Sanskrit language always had the same pronunciation. *"There was no 'sound shift,' no change in the vowel system, and no addition was ever made in the grammar of the Sanskrit in relation to the formation of the words. The reason is its absolute perfection by its own nature and formation, because it was the first language of the world."* **Swami Prakashananda Saraswati.**

Sanskrit is considered as a most wonderful language with clarity, accuracy, exactness and precision. Every letter and word has a vibrant sound and should be uttered without any deviation. It should be pronounced properly and meticulously. Even a slight alteration in their pronunciation can spell disaster. Meaning may change to catastrophic results. If these words are spoken properly with deep knowledge, the benefits would be immense and invaluable. Even if we utter these words properly without knowledge, they will create more vibrations since these words are nothing but Mantras. The sounds of its alphabets are such that uttering them even mentally causes resonant vibration within the Chakras of the human subtle body.

W.C.Taylor, an American Indologist was moved by the richness of Sanskrit language. "It is an astounding discovery that Hinduism possessed, in spite of the changes of realms and changes of time, a language of unrivalled richness and variety .... A philosophy, compared with which, in point of age, the lessons of Pythagoras are but of yesterday, and in point of daring speculation Plato's boldest efforts were tame and commonplace. A poetry more purely intellectual than any of those of which we had before any conception; and systems of science whose antiquity baffled all power of astronomical calculation. This literature, with all its colossal proportions, which can scarcely be described without the semblance of bombast and exaggeration claimed of course a place for itself - it stood alone, and it was able to stand alone."

Sanskrit is a marvelous, majestic, scientific and spiritual language. Its depth, fullness, splendor, simplicity and complexity at the same time is peerless. **A. L. Basham,** former professor of Asian Civilization in the Australian National University, Canberra, writes in his book The **Wonder That Was India**: *"One of ancient India's greatest achievements is her remarkable alphabet, commencing with the vowels and followed by the consonants, all classified very scientifically according to their mode of production, in sharp contrast to the haphazard and inadequate Roman alphabet, which has developed organically for three millennia. It was only on the discovery of Sanskrit by the West that a science of phonetics arose in Europe."*(P:390)

Basham goes on to say *"It will be seen that this alphabet is methodical and scientific, its elements classified first into vowels and consonants, and then, within each section, according to the manner in which the sound is formed. The gutturals are formed by the construction of the throat at the back of the tongue, the palatals by pressing the tongue flat against the palate, the retro-flexes by turning up the tip of the tongue to touch the hard* *palate, the dentals by touching the upper teeth with the tongue, and the labials by pursuing the lips."* (p: 509)

Many scholars have recognized that Sanskrit is the mother of many European languages. Similarly, all the Indian local languages came out of the womb of Sanskrit. It spread far and wide across the globe and touched almost all the languages. It is believed that nearly 97 percent of all languages have been either directly or indirectly influenced by Sanskrit. **Sri Aurobindo (1872-1950)** observed that, *"The Ancient and classical creations of the Sanskrit tongue both in quality and in body and abundance of excellence, in their potent originality and force and beauty, in their substance and art and structure, in grandeur and justice and charm of speech and in the height and width of the reach of their spirit stand very evidently in the front rank among the world's great literatures .... The language itself, as has been universally recognized by those competent to form a judgment, is one of the most magnificent, the most perfect and wonderfully sufficient literary instruments developed by the human mind, at once majestic and sweet and flexible, strong and clearly-formed and full and vibrant and subtle, and its quality and character would be of itself a sufficient evidence of the character and quality of the race whose mind it expressed and the culture of which it was the reflecting medium."*

Sanskrit is not only amenable to spiritual, philosophical and literary fields, it is equally adept to the computer language. Because of its extremely logical, comprehensive, conciseness and preciseness nature, it is more suitable to develop computer language. **Rick Briggs**, a NASA researcher, has written: **"In ancient India the intention to discover truth was so consuming, that in the process, they discovered perhaps the most perfect tool for fulfilling such a search that the world has ever known -- the Sanskrit language.** There is at least one language, Sanskrit, which for the duration of almost 1000 years was a living spoken language with a considerable literature of its own ... The discovery is of monumental significance. It is mind-boggling to consider that we have available to us a language which has been spoken for 4-7000 years that appears to be in every respect a perfect language designed for enlightened communication. But the most stunning aspect of the discovery is this: NASA the most advanced research center in the world for cutting edge technology has discovered that Sanskrit, the world's oldest spiritual language is the only unambiguous spoken language on the planet. Considering Sanskrit's status as a spiritual language, a further implication of this discovery is that the age-old dichotomy between religion and science is an entirely unjustified one."

There is a report by a NASA scientist that America is creating 6th and 7th generation super computers based on Samskrit language. Project deadline is 2025 for 6th generation and 2034 for 7th generation computer. After this there will be a revolution all over the world to learn Sanskrit. (Shanti Yadav)

St. James Independent Schools of London has for more than three decades made Sanskrit as an integral part of their syllabus – indeed a compulsory subject for junior pupils – citing the benefits of the language for children's development. The school has a mixture of Indian and English students, and is a Christian establishment; its interest in Sanskrit derives from the language's intrinsic merit as a 'perfected language' (as the term 'samskrita' of course denotes) rather than any religious agenda.

BENEFITS OF LEARNING SANSKRIT

Learning of Sanskrit improves brain functioning. Students start getting better marks in other subjects like Mathematics, Science etc., which some people find difficult. It enhances memory power. Our ancient rishis have analyzed the various chakras (energy centers) in the human body and their association with Sanskrit alphabets. Reading, reciting and chanting of the Sanskrit words will stimulate these points and raise their energy levels, whereby resistance against illnesses, relaxation to mind and reduction of stress are also achieved.

Sanskrit is the only language that uses all nerves of the tongue. By its pronunciation energy points in the body are activated that causes the blood circulation to improve. This, coupled with the enhanced brain functioning and higher energy levels, ensures better health. Blood Pressure, diabetes, cholesterol etc. are controlled. (American Hindu University).

Research has shown that the phonetics of this language has roots in various energy points and chakras of the body and reading, speaking or reciting Sanskrit stimulates these points and raises the energy levels, whereby resistance against illnesses, relaxation to mind and reduction of stress are achieved.

There are reports that Russians, Germans and Americans are actively doing research on our sacred books and are producing them back to the world in their name. Seventeen countries around the world have a University or two to study Sanskrit to gain technological advantages.

T. R. Seshadri in his book '**The Curative Powers OF the Holy Gita**' reveals that most of the modern-day diseases are psychosomatic – caused by mind. Emotional disturbances like hatred, anger and fear destroy not only our peace of mind but our health as well. They are often caused by the over-or-under secretion of the endocrine glands which secrete chemical hormones into the blood stream, which affects body functions like growth, digestion and energy levels, etc.

The author identified about 30 shlokas which have curative powers. It also mentions the method in which the shlokas have to be recited. To quote from the book "…advocate reciting/chanting the specific Mantras three times, once in the morning and once in the evening, and towards the close of Yogic practice…." The shlokas are to be chanted in Sanskrit.

For example, that by chanting 2:56 sloka in Bhagavad Gita, one may get relief from blood pressure (hypertension, hypotension), depression, impotency, neurosis, sexual disorders, stress, syphilis and venereal infections. Sloka 2:61 would have impact on AIDS, alcohol and drug addiction, blood pressure, brain disorders, depression, mental disorders, mind control, neurosis, psychic and psychosomatic illness, sexual disorders, stress, stroke and tension. Similarly, by chanting sloka 9:18, one may get some help during child birth, conception, delivery, gynecological disorders, menstrual problems and pregnancy.

Rutger Kortenhorst, a Sanskrit teacher in John Scottus School in Dublin, Ireland, invited the parents of the children who enrolled in Sanskrit class and spoke to them about the value of teaching Sanskrit based on his own experience with the language. He is confident that the children will be fortunate to have taken this extraordinary language as a part of their curriculum. He said, "Sanskrit can help your child to express universal, harmonious and simple truths better. As a result, you will really have done your duty as a parent and the world will reap the benefits in a more humane, harmonious and united society. Sanskrit can do this as it is the only language that is based in knowledge all the way. Nothing is left to chance."

THE POWER OF MANTRAS

Every word, a combination of words, a sentence, or a verse when uttered in a particular manner will become a powerful mantra. Mantra means "revealed sound." "Man" means mind and "trai" means liberate. Mantra also means to liberate the mind. They are revealed to the ancient rishis and other enlightened people when they are in deep meditation. They are uttered for spiritual as well as material purposes. The aim of chanting the mantras is to achieve the purushardas in life such as Dharma (religious righteousness and duty), Artha (economic needs and fulfilment desires), Kama (procreative needs and sensual satisfaction) and Moksha (salvation from birth and rebirth). These mantras possess magical or divine power enabling the utterer to achieve the potential desires.

Heinrich Zimmer defined mantra as "A word or formula .... Which represents a mental presence or energy; by it something is produced, crystalized, in the mind. The term mantra Shakti is employed to denote this magic power possessed by words when they are brought together in a formula." Sanskrit mantra, when chanted with proper sound vibrations and proper utterance, will have specific effect on the mind and body.

The **Power of Mantras** is amply described by **Judith Tyberb**. She observed that, "Its every alphabet is a Mantra, a sound or phrase of spiritual significance and power... The language is constructed inharmonious relation with the very truths of existence, hence its power of illumination ... that every word or sound (shabda) has a power (Shakti). This intrinsic power can always convey the sense that is inseparably related to the sound ... In the sacred Sanskrit scriptures, this power was not only intuitively expressed but consciously wielded. And the power was not only of the human mind but of the Spirit." As per the tradition, initiation into mantra is given by the guru, one's mother or revelation. A mantra can never be bought or sold. When a guru gives a mantra, it is never based on a monetary transaction. A mantra obtained in such a way will never have any power.

Mantra is a condensed form of spiritual energy of the divinity. **Pandit Rajmani Tigunait** says, "The yogic scriptures often compare mantra to a boat or a bridge that an aspirant can take to cross the mire of delusion created by the external world and reach the center of consciousness within. Mystics and yogis say that mantra is an eternal friend who accompanies the meditator even after death, lighting the way in the realm where the light of the sun and the moon cannot penetrate. According to the more esoteric literature of the yoga tradition, mantra is the essence of guru Shakti, the power of the spiritual master. In other words, the mantra is itself the guru. Mantra, God, guru, and one's highest self are identical."

Sanskrit mantras are recited by millions of Hindus – they could be just one letter mantra or a combination of any number of letters. All temple functions are conducted entirely in Sanskrit starting from waking up the Deity until the night where the Gods are retired for the day. Homas are conducted on a regular basis. Agnihotras are conducted across the globe by chanting appropriate Sanskrit mantras. Similarly, mantras are chanted during all sixteen Samskaras starting with the birth of a child to the last stage of life.

Even chanting of one word **"OM"** creates sound of cosmic creation that pervades the universe. Chanting of a given mantra "activates the stomach, spinal cord, throat, nasal and bran regions. It activates prana that will move from the base all the way up to the brain, thereby channelizing energy and activating the spinal cord and brain. Its continuous chanting will shift the attention and echo the harmonic relationship of every vital organ, our heartbeat, breathing, brain wave pulsing, neuron cells, metabolic, enzymatic and hormonal rhythms, and will bust stress, addictions and improve behavior. It acts as brain stabilizer, and by practicing it, one can enter into one's own natural state." **(Vijay Hashia)**

BENEFITS OF CHANTING OM/SLOKAS

⅄ Gives strength & stability to the mind to handle conflicts;

⅄ Fills the mind with light and brings in a ray of hope;

⅄ Helps in dealing with unexpressed emotions by opening the channels of communication;

⅄ Helps in stress management by bringing about creative will, abundant wisdom and right action;

⅄ Eliminates the root cause of Stress, Anxiety and Depression;

⅄ Stimulates both the used and unused cells of the brain and increase your memory;

⅄ Enhances the capabilities of the mind to focus, retain & recollect information;

⅄ Enhances Intelligence and improves memory power;

⅄ Helps cultivate superior thoughts;

⅄ Rejuvenates the brain and helps shed unnecessary stress and mental fatigue;

⅄ Reduces stress by maintaining blood pressure;

⅄ Immunity of the body gets stronger;

⅄ Improves the production of endorphins and makes you feel relaxed;

⅄ Decreases adrenaline levels and reduces stress by providing more oxygen to the body;

⅄ Slows down heartbeat and dilates the blood vessels to provide more oxygen to the body;

⅄ Creates vibrations in the body which increase the effectiveness of the spinal cord;

⅄ Creates vibrations in the throat and benefits the thyroid glands;

⅄ Revitalizes the mind by improving memory, concentration and grasping power;

⅄ Provides relief from stress-induced headaches.

WHY BHAGAVAD GITA?

Of all the thousands of scriptures, why did **Sadhguru Sri Ganapathy Sachchidananda Swamiji** select Bhagavad Gita to be chanted by children? It reflects one of the forms of the perennial philosophical systems that embodies those universal truths that are eternal with no physical boundaries and no time limitations. Sri Swamiji with His divine vision, felt that the Bhagavad Gita would equip the children and youth to cope with the challenges they face in life; trials and tribulations they encounter daily; problems they meet in the modern world; frustrations they may bump into in the competitive world of work; and adjustments they have to make in the family life. Bhagavad Gita would enable them to utilize the ancient wisdom that might help them to differentiate between the dharmic and adharmic values; exercise their freedom to make wise decisions; and cope with the stress they might face in their hectic, hurried and materialistic world. Bhagavad Gita would teach the high morals that promote peace and harmony. Bala Gangadhar Tilak observed, *"The most practical teaching of the Gita, and one for which it is of abiding interest and value to the men of the world with whom life is a series of struggles, is not to give way to any morbid sentimentality when duty demands sternness and the boldness to face terrible things ... It is my firm conviction that it is of utmost importance that every man, woman and child of India understands the message of the Gita."*

Sri Swamiji wanted to impress upon the children the timeless and universal Gita can offer them for the rest of their life by learning the basic principles of life that will shape, guide and mold their personalities. One would learn about discharging one's own dharma, discharging responsibilities without attachment to the fruits of the action, establishing a balance between material and spiritual fields, realizing the importance of a Sadguru in one's own life, learning the art of maintaining Stithipragna (controlling the mind), the virtues of freedom and independence, acquiring the courage and strength in face of distraught and hopelessness, and be adept at handling the confusion and troubles that beset the modern world.

The relevance and importance of Bhagavad Gita is emphasized by
Ananda K Coomaraswamy, "....We must, however, specially mention
the Bhagavad Gita as probably the most important single work ever
produced in India; this book of eighteen chapters is not, as it has been
sometimes called, a "sectarian " work, but one universally studied
and often repeated daily from memory by millions of Indians of all
persuasions; it may be described as a compendium of the whole Vedic
doctrine to be found in the earlier Vedas, Brahmanas, and Upanishads,
and being therefore the basis of all the later developments, it can be
regarded at the focus of all Indian religion."

DHARMA REIGNS

Bhagavad Gita starts with the word Dharma which is defined as duty,
responsibility, principle, and to hold together. When Sanjaya started
narrating the story, he used the word dharma to make Dhritarashtra
reflect on his responsibility in this Kurukshetra where a number of
religious activities have been conducted to preserve the customs and
traditions. When Arjuna was despondent of the consequences of the
war that may result in the death of many people, he seeks the advice
of Lord Krishna who recognized Arjuna's weakness of heart and
feebleness. The Lord tells Arjuna that it is his responsibility to fight by
saying, "And even considering your personal dharma as well, it is not
right for you to hesitate. There is nothing better for a warrior than a
fight based on dharma." (2.31). If you fail to execute your dharma for
personal reasons, you shall incur sin. Those who perform their duty
are very close to the Lord. "But those who fully honor this immortal
nectar of dharma as it has been spoken [by Me], having faith, taking
Me as supreme—those devotees are exceedingly dear to Me." (12.20)

In the first chapter it is clearly stated that there is a conflict of duties
within all of us not knowing which course of action to take. Arjuna
was in confusion and agony and not in a position to make a righteous
decision. Lord Krishna talks about the eternal nature of soul, and says
that one is not responsible for the consequences of discharging his
dharma. "Even a very small amount of this dharma saves one from
great danger, for there is no loss in such an endeavor, and it knows

no diminution." (Bg. 2.40). One has to follow his dharma in order to preserve and protect the very nature of existence.

IMPORTANCE OF SADGURU

Sadguru Tattva permeates the entire cosmos as per Hindu scriptures. Guru is essential for spiritual growth and his advice, guidance and knowledge is sought by the disciples for many millennia. Guru is the one who can remove the ignorance by lighting the lamp of knowledge in the heart of the disciple. **Sadhguru Sri Ganapathy Sachchidananda Swamiji** says, "By mere touch the Guru transforms "Manava" (man) into "Madhava" (God). By his mere look "nara" (human) becomes "Narayana" (God) and "Jeeva (soul) realizes its identity with "Ishwara" (God). The land trodden by the Guru becomes a place of pilgrimage. By mere sight he transforms mud into delicious food and stone into glittering gold ... There is nothing in this world that cannot be obtained by Guru's grace." Guru is indeed a friend in need, especially when our mind is fogged by ignorance, confused by turmoil, and disoriented with indecision. Guru is the only person who can come to the rescue.

When Arjuna approached Lord Krishna by saying, "My heart is overpowered by the taint of pity, my mind is confused as to duty. I ask Thee: tell me decisively **what is good for me**. I am Thy disciple. Instruct me who has taken refuge in Thee." (2:7). Knowing fully well about the nature of Guru who knows about both illusion and truth, and whose mission is to help his devotees to overcome the ignorance and darkness by imparting the knowledge and truth, Lord Krishna tells Arjuna the method to find a Guru and surrender. Sri Krishna Himself tells that, "Just try to learn the truth by approaching a spiritual master. Inquire from him submissively and render service unto him. The self-realized soul can impart knowledge unto you because he has seen the truth."(4:34).

If we are very serious about understanding the science of God is a guru required. We should not try to keep a guru as a matter of fashion. One who has accepted a guru speaks intelligently. He never speaks nonsense. That is the sign of having accepted a bona fide guru. We should certainly offer all respect to the spiritual master, but we should also remember how to carry out his orders.

Following Lord Krishna's message to Arjuna to carry out his dharma in discharging his duties, Arjuna's ignorance due to delusion, passion, attachments and perception of consequences was removed. He realized that it was his foolishness and childishness to think that he would be responsible for the death of his kith and kin, not knowing that everybody who is born is destined to die. Lord Krishna's Vishwarupa convinced him of the inevitability. With that realization, Arjuna says, *"My delusion is destroyed. I have regained my memory through Your grace, O Achyuta. I am firm. I am free from doubt. I shall act according to your word."* (18:73).

GURU SISHYA SAMPRADAYA.

Since ancient times, the Guru-Sishya relationship existed in Bharat where mentoring of a student by a spiritual teacher is undertaken. Selfless transmission of information by a genuine, dedicated and committed teacher to a student who is expected to receive the knowledge with committed, faith, devotion, respect and sincerity. The tradition of dialogue, discussion, debate, questioning, dissecting and deciphering is the hallmark of exchange of opinion. No WORD is taken for granted. Tradition of un-questioning the scriptures is unheard of this tradition. It is this kind of questioning that encouraged the freedom that is essential for the intellectual growth and survival of humanity. Just imagine how much valuable, eternal, immortal and everlasting message was rendered by Lord Krishna to Arjuna who asked a simple question about his confusion and dilemma about waging a war that might kill all his relatives and gurus?

REMOVING CONFUSION AND INDECISION.

In the Gita, Lord Krishna delivers the message in order to remove the confusion and sorrow that engulfed Arjuna, who asks the question: "With a heart contaminated by the taint of helplessness, with a mind confounded as to my duty, I ask you to tell me what is assuredly good for me. I am your disciple. Instruct me who have thrown myself on your indulgence."

Lord Krishna says: "Undoubtedly, O Arjuna, the mind is restless and difficult to restrain, but it is subdued by any constant vigorous spiritual practice -- such as meditation -- with perseverance, and by detachment" (6.35). Lord Krishna tells Arjuna to gain clarity on any given situation, ponder over it and develop clear, calm and collective mind to do your duty with no attachment.

BALANCING

Samatvaṁ yoga ucyate (Gita 2.48): Equilibrium, evenness, harmony, adjustment, adaptability, unity, the blending of the subject and the object in harmony is Yoga. In everything that we do, we must be able to balance between various facets of life. Balance must be maintained in our daily life with regard to work, family, leisure, friends, opportunities, children and other pursuits. Decisions must be made based on dharmic values as priority without expectation of rewards or fruits. Let us remember the words of Lord Krishna:

"Fixed in yoga, do thy work, O Winner of wealth (Arjuna), abandoning attachment, with an even mind in success and failure, for evenness of mind is called yoga"(2:48).

NISKAMA KARMA

Bhagavad Gita is the source of for one's ethics with regard to the discharge of his duty without expectation to the fruits of action. Performing duty without motivation, thinking, deliberating and calculating about its outcomes tends to purify one's mind and see the value of desire less action. These concepts are vividly described in the following verses:

To action alone hast thou a right and never at all to its fruits; let not the fruits of action be thy motive; neither let there be in thee any attachment to inaction. (2:47).

The Gita advocates action, relentless action regardless of the rewards. It preaches the mantra of karma yoga and defines it as dexterity in action; 'yagahe karmasu kaushalam' gives new dignity to work.

STITHIPRAGNA

In life, many decisions are made with vagaries of mind. Mind is always fickle, not stable. Decisions made without an agitated state of mind yields better results. Lord Krishna says that one should be able to make decisions effortlessly, naturally and calmly based on the pros and cons of the situation with no attachments. One has to do sadhana to reach that state known as Stithipragna. It is the stage where one will be able effective control on Mind and the Indiriyas (sense organs). Just like a driver of Charioteer can control the horses, mind should be able to control all the sense organs. To achieve this stage, one has to be trained by a living guru and practice mind control under his guidance. Stithipragna is always alert, wakeful, efficient, attentive and careful. Whatever we do in this state is done with full control of the mind and control of all the Indiriyas (senses) based on wisdom; and not based on whims and fancies. Decisions must be made without attachment, fear and anger. A steady mind is a prerequisite for making rational decisions.

THE VALUE OF FREEDOM

Arjuna was distraught about the potential demise of his kith and kin, his Gurus and the dynasty itself and expressed his desire not to fight. Lord Krishna, realizing the despondence of Arjuna, delivers the eternal message of individual dharma to uphold harmony in the society. Lord Krishna talks about the Supersoul, dharma of each person, the inherent nature of creation, the karma theory, importance of devotion and knowledge, and how to remain balanced in the society faced with turmoil and turbulence. He even shows his Vishwarupa to convince the inevitable nature of the existence itself. Arjuna is a Kshatriya and his natural duty is to fight for justice. Through Viveka (discrimination), one should surrender to the Lord. Whoever engages himself under the direction of the Supreme Lord, he becomes glorious. One should not think of himself as independent from the Lord, since he abides in very living creature. Lord Krishna tells Arjuna in sloka 18:62 that he should surrender to Him completely. By doing so, one will attain transcendental peace and an eternal abode.

Finally, the Lord says, "Thus I have explained to you, knowledge still more confidential. Deliberate on this fully, and **then do what you wish to do.**" The hall mark of Bhagavad Gita and Hinduism is the concept of freedom. It is only with unflinching freedom, one can excel in his talents and skills and contribute to the welfare and prosperity of the society. Any imposition by or interference from external authority would not be conducive to a healthy society. That is the reason, Lord tells Arjuna that he should deliberate on His message with all his intelligence and decide by himself. No external pressure was imposed on Arjuna and Lord Krishna did not ask him to what wanted to him to do. Lord gave him full freedom to choose what he wanted to do.

MUCH MORE TO LEARN

The sessions conducted at IIM Indore can serve as guiding principles that can be introduced at different levels of the educational system subject to the level of knowledge. Ten modules developed by Swami Samarpananda of Ramakrishna Mission are appropriate for proper discussion to be included in the curriculum: (1) Harnessing mental energy (2) Values in leadership and administration (3) Philosophy of life and its importance (4) Acquiring excellence (5) Managing stress, (6) Duty (7) Karma Yoga; (8) Dynamics of work (9). Self-Upliftment (10). The goal supreme and looking back.

Finally, the Lord says, *"He is dearest to me who imparts this knowledge to earnest spiritual students"*. Study of the Gita is a great yajna or sacrifice because the student offers his ignorance to be burnt up in the fire of knowledge. Even those who listen to the Gita with faith in the Lord reach the land of the meritorious, the world of peace and joy, for the reaction of their past misdeeds will not act upon them.

GREATNESS OF BHAGAVAD GITA

The Gita concludes with Sanjaya's assessment of the message of Lord Krishna to Dhritarashtra. Sanjaya says that his hair stood up as he listened to the dialogue between Vasudeva and Arjuna through the grace of Sage Vyasa who blessed him the vision of Cosmic form of Lord Krishna. He concludes with the statement: "Wherever is Krishna, the Lord of Yoga, wherever is Partha, the wielder of the bow, there prevails prosperity, victory, glory and righteousness; that is my conviction." (18:78). This verse is called ekashloki Gita and is Sanjaya's answer to Dhritarashtra's question about the war. Sanjaya says indirectly that there is no doubt that the Pandavas will win the war.

The Mahabharata says "*sarva shaastramayii giitaa*" meaning that the Gita comprises all the scriptures. Sage Vyasa has said that the Gita alone should be sung, heard and assimilated and there is no use of any other scripture when one has the Gita because it has originated from the lips of the Lord Himself in the following words. **Gita Mahatyam** or the Glory of Gita says that Gita contains the essence of all the four Vedas and yet its style is so simple that after a little study, anyone can easily follow the structure of the words. As a reader grows in maturity, the same words reveal more and more facets of thought and hence the Gita remains eternally new. The Lord Himself says in the **Varaha Purana** that, "Where the Gita is read, forthwith comes help. Where the Gita is discussed, recited, taught, or heard, there, O Earth, beyond a doubt, do I Myself unfailingly reside."

The Bhagavad Gita has lessons for the young and old of any caste, creed and religion and teaches the technique of perfect living. It is for all ages; and it is universal. Where the Bhagavad Gita book is kept and the study is conducted, there all the sacred places, the sacred rivers and all holiness are present. It is also said, where the Gita is read, there help comes quickly. It became a source of inspiration to **Mahatma Gandhi** to lead the Independence movement and became a good friend during his imprisonment. "When doubts haunt me, when disappointments stare me in the face, and I see not one ray of hope on the horizon, I turn to Bhagavad-Gita and find a verse to comfort me; and I immediately begin to smile in the midst of overwhelming sorrow. Those who meditate on the Gita will derive fresh joy and new meanings from it every day".

HISTORY WAS MADE

Sadhguru Sri Ganapathy Sachchidananda Swami has made a history by inspiring, encouraging, guiding and blessing 43 children of ages 6 thru 14 to memorize all 700 verses of Bhagavad Gita and chant in His presence. On July 17, 2016, these children chanted Bhagavad Gita without looking at the book sitting more than four hours creating vibrations and spreading the energy waves across the space. These children's lives have changed forever as these verses have permeated their body, mind and soul. It is also time remember that Lord resides in each of these verses to mean that Lord Krishna will be there with them and in them. By memorizing, they have absorbed the eternal message, improved their intelligence and expanded their memory bank. The power of the Sanskrit and vibrations created by chanting the mantras (verses), would live with them forever. Bhagavad Gita will help them to face numerous roadblocks with little difficulty. The eternal universal message will guide them throughout their lives. Bhagavad Gita equipped them with a lifelong friend who travels with them wherever they go. It will never fail them. Many scholars, researchers, philosophers, politicians reaped benefits in their daily pursuits as well as their academic pursuits. By commanding the children to learn Bhagavad Gita, Sri Swamiji instilled curiosity in them, helped them memorize all its 700 verses, implanted courage in them, infused confidence, helped expand their memory power, and shaped their personalities for life. With Sri Swamiji's blessings, these kids will be role models for all other children and their parents to pursue their talent and become ambassadors to the richness of Sanatana dharma.

GURU TATTVA
QUINTESSENCE OF KNOWLEDGE AND CULTURE.

WHO IS GURU?

From times immemorial, a Guru or a spiritual teacher has been given the highest place of honor in India and elsewhere. It is very difficult to define, describe, elaborate, and understand the concept of Guru. It becomes even more difficult to understand when we examine different types of Gurus. One should learn at the outset that there are different kinds of Gurus. On one end of the spectrum any teacher is a guru, whereas on the other end we will find incarnations of God in a human form with super natural powers. Most people, however, forget that this has been said from the spiritual angle, and never from the physical point of view. Guru Tattvam is even far more difficult to define. It is beyond description, perception, and understanding. However, our attempts to define Guru Tattvam should recognize the fact that it is limited to our perceptions, knowledge, time, and language. Sri Ganapathy Sachchidananda Swamiji emphasizes this point by saying that "Guru Tattvam is not like an object which can be purchased or possessed, nor it is found or discovered as it has not been lost, stolen or hidden in a safe. It is everywhere provided you know the secret to find it."

The most well-known Sanskrit verse on the concept of Guru is:

> *Gurur Brahma Gurur Vishnuh Gurur Devo Mahesvarah;*
> *Guru Sakshat Param Brahma Tasmai Sri Gurave Namah.*

This is a very powerful and profound statement. It says that the Guru is the Creator Brahma, the Protector Vishnu and the Destroyer or Rejuvenator Siva. Furthermore, in reality he is **Transcendental Absolute** (*Param Brahma*) himself. To that Guru we prostrate. Thus, Guru is not just one of the Trinity, not even just all three of them. He is all three manifestations and something beyond. Each one of them has just a specified function in the milieu of the Hindu mythology,

Vedanta as well as orthodoxy. Any time you pray to one of them about your problems - they seem to help you only to a certain extent. But each one of them says that there is a Supreme Absolute beyond them and it is He, She or It, which prescribes what should be and what should not be; they only carry out the Supreme Will! The fact that the Guru is equated with *Param Brahma* places him beyond the Trinity.

A Guru is a god on earth. He descended to earth on his volition only to guide the humanity, uplift them from their doldrums, remove their ignorance and show the path to emancipation or self-realization. To him, pleasure and pain, happiness and sorrow, heat and cold, gold and stone, rich and poor, men and women are the same. A guru lives in bliss, cosmic consciousness. He is God Himself. He is one with God. They serve as ambassadors of God on earth.

Sadhguru Sri Ganapathi Sachchidananda Swamiji says, "Guru means heavy, who cannot be bought by money, lust, position, publicity, or power. To keep the papers in proper place we use a paperweight. Similarly, we need Guru to keep ourselves at a proper place as a human being and when the winds of Kama, krodha, Lobha, Moha and Matsarya try to deviate us from our journey of salvation, Guru keeps us under control."

Swami Muktananda describes an ideal guru: "A true guru breaks your old habits of fault finding, of seeing sin, of hating yourself. He roots out the negative seeds that you have sown as well as your feelings of guilt …. You will never hear him criticize you. Instead, when you are in his company, you will experience your divinity. You will never be found guilty in the guru's eyes. You will find in them only praise of your hidden inner God."

Guru Gita defines the Guru in this sloka:

"Gu" means ignorance, "Ru" means dispeller, thus Guru is the Supreme Light

Guru is the great Self in the heart of all beings, Guru is the wisdom light

Guru is the absolute knowledge, sacred secret, O Shakti

He is effulgent, inspiring Truth, one who bestows final Mukti.

Guru Stotram talks about Guru who removes the ignorance:

Ajnaana-Timiraandhasya / Jnanaanjana-Shalaakaya

Chaksur-Unmilitam Yena / Tasmai Shri-Gurave Namah

Salutations to that Guru who applies the collyrium of knowledge with a sharp needle to open the eyes blinded due to ignorance (lack of spiritual knowledge).

Kularnava Tantra says, "Shiva is all-pervasive, subtle, beyond the mind, without attributes, imperishable, eternal and infinite. How can such a one be worshipped? That is why, out of compassion for His creatures, He takes the form of the Guru and, when worshipped with devotion, grants liberation and fulfilment …. The Guru is supreme Shiva clothed in flesh, walks on the earth, concealed and bestowing grace."

Guru Tantra states: "If Guru be pleased, Siva Himself is pleased; if Guru is displeased, the three-eyed Deva is displeased; if Guru be pleased, the all-good Devi is pleased; and if Guru be displeased, Tripurasundari becomes displeased. Hence, O Maheswari! For the crossing of the sea of Samsara, Guru is the only master, protector and destroyer, and he also is the grantor of liberation."

Rudrayamala says: 'Guru alone can in a single moment destroy the mass of his sins, for in the Tantra Shastra none but Guru has any competence. One should therefore take as one's Guru a very good man."

Yogini Tantra says: "The place where Guru resides is Kailasa. The house in which Guru lives is Chintamani house. The trees in the Guru's house are Kalpa trees. The creepers are Kalpa creepers. The water even in ditches is Ganga. In short, O Devi, everything in that sacred place is sacred. The female servants in the Guru's house are Bhairavis, and the male servants are Bhairavas. In this manner, it is that an earnest Sadhaka should think of his Guru. O Maheswari, He who has gone around his Guru but once has circled the whole earth with its seven islands."

Kesavadas observed, "Guru is Master. He is the dispeller of the darkness of ignorance. He is a realized soul. He is simple, humble, serene, and still unique. He is ever united with God. Ego has no place in him. Arrogance has disappeared from him. Lust, rage, greed, infatuation, arrogance and jealousy - the six enemies of man - are totally converted into love, compassion, benevolence, auspiciousness, selfless action and forgiveness in him."

QUALIFICATIONS OF A GURU

Who is an ideal guru? What are his characteristics? What are his qualifications? How do you recognize him? Many scriptures define Guru and identify the qualifications. Multitude of Gurus, Sadgurus and Paramagurus have also described them even more realistically and with more passion and direct experience of the bliss they received from their respective gurus.

Saradatilaka Tantra defines the qualification of the guru as follows: "The Guru must know the essence of all *Agamas* and the principles and meaning of all *Shastras,* he must be one whose words come out true, who has a quiet mind, who has profoundly studied the Vedas and its meaning, who follows the path of yoga and whose bearing is beneficent as that of a deity ... A body which is pure both on the mother's and father's side; purity of thought; mastery over the senses; knowledge of the substance of all Tantras; knowledge of the purpose of all *Shastras*; a doer of good to all others; devoted to *Japa, Puja,* and so forth; truthfulness of speech acquired by Tapas; calmness; proficiency in Vedas and the Vedangas; eagerness to know the truths of the Yoga path, and who feels the presence of Devathas in the heart, and so forth."

Ramadas described the Guru: "He alone can be called a Guru who has no desires left in him, and whose determination is as steady as a mountain. He must have extreme passion, and his actions should be beyond censure. With him, spiritual discussion must be a constant pastime. He uplifts the world and becomes an exemplar for the various kinds of Bhakti. Knowledge, dispassionateness, devotion, rightful conduct, Sadhana, spiritual discussion, meditation, morality, justice, and the observation of Dharma constitute the characteristics of a Guru."

Swami Sivananda Saraswati described the characteristics of a real guru: "He has full knowledge of the self and Vedas. He can remove the doubts of aspirants. He has equal vision and balanced mind. He is free from egoism, anger, lust, greed and pride. In his presence one gets Shanti and elevation of mind."

Adi Sankara *said in Vivekacudamani:*

Durlabham Trayamevaitat, Devanugraha Hetukam;

Manusyatvam Mumuksutvam, Mahapurusa Samsrayah

"Three things are difficult to obtain and, if obtained, they are to be treated as the result of the Grace of the Divine; these are: human birth, desire for spiritual emancipation, and guidance and help from a *Mahapurusa*, great man."

"This splendor of the empire of spiritual freedom I have achieved through the blessings of Thy grace; salutations to Thee, O glorious high souled teacher; I salute Thee again and again. (Verse 517).

Adi Sankara also defines Guru in the *Sarva Vedanta Siddhanta Sangraha* as follows:

Srotriyo Brahmanishto yah Prazntah Sama-Darsanah /
Nirmamo Nirahamkaro Nirdvandvo Nishparigrahah //
Anapekshah Sucir-dakshaH karuNAmRta-sAgaraH /
evam lakshaNa-sampannaH sa gurur-brahma-vit-tamaH //

He must be an adept in all the Vedas. He must be a realized Soul who is always rooted in the Absolute Brahman. Calm and serene, Equanimeous to the core, free from Ego, and from the evil of 'mine' and 'thine', he is devoid of all delusions of duality like happiness and misery, pleasure and pain, like and dislike, honor and dishonor, cold and heat, friend and foe and even cause and effect. He has no desire for possessions; he has no wants, is always pure in heart and mind and is at the top of his efficiency. He is an ocean of compassion and grace.

These are the qualities that make up the model guru. Adi Sankara himself was a Guru of such standards. Everyone who has come in the disciple's lineage from him has lived up to that standard, each in his own unique way. The biographies of each of the Sankaracharya's who have held the position of the pontiffs of the various Sankara Mutts, even up to the present time, are full of anecdotes which bear testimony to these characteristics of an ideal Guru.

IIn the *Vivekacudamani* (verse 33), **Sankaracharya** gives the qualifications of a true guru:

"Who is well versed in the Vedas, sinless, unsmitten by desire, and a knower of Brahman par excellence, who has achieved tranquility in Brahman, who is calm, like the fire that has consumed its fuel, who is a boundless reservoir of mercy that knows no motive, and a friend of all good people who prostrate themselves before him?" A true guru must know the spirit of the scriptures. He must be completely free from selfish desires; the only selfish desire is to serve and do good to others. He must be tranquil in order to bring tranquility among others.

1 Many Upanishads, especially Manduka and Brihadaranyaka Upanishads, and other scriptures have praised the following four qualifications of a true Guru: The Guru should be Stotriyas, i.e., well versed in scriptures. If he is to teach religion, he must have a proper grasp of the subject as expounded in genuine ancient texts and books. This does not mean mere book knowledge, but the Guru must have imbibed the Truths of the scriptures in his daily life. His actions, speech, and thoughts must express these truths in his day-to-day behavior. Without uttering a single word, he should convey the spirituals truths all around him. The Guru must be able to handle all types of minds, which may come to him, which is why he must keep up the scriptural tradition and continue his study and Sadhana throughout his life.

2 The second qualification of a Guru is more important than the first, and that is: The Guru must be a Brahma-Jnani. He must be a realized soul, which means he must be established in Brahman, ever living in God. If he is ignorant how can he guide the aspirants beyond ignorance! How can a blind man lead another blind to the goal? Chances are both would fall

in a ditch. This separates the Vedanta Guru from teachers of secular sciences where instructor has no particular need of virtue or good character. The subject taught here is pure, blissful God and hence the Guru must be pure and god-drenched. Anyone and everyone can't be a Guru. A huge load of solid timber floats on the water and can carry men and animals across the bank, even in rising waters. But a piece of worthless ordinary wood sinks as soon as one steps on it and drowns the person. Therefore, in every age God incarnates Himself as the Guru, to teach humanity. Sachchidananda alone is the Guru.

3 The third qualification of a Guru is that he should be 'Akaamahata', not smitten by desires selfishness. His character must be spotless and clean. He should have such virtues as compassion, love, generosity, and altruism. He sees divinity all around and can understand its variable manifestation in his various disciples. Therefore, he does not hate or look down upon any Sadhaka for he knows that in many aspirants' divinity is covered with dirt of ignorance. In every case, he guides the disciples to the same goal of Self Realization.

A Guru considers the nature of the people before making them his disciples. All men look alike but have different nature. Some have an excess of Sattva, others excess of Rajas, and still others an excess of Tamas. Accordingly, Guru gives differing instructions for spiritual aspirants. Therefore, faith in Guru's words and instructions is the most vital part in the progress on the spiritual path; howsoever, odd or contradictory his instructions may appear!

4 The fourth qualification is linked with the third. The Guru should be Avrijina, stainless and pure. He should be simple and guileless. He should have to totally overcome lust for flesh and gold. We see this in the holy lives of all the saints.

The Guru should be **truthful**. Under no condition should he deviate from **righteous path**. This **purity** comes through constant discrimination between real and unreal and giving up the unreal. Thus, the Guru should be well established in the highest Truth that God alone is Real and rest all is transitory. Therefore, the Guru renounces all worldly pleasures and carvings of the sense. Privilege and prestige, name and fame should not affect the character of the Guru in the least. He should be easily accessible and approachable to his all the minor and major disciples.

Without Guru one can also proceed on the royal path of self-realization. But then the journey would be full of obstacles and pitfalls. It would take long time to reach the destination. This Sadhana is like trying to cross the ocean in a small boat. Guru is like a huge steamer to which one ties one's boat and relaxes. That huge steamer is sure to take the disciple to other shore. The dangers are minimized and the delays are cut down.

Muktananda: He should be learned; he should have studied many scriptures and spiritual philosophies, and he should know them perfectly. The knowledge of the ancient scriptural authors was unsurpassed... Siva told Brahma, "He who indulges in mere reasoning, who entangles his disciples in a net of gossip, complicated words, and arguments, can never be a true Guru." A genuine Guru has full knowledge of the Truth embodied in the Upanishads and other great scriptures, and his teachings are same as the teachings of the ancient sages.

But, it is not enough to know the scriptures. He must also be **well versed in mundane arts and skills**. He must be knowledgeable about every area of life. It is all right if an ear specialist knows only about the ear or if a heart specialist is an expert only on the subject related to heart. But a Guru cannot be specialist in just one area. If a Guru is to guide seekers who are living in this world, he must be familiar with all their joys and all their problems.

A Guru must have had the **direct experience of God**. A true Guru has seen God just as one sees any object in the outer world. By meditating on the supreme truth, he has experienced the Truth within himself and has merged his individuality into it.

Sant Namdev describes the qualities of a True Guru as thus: "You can know a saint by his indifference to worldly life, his perennial love, his incessant remembrance of God's name, his humanity, his constant divine contemplation, his effacement of egoism, his disregard of money, his absence of sensuousness and anger, his peace and forgiveness, his equality, his indifference to pleasure and pain and his eagerness to show men the path of devotion."

Guru is **holy mother** and disciplined father. Guru acts in both ways. He pampers the child, nourishes the child in a motherly manner and at the same time punishes the child whenever he goes astray. He is a strict disciplinarian and a man of principle. He never budges an inch where his teachings are concerned. Qualities of both the mother and father are incorporated in him. Disciples should bear it in mind that when they receive the blessings of their guru, they are in safe hands. Their lives are safe in a firm hand and the disciple should behave accordingly. When child comes of age every father and mother prefer their child to take their responsibility. (**Indian Express Article**)

Osho, while explaining the role of a *Guru*, says, "Role of a *guru* is to give you a glimpse of the real, not a teaching but an awakening. The *guru* is not a teacher but he is an awakener…. The allegorical lesson being that the *guru*, an embodiment of divine wisdom, is all pervasive. We therefore need to conduct ourselves virtuously, learn to appreciate the beauty of natural phenomena and live simply before we can expect to find a *Satguru*. A *guru* can only guide us along the path of learning; but the effort and toil have to be disciple's efforts. In a way, you are your own *guru*. Only when you learn to seek divinity within yourself, live a disciplined life and follow the advice of your *guru*, will you find the light within."

SIDDHA YOGA CONCEPT

"A true guru is one whose mere presence brings about a deep transformation, whose voice, more than words, serves as a vehicle to lasting inner bliss and who with ease instils a state of calmness. Such a one whose identification with the Supreme is complete, and who, with authority from the Guru's lineage, enables us to retrieve our identification with Divinity, is a true guru."

SWAMI KRIPANANDA

"The closer we come to the nature of the Guru, the more mysterious it seems. "The embodiment of the Absolute, grace-bestowing power, giver of knowledge, purifier, remover of sorrow, conqueror of the obstacles that hold us back from the experience of our own true nature — all these, as we have seen, coalesce in the Guru." (*The Guru Sandals*)

GREATNESS OF GURU

To be able to transmit spiritualism one must first be a spiritual powerhouse oneself. They should possess some extraordinary powers like Ashtasidhis. These realized souls would know how to communicate, how to transmit energy, how much energy to transmit, and the receptivity level of the spiritual aspirants. Only an enlightened soul can recognize a worthy soul for spiritual transmission of knowledge and spirituality. Ramakrishna Paramahamsa knew that Vivekananda was one such worthy soul, long before the former met him at Dakshineshwar. All the realized souls can recognize the worthy souls and will be waiting for them to come to them. There are numerous instances the authors can cite where Sri Ganapathy Sachchidananda Swamiji predicted the arrival of certain individuals, sometimes years before. Sri Swamiji predicted our meeting with Sri Swamiji two years before we met him in 1990.

Dr. Paul Brunton from London has written in the book, **A Search in Secret India**, about his first meeting with Ramana Maharishi: "For it does not now seem to matter whether they (the questions he has prepared to ask) are asked or not, and it does not seem to matter whether I solve the problems which have hitherto troubled me, I know only that a steady river of quietness seems to be flowing near me, that a great peace is penetrating the inner reaches of my being". He further observed, "The most important part of his utterances, the subtle and silent flavor of spirituality which emanated from him, can never be reported. **Our best philosophers could not hold a candle to him**".

Similarly, **Duncan Greenlees** writing about the Maharishi, says, **"I have found no other human being who so emanates his grace that**

it can catch away the ordinary man from his stillness and plunge him deep in the ecstasy of timeless omnipresent being".

The spiritual ecstasy was experienced in Maharishi's presence by many aspirants who had quietened their mind and opened their heart to receive the outpouring of the divine grace.

The Maharishi suggested self-inquiry and the elimination of "I" as a method of spiritual discipline. All other paths culminated according to him in the Jnana Yoga.

HOW DOES GURU INFLUENCE YOU?

A guru can transmit Shakti or spiritual power in **five ways**. The authors of this book have experienced these five ways and more when they met Sri Ganapathy Sachchidananda Swamiji for the first time in 1990.

One, is by touch. The teacher/Guru accumulates power of spirit through intense sadhana over years. He bestows this power on the deserving disciple by direct transmission in a place and time chosen by him.

Second method of initiation the Guru transmits his energy into the disciple through a word or Mantra that is charged with power through Guru's Sadhana.

The **Third** takes place through Guru's look.

In the **Fourth**, Guru transmits his spiritual power into the disciple through a thought - as it mostly happened in the presence of Ramana Maharishi.

In the **Fifth**, a Guru can guide you in dreams.

In all five cases, it is essential that the receiver should be in a state of readiness. As narrated in a Zen story, you can pour tea only into an empty cup.

WHO IS A SADGURU?

A Sadguru is one on whom the spiritual powers descended through Guru Parampara in an unbroken chain of discipleship according to Swami Vivekananda. He further continues that only an Avatara but not an ordinary Guru can make the spiritual aspirant fit. Guru is the means for realization of liberty. There is no knowledge without a Guru.

The prefix "Sat" means truth. Sadguru is known to tell the truth. He is not the one to make the listeners comfortable and appreciate him. He is not there to please and entertain them. He is not worried about the reaction of the disciples. He is known to tell the truth. His words will be harsh and difficult to swallow. He may even chastise the listeners for not fulfilling their responsibilities and their indifference to follow the Dharma. He keeps reminding them that the road to spiritual development is filled with many thorns. They must endure suffering and pain, and fulfill their Karmas. Sadguru is never worried about the number of people attending his lectures, Bhajans, concerts and workshops. He knows that only few souls are spiritually oriented.

A Sadguru is also known as one who answers a disciple's need for surrender and quest for liberation. There are a number Gurus: there are teachers in the field of music, dance, education, politics, sports, wrestling and others. But one has to be careful about selecting a Sadguru. If you find anyone whose line of succession goes back to generations and generations, you can consider the occasion to be a divine opportunity to embrace. Everyone is not ready for a Guru. It all depends on one's level of religiosity, spirituality and burning desire for self- improvement. Unless we know the value of a Guru, the concept of Guru Tattva would not make sense and would seem useless. One must be physically and mentally ready for self-surrender. Unless we know the value of gold, it will be considered as any other metal on the road to pass by. Even if a Guru is next door, in the same place, and sitting face to face, if we are not ready spiritually and mentally, he would look like any other ordinary person.

The **Guru Gita** says about Sadguru as follows:

"I bow to the Sadguru who is the source of bliss, giver of great comfort, form of pure knowledge, beyond all dualities, sky - like the essence of the Mahaavaakyas like Tatvamasi, unique, eternal, pure, steady, witness to all intellect, beyond the intellect and who is without the three qualities Sattva, Rajas and Tamas." (87)

I bow to Sadguru who is the embodiment of bliss, bliss-giver who is gracious, embodiment of knowledge, self-realized, supreme Yogini, and praise worthy and the doctor of all diseases of Samsara. (88)

Take refuge in Sadguru, the all-merciful Master

Make every effort to take shelter in Guru who saves you from disaster

If God is angry, Sadguru protects you with His boundless compassion

If Guru is angry, none can save you, therefore serve Him with great devotion

Swami Sivananda:

"A Sadguru is endowed with countless Siddhis (psychic powers). He possesses all divine Aisvarya (powers), all the wealth of the Lord.

Possession of Siddhis, however, is not the test to declare the greatness of a sage or to prove that he has attained Self-realization. Sadgurus generally do not exhibit any miracle or Siddhi. Sometimes, however, they may do so to convince the aspirants of the existence of super physical things, give them encouragement, and instill faith in their hearts.

The Sadguru is Brahman Himself. He is an ocean of bliss, knowledge, and mercy. He is the captain of your soul. He is the fountain of joy. He removes all your troubles, sorrows, and obstacles. He shows you the right divine path."

WHY DO WE NEED A GURU?

If you want to experience unparalleled compassion, receive the boundless love, experience the inexpressible silence, receive the Himalayan mountain size support, experience the indescribable miracles in life, receive infinite joy and bliss that we never received before, receive the unlimited grace, understand the real meaning of life, feel the presence of divine - god himself, uplift your spirits, subdue your ego, elevate your mind, tread the path toward Vairagya (renunciation), bathe in the company of the holiest of the holiest, cleanse the impurity of thought, show compassion toward others, you need a Guru.

If you want to open your inner eye to see the self inside instead of seeing outside only through outer senses, if you want your life to be directed toward spiritual growth, if you want your heart to be filled with Amruta (ambrosia), if you want your suffering to be minimized and cushioned, if want your problems to be diminished, then you need a Guru.

Guru is a veritable treasure house containing rubies of wit and humor and emeralds of truth and divine grandeur. He is deep and sublime but simple and approachable. He is a fire burning the bad karma of his devotees. Guru has the greatness of water to purify and quench the parched thirst of his disciples. He punishes through his silence and teaches through his action. His ways are as mysterious as the body and shines through his lustrous eyes. "It is impossible to attain Mukti (emancipation) without the grace of a guru," says Purandaradas. A man might be well-versed in all scriptures. He might have renounced the world and might have crucified his flesh, but truth is revealed only to him who has become slave to the great Master.

For a beginner in the spiritual path, a Guru is necessary. To light a candle, you need a burning candle. Similarly, an illumined soul alone can enlighten another soul. Many people practice meditation thinking that they can become enlightened persons. Then they face many problems and encounter many difficulties that cannot be resolved by them. It is difficult to obviate the obstacles and road blocks they encounter in their independent search for God within. Slowly they will be looking for a Guru and feel the necessity for a Guru.

Only the man who has already been to the forest can help you to find the short cut to the exit. Otherwise this man will be going round and round unable to find the way out of the forest. Anybody who has gone to on a pilgrimage, can tell you the way to go without wasting much of your time. In the case of the spiritual path, it is still more difficult to find your way. The mind will mislead you very often. The Guru will be able to remove pitfalls and obstacles, and lead you along the right path. He will tell you: "This road leads you to Moksha; this one leads to bondage." Without this guidance, you might want to go to Badrinath, but find yourself in Delhi!

In Hinduism, you will find thousands and thousands of books. The more you read, more confusion you may encounter. They may look contradictory, ambiguous, confusing, vague and inconsistent. In many cases the passages are very difficult to grasp and understand. The meanings and definitions may be changing and some may have hidden meanings. You will be at a crossroad not knowing which direction you must go to reach the destination. This is the time you need a guide, a Guru or a Preceptor who can explain to you the real meaning of the scriptures in simple language by clearing the doubts, dissipating the contradictions and removing the ambiguities.

All the scriptures and Gurus have emphasized the need for a Guru for nay spiritual aspirant to travel on the spiritual path. It is only the Guru who will find out your defects, tap your agony, discern your anguish, and grasp your dilemmas. Our ignorance and ego usually comes in the way to find our own defects. Guru can help you to find the real you unmasking the clouded character. Constant association with Guru will help remove the thorns that are preventing you to tread the spiritual path.

All great ones had their teachers. All the sages, saints, prophets, world teachers, incarnations, great men have had their own Gurus, however great they might have been. Govindacharya learned from Gaudapadacharya; Sankaracharya from Govindacharya; Suresvaracharya from Sankaracharya; Gorakhnath from Matsyendranath; Nivrittinathom Gorakhnath; Jnanadev from Nivrittinath; Sri Ramakrishna from Totapuri; Swami Vivekananda from Sri Ramakrishna.

Svetaketu learnt the nature of Truth from Uddalaka, Maitreyi from Yajnavalkya, Bhrugu from Varuna, Narada from Sanatkumara, Nachiketu from Yama, Indra from Prajapati; and several others humbly went to the wise ones, observed strict Brahmacharya rules, practiced rigorous discipline, and learnt Brahma-Vidya from them. Lord Krishna sat at the feet of His Guru Sandeepani. Lord Rama had

Guru Vasishta who gave Him Upadesa. Even Devas have Brihaspati as their Guru. Even the greatest among the divine beings sat at the feet of Guru Dakshinamurti, who was a silent teacher.

A beginner must have a personal Guru first. He cannot have God as Guru to begin with. He must have a pure mind. He must have ethical perfection. He must be intensely virtuous. He must be above body-consciousness. Then alone can he have God as Guru.

Upanishads are a gold mine. The more you the more you get. They are the most difficult scriptures to grasp and understand. They emphasize the need for a guru to attain liberation from the cycle of birth and rebirth. You will find continuous discussions between a guru and a disciple or a seeker. A disciple should not approach a guru unless he firmly desires initiation, put aside all the worries, ready to listen without any doubts and makes up his mind to accept his teachings. Everybody is not ready for guru. One must mentally accept the need for and the value of a guru. Unless one knows the value of gold, it is considered as any other metal. According to **Upanishad**: "Arise: awake: approach the teachers and know the Truth. The person who is blessed with a teacher knows the Highest. He whose devotion to the Lord is great and who has as much devotion to Guru as to the Lord, unto him; that high souled one, the meanings of the sacred texts stand revealed."

Sant Ramadasa wrote in the seventeenth century in *Dasabodha* on the absolute necessity of a guru: "Without a guru we can never attain real knowledge. Even though one may study the sciences and attain all kinds of powers, both physical and mental, without the grace of Guru one cannot realize the Self. Contemplation and concentration, devotion and worship would be all useless without the grace of the Guru. Rama and Krishna, and all the saints of bygone times, devoted themselves wholly to the service of their Master." (*Dasabodha V*)

Sri Ganapathy Sachchidananda Swamiji says that, "Those who want to break the bondage of birth and death, and try to attain Dharma, Artha, Kama, and Moksha need a Guru. Nobody in the world can be successful and great in his life without the guidance and of blessings of Guru."

Swami Sivananda: "For a beginner in the spiritual path, a Guru is necessary. To light a candle, you need a burning candle. Even an illumined soul alone can enlighten another soul.

A Guru is absolutely necessary for every aspirant in the spiritual path. It is only the Guru who will find out your defects. The nature of egoism is such that you will not be able to find out your own defects. Just as a man cannot see his back, so also, he cannot see his own errors. He must live under a Guru for the eradication of his evil qualities and defects."

The aspirant who is under the guidance of a Master or Guru is safe from being led astray. Satsang or association with the Guru is an armor and fortress to guard you against all temptations and unfavorable forces of the material world.

All great ones had their teachers. All the sages, saints, prophets, world-teachers, incarnations, great men, have had their own Gurus, however great they might have been. Svetaketu learnt the nature of Truth from Uddalaka, Maitreyi from Yajnavalkya, Bhrigu from Varuna, Narada from Sanatkumara, Nachiketa from Yama, Patardhana from Indra, Indra from Prajapati; and several others humbly went to wise ones, observed strict Brahmacharya, practiced rigorous discipline, and learnt Brahma-Vidya (the science of God) from them.

Lord Krishna sat at the feet of His Guru Sandeepani. Lord Rama had Guru Vasishta who gave Him Upadesa (spiritual advice). Even Devas (celestial beings) have Brihaspati as their Guru. Even the greatest among the divine beings sat at the feet of Guru Dakshinamurti.

A neophyte must have a personal Guru first. He cannot have God as Guru to begin with. He must have a pure mind. He must have ethical perfection. He must be intensely virtuous. He must be above body-consciousness. Then alone can he have God as Guru.

Kabirdas, the fifteenth century mystic, clearly records the status of Guru as follows: "In the midst of the highest heaven there is a shining light; he who has no Guru cannot reach the place; he only reaches, who is under the guidance of a true Guru.

Muktananda: The Guru is absolutely necessary in one's life – as necessary as the vital force. "The Guru is more necessary than a friend, a son, a husband, or a wife; more necessary than wealth, machines, factories, art, or music. What more can I say? The Guru is more necessary than health and prana itself. By his grace alone, the inner Shakti is unfolded. The glory of the Guru is full of mystery and is supremely divine. He gives a new birth to man, he gives him the experience of knowledge; he shows him Sadhana and makes him a lover of God."

Saint Sundaradasa said "Without Guru there is no meditation. No high knowledge can arise without him. There is no love without the Guru, no wealth without the Guru, no equanimity of mind without the Guru....He takes away the disciple's wrong understanding, his delusion of imperfection, and grants him the highest wisdom.

He does not need anything from anybody, because he has everything he wants within himself. His eyes are not attracted by beautiful forms, nor his tongue infatuated with delicious flavors, nor do his ears long to hear sweet sound. He is completely free from the pull of senses; because he is constantly drinking ecstasy of the inner Self, his senses have turned within and take the delight only in that inner ecstasy. Unlike the mind of an ordinary person, the mind of the Guru is always steady. Just as a flame does not flicker where there is no wind, the Guru's mind never moves from the Self. The Guru is as deep and serene as the ocean. In his heart, there is only compassion and love for all beings; there is no desire, anger, pride or jealousy. For him, all religions, all actions, all countries, and all beings are equal.

The Guru is the supreme benefactor. He destroys our confusion and shows us our true nature and the purpose of our lives. He helps us to develop love for God and reveals God to us from within. The mystery of the Guru is very great. Just by keeping His company, we can experience God directly.

Eknath Maharaj said, "O my friend, since I received the lotion of the Guru's grace, I see only God wherever I look. Inside I see God, outside I see God. Whatever I see in this world is only God. This is the power of the Guru's grace."

Sant Kesavadas: "The necessity of a guru, a man of God-realization, is felt by all seekers after reality. Even in material matters, the necessity of a teacher is felt; how much more it should be in the case of spirituality for the path is very subtle .... In the ocean of rebirth, lust and rage are two big rocks through which the boat of life cannot pass unscathed. The thieves of greediness are waiting to steal the spiritual wealth of an individual. There will be sharp showers of arrogance and jealousy and the hurricane of illusion which overturns the ship. Guru alone knows the proper way to escape these dangers and reach the other shore, for he has already reached the other shore. He has come, out of compassion, to take others across the ocean of Samsara, the cycle of birth and death."

Sant Tukaram says: *"Without the Satguru, all talk of liberation is the whispering of ghosts. Vyas, other sages, and scriptures, too, sing the glory of the Master."*

Consider the one without a Guru as ever in mourning;

> Do not even glance at his face. *
> No efforts will ever liberate him from birth and death;
> Know that his human life will go to waste.
> Holy books have stated thus, O Tuka,
> And thus, have declared all Saints in the past.
> (Gatha, 4341)

Spiritual initiation is a necessary factor in the path of spirituality. During such an initiation, a spiritual power is transmitted from the guru to disciple. One who receives such transmitted power is a disciple and one who transmits it is a guru. This power is very subtle but powerful. It clears doubt, extinguishes confusion, settles the mind and the disciple reaches stability and equanimity. He finds his safety in the pouch of its mother. He could stare at death without any fear, for he has reached immortality by the all-encompassing love and protection from the guru.

Paramahamsa Yogananda also talks about the need for an illumined soul to guide the disciples.

"A true, God-illumined guru is one who, in his attainment of self-mastery, has realized his identity with the omnipresent Spirit. Such a one is uniquely qualified to lead the seeker on his or her inward journey toward perfection.

The blind cannot lead the blind. Only a master, one who knows God, may rightly teach others about Him. To regain one's divinity one must have such a master or Guru. He who faithfully follows a true guru becomes like him, for the Guru helps to elevate the disciple to his own level of realization."

Swami Muktananda says that a Guru is more important than wealth, family members, friends, health, Prana and any property one can possess. A Guru who is endowed with spiritual powers is important for awakening the inner eye and changing the external worldly bondages. He is more likely to give new and second birth that takes the disciple to a higher level. It is through speeches and silence he can change the disciple. "The Guru is true, the Guru is perfect, the Guru is simple, direct, and loving. He is the well-wisher of his disciples. He doesn't steal his disciples' money; instead, he takes their ignorance, or nescience. He doesn't seize their wealth and property, but he takes their sins and anxieties. The greatness of the Guru is that he can lead his disciples to the vision of God without severe asceticism. He brings the peace of a cave and the experience of solitude right into people's houses. He shows the spiritual path in the midst of the world. He lets you see the Himalayas in everyday life and Mount Kailas in meditation."

GURU COMPARED TO GOD

Scriptures, saints and disciples have fondly described the relationship between Guru and God. Some of them described Guru as the highest spiritual Master, depicted his as the liberator of the embodied souls, and equated Guru with God, while others gave higher status to Guru than God.

God is known to perform three main functions. Trimurthies - Brahma, Vishnu and Siva - perform these functions, namely, Creation, Sustenance and Dissolution respectively. In case of a Guru, in addition to these three functions, He performs two additional functions namely

*TirodhAn*a (concealment, eradication, vanishing) and *Anugraha* (Grace).

These five-fold phenomena constitute the entire cosmic cycle of events. Though the third function, dissolution, puts an end to everything, it does not put an end to the sins - why sins, in fact all karma - in the bank-balance of individual *Jivas*. They remain in latent form till the beginning of the next cycle of creation. It is only the *TirodhAna* function of the Lord that eradicates the latent *Vasanas* stored up by past karma. This '*TirodhAna*' is the function of the **'placed foot'** of the Divine. On the other hand, *Anugraha* - Grace, the award of *Moksha* is the function of the **'raised' foot** of the Lord. That is why one surrenders to the '*Tokay Tirade*' of the Lord for Him to grace us so that *'we are no more thrown in the deep abysses of the feminine womb to be born again'*. In the Advaita tradition, this '*tokay tiruvaDi*' is equated to the Guru. He is the One on Earth who can grant the same Grace. The small poem *Bhaja-Govindam* of Adi Sankaracharya extols the lotus feet of the Guru for this very purpose. Incidentally the folklore is that Sankara immortalized the name Govinda in that *Stotra* because it was the name of his Guru!

Guru Gita describes in greater details the significance of guru and his relationship with God.

"Guru is Brahma, Guru is Vishnu, Guru is Maheshwara (Lord Shiva). Guru is verily Brahman, the transcendental reality, salutations to the Guru who saves us from duality. (Sloka 32)

"Guru is Brahma. Guru is Vishnu. Guru is Shiva. Know this Guru is Trinity, Guru is unity, Guru is the whole universe. Adore the Guru, worship the Guru, and surrender to the Guru with Bhakti; nothing is higher than the feet of Sadguru that brings the blessings of Mukti." (Sloka 80)

The Guru Gita also describes the Guru as being identical with God:

Brahmananda paramasukhada kevala jnanamurtim

Dvandvtitam gaganasadrsam tattvamasyadilaksyam

Ekam nityam vimalamacalam sarvadhi-saksi -bhutam

Bhavaatitam triguna-rahitam sadgurum tam namami

"I bow to the divine Guru, who is the bliss of the supreme Absolute, the embodiment of the highest joy, who is supremely independent and the personification of pure knowledge. There is no trace of duality in him. He is perfectly detached and all-pervasive, like the sky. He is the goal of the wisdom of the great statement 'Thou art That.' He is the One without a second. He is eternal, pure, and taintless. He is steady and the witness of all. He is beyond all modifications and devoid of the three gunas."

Gupatsadhana Tantra also accorded supreme place to Guru: "Guru is Brahma. Guru is Vishnu. Guru is Deva, Mahadeva himself. Guru is the place of pilgrimage. Guru is the sacrifice. Guru is charity. Guru is devotion and austerities. Guru is fire. Guru is Surya. The entire Universe is Guru."

According **Vivekananda,** "The Guru must be worshiped as God. He is God; he is nothing less than that. As you look at him, gradually the Guru melts away, and what is left? The guru picture gives place to God Himself. The Guru is the bright mask, which God wears to come to us. As we look steadily on, gradually the mask falls off and God is revealed."

Sri Ganapathy Sachchidananda Swamiji says "God has given his judgment that we should be punished for our wicked actions but merciful Guru will give asylum under his kingdom and offers a special protective shield of bliss to his disciple (Sishya). Once we accept asylum of Guru even God will not punish us for our misdeeds."

Ramadasa's admiration for guru was great: "He who regards God as superior to the Guru is a fool. Before the greatness of the Guru, the greatness of God is nothing. God is made God by the power of Mantras; but the Guru cannot be made even by God. The power of God is the power of illusion; the power of the Guru carries everything before it." (Dasabodha V, 3)

Yogashikha Upanishad explains the relationship between Guru and God as follows: Brahmavid-Brahmaiva Bhavati, "One who has known

Brahman completely and has merged in Him is Brahman Himself."
Further it states:

Yatha gurustathaiveso yathaivesastathta guruh I
Pujaniyo mahabhaktya na bhedo vidyatenayoh II

"The Guru is God and God is the Guru. Therefore, considering
the Guru to be God, one should worship him with all one's
heart, with great devotion, respect, and love."

GURU TATTVAM

Guru Tattva means the essence, the principle or the spirit of a Guru.
The process by which a Guru uses to make an ignorant disciple lead
to self-realization. The methods that a Guru uses to bring changes
in a disciple are part of the concept of Guru Tattva. Similarly, the
teachings, the bhajans, personal interviews, looking after his disciples,
protecting them from impending dangers, providing security, and
showing affection and love by a Sadguru are part of that Guru Tattva.
Without these kinds of functions being undertaken by a Guru, the
humans will be in deep ignorance. The fact that our Rishis developed
this mechanism to transmit the rich, ancient culture to next generation
is a testimony to the significance of Guru Tattva.

Sri Ganapathy Sachchidananda Swamiji describes Guru Tattvam as
follows:

- Guru's grace is the most valuable thing of life, it helps, provides, protects and uplifts. It finally leads to liberation even while living.
- Whatever is available to you by God's grace, share with others as far as possible. You will feel no scarcity, instead, you will get more, "this is the law of nature."
- God is one, though, He has different names and forms, He is all powerful. Similarly, saints look different but their mission is common, the welfare of mankind. Respect all saints but follow your own Guru.
- Guru appears in life by the grace of God. You do not know how and when He graces. Surrender to Guru with faith, love and devotion.

⼊ Selfless service to Guru is the only method to please Him. (Mystic Glimpses of Sri Guru's Grace by Prem Kishan Kapoor).

According to **Bhakti Rasamrita Sindhu**, finding a spiritual master, learning with faith, discharging the service to Guru and **follow the master** are essential components of Guru Tattva.

Guru-padashrayas tasmat

Krishna-dikshadi-shikshanam

Vishrambhena guroh seva

Sadhu vartanuvartamanam (1.2.74)

[1] Accepting the shelter of the lotus feet of a bona fide spiritual master,

[2] becoming initiated by the spiritual master and learning how to discharge devotional service for him,

[3] obeying the orders of the spiritual master with faith and devotion, and

[4] following the footsteps of great *Acharyas* [teachers] under the direction of the spiritual master"

A disciple should have abiding faith in his Guru and surrender to him with the firm belief that Guru will protect you, he is *Kripa Sindhu* (ocean of kindness), he is *Daya Sagar* (sea of piety), *Prema Murthy* (embodiment of love), and *Sarva Deva Mayo Guruh* (representative of all Gods) exemplifies the true nature of experiencing *Guru Tattvam*.

ASHTASIDHI

There are different types of Gurus and Swamis. One must be very careful in selecting the right one. You must observe, watch, listen and ask many unanswered questions before you select your own Guru. For all the Gurus, *Ashtasidhi's* (eight mystic powers) are recognized as powerful. *Bhagavat Purana* describes the Ashtasidhis as follows:

⼊ Anima (reducing the body to the size of the atom)

⼊ Mahima (magnifying the body to a gigantic size)

⼊ Laghima (extreme lightness of the body)

⚔ Prapti (establishing contact with the senses of the entire creation in the form of deities presiding over the senses)
⚔ Prakamya (the capacity to enjoy pleasures heard of and enjoyable only in heaven and the subterranean world)
⚔ Isitva (the capacity to arrest Maya and other potencies from functioning)
⚔ Vasitva (absence of attachment to pleasure s of the senses)
⚔ Kamavasayita (ability to enjoy whatever pleasure he desires in the highest measure)

Other powers are:

⚔ absence of hunger, thirst, old age etc.
⚔ capacity to see distant things
⚔ capacity to hear from unusual distance
⚔ moving at any speed
⚔ taking any form at will
⚔ leaving one's body and entering any untenanted body
⚔ giving up body at will
⚔ participate in the sports of gods
⚔ attaining any desired object
⚔ exercising unobstrued authority anywhere
⚔ knowing past and future
⚔ remaining unaffected by heat and cold, joy and sorrow
⚔ reading other people's mind
⚔ neutralizing the power of fire, sun, poison etc. and to suffer no defeat at the hands of anyone.

Very rare indeed art the Gurus who possess such miraculous and mystic powers. Once we find such a teacher, it is better to hold on to him, accept him and get into his fold. He is no ordinary person. He is endowed with extraordinary powers that transcend our perceptions, reasoning, objectivity and judgment. He is an Avatara who descended on this earth only to lift the humanity to a higher level by infusing dharmic values embedded in the scriptures. Surrendering ourselves to such Sadguru is first step to traverse on the road to self-realization.

Swami **Vivekananda's** two verses from his hymn to his Guru Sri Ramakrishna are very touching and inspirational to follow:

"I take refuge in the Guru, who is like a wave rising out of the ocean of cosmic energy, who enacts His manifold divine play out of pure love, who is the great arrow to destroy the demon of doubt, who is the divine healer of the disease of worldliness."

*"I take refuge in the Guru, who is well-established in the knowledge of the Truth of Non-duality, whose life is wrapped in the glowing garment of **Bhakti,** or loving devotion to God, whose body is ever active in the wonderful work (of doing good to mankind), and Who is the divine Healer of the disease of worldliness."*

SWAMI YATISWARANANDA

There is a saying that the human Guru utters a Mantra in the ears of a disciple, while the world Teacher speaks in the heart of the devotee. Real initiation takes place when God awakens the spiritual consciousness of a seeker. The real Guru is the immanent God, the indwelling supreme Spirit who is the Goal, the Controller, the Lord, the Witness, the Abode, the Refuge, the Friend, the Origin and Dissolution of the universe, its Substratum, the Repository of all knowledge and the Eternal Seed.

ADI SANKARA

The disciple looks upon the teacher as a visible manifestation of the supreme Spirit, the teacher of all teachers, as a channel for the flow of the divine Grace. It is in this spirit that he serves him, obeys him and worships him. This idea is expressed in well-known verses of *Dakshinamurti Stotram:*

"I bow to the divine Guru who, by the application of the collyrium of Knowledge, opens the eyes of one blinded by the disease of ignorance. I bow to the divine guru who imparts to the disciple the fire of Self-knowledge and burns away his bonds of karma accumulated through many births.

I offer my salutations to the beneficent Being who is incarnate in the Guru, the Light of whose absolute Existence shines forth in the world *of appearance, who instructs the disciples with the holy test, `That thou art', realizing whom the soul never more returns to the ocean of birth and death.*

WHY WORSHIP GURU'S PADUKAS

One may ask why worship Guru's feet. Why not the Guru's face, the hands, the eyes? Swami Muktananda once said, "The Guru's feet are worshiped or revered because all the Guru's Shakti dwells in the feet. If one does research into this with modern instruments, you would find that vibrations of the inner Self constantly flow out through the feet. The nerves of the subtle body that come from Sahasraara reach right down to the feet. The feet serve as the support for the whole body. This is the reason that feet are given so much importance. More Shakti flows from the feet than any other part of the body. The glory of the Guru's feet or the Guru's sandals is great." (P: 54) That is why the scriptures glorify the Guru's sandals. For example, the Kularnava Tantra says: "Remember the Guru's sandals .... They provide protection against diseases, great disturbances, great evils, great fears, great calamities, and great sins." ...." The Guru's feet refer to the Being in whom the Guru stands rooted, and that Being is the supreme Being, that Being is the highest Truth.... The lotus feet of the Guru are the most sacred centers for the disciple. They encompass all sacred centers. If a disciple worships this sacred place, he worships all sacred. **(Extensive explanation is provided in a chapter on "Speech on Guru Paduka Puja on Guru Purnima Day in this book)**

WHAT IS SATSANG?

"Sat" means truth, and "Sang" means association. Satsang means association with people who embody truth and who represent the absolute existence. An aspirant should always be in the company of good people. Association with good drenches you in good thoughts, good speeches and good deeds. There is a well-known saying in Sanskrit: `It is far better to roam in the forest with the hill tribes than to live with fools even in heaven."* It admonishes us to associate only with good company and avoid the people with mere worldly desires.

Holy association is an antidote for egoism, selfishness and pride. Through holy association one's bad thoughts and habits are curtailed and good Samskaras are awakened. In Bhagavata Purna there is a famous statement: "Holy sages are the **greatest purifiers**." It means holy saints can free one from impurity in no time. In fact, these Sadgurus make the religious places holy and sacred by their mere presence and by their Padukas and their bare feet.

If you come into intimate contact with an illumined soul you should realize that God's grace has been showered on you. That grace may be taken away any day and perhaps forever; some of you may not be given a second chance. Sankaracharya's composition, *Vivekacudamani* says, 'A human birth, the longing for liberation, and the company of illumined teachers are extremely difficult to get through God's grace.

In Satsangs, the spiritual leaders deliver lectures on various topics that help mold the minds and body of the disciples, conduct bhajan sessions where the disciples are given chance to participate and sing to their hearts content, conduct numerous Pujas and Homas to generate good vibrations, encourage disciples to arrange numerous cultural programs to develop appreciation for the richness of our culture, encourage them to chant the holy names of gurus and gods, and transmit the energy and power to the attending disciples. It is a kind of new experience for many people to change both internally and externally to face modern day challenges.

In these associations with extraordinary holy people, the seekers experience love, peace of mind and new way of thinking. This is expressed in one of the ślokas:

> *Sadhunamdarshanam Punyam*
> *Sparsanam Papanasanam*
> *Sambhashanam kotiteerdham*
> *Vandanam Moksha Sadhanam*

The Darshan of a Sadhu (realized souls) gives spiritual merits; their touch removes the sins, a dialogue with them gives the merit of visiting a crore of sacred places and our obeisance paves the way for liberation.

The mere looks of a Sadguru, casual deliverance of a message and a simple word can have alchemic effect in transforming one's life.

Satsang - Association with Great Souls

"O Shri Rama, an aspirant should take recourse to Satsang (good association). He should nourish his intellect by receiving instruction from the sages and reflect upon them. Gradually, he should cultivate the great qualities that manifest in enlightened personalities" —Yoga Vasishta

Swami Sivananda says, "These holy men are like live electric wires which are connected to a power house. They are always in conscious contact with the Divine. Their finite personalities are always in touch with the infinite. When you touch a live wire, you get a tremendous shock. When you touch these pure souls, you touch the Lord ever present in them."

Narada Bhakti Sutras also praises the effect of Satsang on the seekers. "Noble thoughts are given to a society in which God's glory is always heard and recited. Our ears should be engaged in listening to the *Nama* and glory of God, our tongue in the repetition of the Divine name, and our heart in the remembrance of the Divine Form."

Whoever comes in touch with a holy man, and can receive what he gives, comes in touch with the Infinite also. But the important point to note is that one should have the ability to receive, should have an open mind, should go with empty glass and should have the capacity to experience the divine. Otherwise, as **Sri Ramakrishna** used to say: `The Sannyasin's Kamandalu (water pot made out of a large kind of bitter gourd) goes with him to all the places of pilgrimage, yet does not lose its bitter taste. When we approach holy men, we should be in the right mood, open to receive their blessings. God may grant us the company of holy men but if we are not open, not ready to receive, nothing will happen to us. You must know how to derive benefit from such contact. If you have full trust and faith in a holy man and leave all your problems to him, he will do what is necessary for you. He will lead you along the right path.

Let us digest one of the powerful Slokas about the effect of Satsang on the mind of an aspirant.

Satsangha twe nisangha twam.

Nisangha twe nirmoha twam.

Nirmoha twe nischala ta twam.

Nischala ta twe, jivamukti.

When you are in good company, you are not in bad company.

When you are not in bad company, you don't fall into delusion.

When you don't fall into delusion, the mind becomes steady.

When the mind becomes steady, you are liberated.

Bhagavata Purana has a beautiful story about the need for Satsang and how one can come close to the holy feet of the Lord. Following rigorous meditation, Bhagawan appears and stands in front of Dhruva, then He told Dhruva to ask Him for a boon. Instead of asking for a boon Dhruva instead asked for His holy feet. He further says, "The easiest way to attain your holy feet is listening to your divine glories". Dhruva asked the Lord to bless him with satsanga.

It is said very beautifully in one of his slokas, -

> *"Bhaktim Muhu Pravahataam Tvayime Prasango*
> *Buyath Anantha Mahatham Amalsayaanam*
> *Enancha Solbanam Uru Vyasanam Bhavabtim*
> *Neshye Bhavat Guna Kathamrita Panamathah"*

What is the panacea for the misery from mundane cycle of existence? It is verily listening to the Divine glories of the Lord. It alone will alleviate the souls from the suffering in the mundane world. By listening to the stories of the Lord, we become intoxicated by drinking the nectar of the Lord's divine glories. To get that intoxication, one needs to be in the abode of a Sadguru. The Sadguru is always immersed in and reminisces the divine glories of the Lord and incessantly chants the Divine Names of the Lord.

Association with wise and holy men is stressed heavily in Hinduism than any other religion. In order to progress spiritually, it is very essential to come under the shadow of these holy men. For a beginner, it is one of the most essential factors in one's life. Sadgurus are sought after for spiritual development by many spiritual aspirants.

Ramakrishna Paramahamsa talks about the need for association with God men.

> *"It begets yearning for God. It begets love of God. Nothing whatsoever is achieved in spiritual life without yearning. By constantly living in the company of holy men, the soul becomes restless for God.... There is another benefit from holy company. It helps one to cultivate discrimination between the Real and the unreal. God alone is the Real the eternal Substance, and the world is unreal transitory ... In other words, company of holy man fosters in us a spirit of renunciation. By living with holy men who have renounced everything, others learn the value of renunciation and acquire strength to practice it."*

How do we know that a disciple is touched by a Sadguru? He keeps thinking always, remembering his moments with him frequently, reminiscing the encounter with the guru, reflecting on the words and discourses, recollecting his magnetic and magical personality, and starts developing good habits. His joy wells up and sorrows diminish. Also, you will notice that devotee wants to hear and speak only of the Divine, and spiritual matters. Internal churning starts inside his mindset which will influence his outward behavior also. His manners will change, his demeanor changes, and his association with the friends will also change. It is something like the birds of the same feather flock together. An aspirant who is on his path to spiritual realm would not enjoy the talk of worldly and materialistic matters.

Adi Sankara captures this change in Bhaja Govinda Stotram:

> *"By keeping the company of great Mahatmas, one becomes dispassionate. He gets Vairagya. He does not like the company of the worldly people. Then he develops the state of Nirmohatva. He becomes free from infatuation or delusion. Then his mind becomes steady and one-pointed and rests on the Swarupa or essence. Then he attains liberation or freedom."*

Goswami Tulasidas also discusses the importance of Satsang in his book Sri Ramacharita Manas:

"The intuition of wisdom or the power of discrimination does not come without having Satsanga which is enjoyable or attainable only by those whom Lord Rama chooses or upon whom He bestows His Grace. Even the worst rogues are changed into virtuous men only through the association or Sanga of the seers and sages, as Satsanga is itself an ever-beneficial joy-giver."

One can receive benefits of associating with holy people provided that a disciple has a receptive attitude, no preconceived notions, desire to cross the ocean of samsara, interested in asking only pertinent questions, participate in seva activities, able to control the wavering mind, and willing to cleanse his body and soul to elevate himself.

GURU AND SISHYA

Who is sishya and how do you define? Sishya is defined as *Saasanaat sisyate yah sah sishya*, meaning the one who is ready for any kind of discipline that is expected by the Master. It also implies that a disciple has accepted the reality that he is going to be guided, counseled, disciplined and molded. There should not be any kind of hesitation or reservation to surrender oneself to the lotus feet of a Sadguru. In bhakti tradition, this kind of surrender is known as *sharanagati*. When a Sadguru instructs the student to do something, there should be no resistance from the student or conflict within himself. That means unless a student has full faith in the absolute power of the almighty in his Sadguru, he would not receive the full blessings from his Master. Similarly, it is also the Master's responsibility to create trust in his disciples through His compassion, love and caring. Major responsibility rests on the shoulders of the spiritual aspirant. A sishya should possess the qualities such as humility, burning desire, full faith, renouncement of worldly desires, and relative absence of ego to fully surrender to receive Guru Krupa (grace).

Surrender to Sadguru is an essential component of guru-sishya relationship. Once you surrender, you should not look back and have any doubts. You must let the Guru paint the beautiful picture as He wishes. You should let go and give yourself mentally and bodily for Him to shape your destiny because he knows what you need and deserve knowing your past, present and future. Then the question is what is so unique, special and distinctive about the Guru? To sustain the guru-sishya relationship, sishya should have total undivided faith in his Guru. Faith works wonders. Faith can bring down the Almighty from the Heaven on to the earth like Prahalada and Dhruva. Following poem will highlight the significance of full faith.

As children bring their broken toys with tears for us to mend
I brought my broken dreams to God, because He was my friend.
But, instead of leaving Him in peace to work alone,
I hung around and tried to help with ways that were my own.
At last I snatched them back and cried, "How could you be so slow?"
"My child," He answered, "what could I do? You never did let go."

That idea of "let go" is the faith. If we can surrender to the guru with complete faith, he will transform our lives. However, if we keep looking over his shoulders and pestering and thinking that we know better than our Guru does, then we achieve nothing and receive nothing. Faith should let you trust your guru to do his wonders.

Guru's role in helping the disciple to travel on to the spiritual path, initiate him into mantra, instill in him spiritual growth, and make him realize the God consciousness is considered invaluable. Without Guru's guidance, judgment, counsel, discourse, protection, and grace, God realization is very difficult to achieve.

The question, "Is it possible to realize God without Guru?" is answered by **Swami Prabhavananda** where he states that "It is, but it is not easy without a guru. The guru is one who shows the path to God through a Mantram. He gives the secret of spiritual practices. He watches over His disciple and protects him. A guru must be a knower of Brahman."

Sadhguru Sri Ganapathi Sachchidananda Swamiji observed: *"By sitting in the presence of an enlightened soul, we must get peace of mind, relaxation, and indescribable happiness in the heart. Secondly, if you prostrate to a real Guru, his simple touch, sight or thought should put us in trance and spiritualism should awake. There must be some enlightened soul around the Guru. If all the above tests prove affirmative results, do not wait at all for anybody's opinion or approval. You experience yourself.*

Once you are convinced of your experience, then you found yourself a real Guru who can chart you on the spiritual path."

We have emphasized the importance of and need for a competent Guru for a sishya to follow. But we should also emphasize the fact that Sishya must be equally qualified even to have a Guru in his life. He should be spiritually receptive to the teachings of a Guru and should have an intense desire to follow the instructions of a Guru. The most well-known dialogue occurred in the **Kathopanishad** (2:7-9), where Yama, the teacher, addressed a young disciple Nachiketu:

> *That which not many gain through hearing,*
> > *not many know even when they hear it --*
> *Marvelous is the teacher, skillful is the receiver,*
> > *marvelous the knower, skillfully instructed.*
> *When taught by an inferior person it cannot be*
> > *understood even though reflected upon.*
> *Unless taught by another, there is no way, for it is*
> > *inconceivably more subtle than the most subtle.*
> *It is not obtainable by reasoning but taught by someone*
> > *else it may not be known, my dear.*
> *You have obtained it, resolve come true. May we*
> > *Find an inquirer like you, O Nachiketa.*

Guru is always looking at his disciple to help him through various means to help them in the spiritual development. Even though physical closeness is not required and personal intimacy is not necessary, Guru will accommodate the needs of his devotees. Sixteenth Century North Indian Saint Dandu describes the process of imparting knowledge to the disciples:

> *The guru speaks first with the mind*
> *Then with the glance of the eye*
> *If the disciple fails to understand*
> *He instructs him at last by word of mouth*
> *He that understands the spoken word is a common man*

He that interprets the gesture is an initiate
He that reads the thought of the mind
Unsearchable, unfathomable, is a God.

THE DISCIPLE'S QUALIFICATIONS

We have described the qualities of a guru, the kind of powers they possess, the method of guiding his disciples and how he can help the devotee to trek on the path of spirituality. No matter how much he may guide, counsel and teach, if the disciple is not ready, everything a Guru does becomes futile and waste of energy. One must progress incrementally to a higher level as he starts associating with a guru on a regular basis. What distinguishes the advanced student of spiritual life from the beginners? Or, to put the question another way, what are the qualifications for a chela who wishes to begin the most difficult and rigorous path or some people call "the razor-edged path"?

There are four characteristics of the advanced pupil, according to Vedantic teachers. These characteristics, or qualifications, are known as the **sadhana chatushtaya**, or the four instruments of spiritual knowledge; and they may also be called the disciplines necessary to those who seek self-knowledge, or God -realization.

Sadananda Yogindra, in his **Vedantasara**, "the essence of Vedanta" states the four requirements thus:

> *"The means to the attainment of knowledge are these: discrimination between the permanent and the transient; renunciation of the fruits of action, in this world and hereafter; "the six treasures," such as control of the mind, and so forth; and the desire for liberation."*

First, the pupil should have **Viveka, discrimination**. He should be able to separate the permanent from the impermanent, the real from the unreal. He should slowly realize that his body, emotions, and mind, his desires, fears, and ambitions, bind them preventing him to travel to higher realms. He should perceive the difference between changing and unchanging, and permanent and impermanent. His Self within is identical with the Absolute, Brahman, which, Sadananda declares, "alone is the permanent Substance" and "all things other than it are transient." Because of this insight into where truth is found, the pupil is not deceived by mundane distractions.

Second, the pupil's life, both inner and outer, should exemplify **vairagya, renunciation**. He should know that all pleasures, enjoyments and entertainments are transient and these worldly pleasures destroy character, stimulating one's ignorance, impurity, and suffering. Realization should dawn on the disciple's mind that pleasures distract the truth-seeker from his quest for permanence and changeless. He should be nonattached to everything of a temporal nature. He should be detached even in his thought of whatever rewards may accrue to him in the life hereafter. He should renounce every distraction which obstructs his path to God realization.

Third, the pupil should have the **shatsampatti, the six treasures**. These are **shama**, calmness- the inner poise which comes with continuous contemplation of the Supreme Reality; **dama**, self-control - the restraint of the lower nature from every activity except the pursuit of the real; **uparati**, self-settledness - the mental ability to restrain the lower nature, temporarily governed by shama and dama, from again pursuing the unreal; **titiksha**, forbearance - the ability to endure, with detachment, everything arising from any of the pairs of opposites (such as heat and cold, or pain and pleasure); **samaadhana**, perfect concentration- the steady centering of awareness on the nature of the Absolute as interpreted by the scriptures and one's guru; and **shraddha**, faith- the affirmative and intuitive attitude of heart and mind which enables the chela to respond to and accept scriptural truth as his teacher expounds it.

And fourth, the pupil should have **mumukshutwam**, the yearning or a burning desire for spiritual liberation. Only when the foregoing three qualifications have been fulfilled, the disciple may be said to be truly ready to experience absolute knowledge. It is required to have single minded concentration to achieve this fourth stage. It signifies peeling of layers of ignorance to experience the flowering of consciousness. At this stage, a student starts aligning and integrating dots to get connected to the supreme consciousness. He will leave behind intellectual discussions, bookish knowledge and emotional attachments. He must be on his way to experience God-nature. Everything else is left behind, things become insignificant to experience the God realization. No obstacles or bottlenecks should disturb him. For any student *mumukshutwam* would be the ultimate goal.

Once a student passes through these four stages of spiritual development, according to Mukund Upanishad, "To that pupil who has approached him with due courtesy, whose mind has become perfectly calm, and who has control over his senses, the wise teacher should truly impart that knowledge of Brahman through which he knows the Being, imperishable and real." One has to have thirst for knowledge and liberation, yearning to follow the commands of the scriptures and possess the qualities of love, compassion, patience, tolerance, ahimsa, humility etc.

FOUR CLASSES OF DISCIPLES

Whenever disciples approach a guru, their level of devotion, desire to learn, the capacity to learn, and their commitment to follow the spiritual education are different. No two disciples are alike. Swami Sivananda classified the disciples into four classes:

- The best disciple is like petrol or aviation spirit. Even from a great distance, he will instantly react to the spark of the Guru's Upadesa.
- The second-class disciple is like camphor. A touch awakens his inner spirit and kindles the fire of spirituality in him.
- The third class of disciple is like coal. The Guru has to take great pains in order to awaken the spirit in him.
- The fourth class of disciple is like a plantain stem. No efforts will be of any avail over him. Whatever the Guru may do, he remains cold and inert.

Swami Sivananda further stated that two things are necessary to make beautiful image of a God. One is a perfect, faultless, good piece of marble; the second is an expert sculptor. The sculptor should have the piece of faultless and good piece of marble in the hands of a sculptor for him to chisel a beautiful image. Similarly, if a disciple is interested in the spiritual liberation, he must cleanse himself and should be allowed to be molded, carved and shaped into an image of God.

HOW TO SERVE GURU

A disciple should always be ready to serve his guru. He should be mentally and physically ready to serve with no reservations, no ego, and with full of bhakti. Sant Jnanadev has beautifully described the responsibility of a disciple to receive the full benefit of the grace of a Sadguru.

> *[The devotee] regards the Guru as a holy place, his deity, mother, and father, and knows no other path than service to him.*
>
> *It is the joy of his life to live in his Guru's house, and he loves others who serve the Guru as his own brothers.*
>
> *The repetition of the Guru's name is his only prayer, and his only scripture is his Guru's words.*
>
> *For him the water that touches his Guru's feet embraces all the holy places in the three worlds.*
>
> *If he should find some of the leftovers of his Guru's meal, they would be a feast far more sumptuous for him than even the bliss of Samadhi.*
>
> *O Arjuna, he would take a speck of the dust raised by his Guru's feet as the price with which to obtain eternal joy.*
>
> *What more can I say? His devotion is boundless. Out of overpowering inspiration, I have described it in this way.*
>
> *A person who has this kind of devotion and who enjoys nothing but serving the Guru is a treasure house of wisdom. Wisdom is even honored by his existence. He is a god and wisdom is his devotee.*
>
> *Wisdom enters him through open doors and lives in him. It is enough to satisfy the whole world.*
>
> *Jnanadev says, my soul takes delight in serving my Guru. This is why I have explained it in such detail.*

Otherwise, if I am not occupied in serving him, I am helpless even though I have hands, I am blind to worship even though I have eyes, and I am less able than a lame man to walk around the temple.

I am mute in praising his glory even though I have a voice, an idler who eats others' food. Yet in my heart I have the sincere desire to serve him.

It is this kind of obedience, willingness, humbleness, reverence, respect, and disposition that is essential to serve a Guru to experience the bliss. It is the responsibility of a devotee to follow him, listen to him, worship him, love him and surrender to him both mentally and physically. **Sant Kabir** explains the consequence of surrender to a Guru by a disciple. *"When you surrender all your consciousness, all outer forms will vanish from your sight and you will see nothing but Master everywhere. Such is the greatness of a perfect Master, and if the world were turn to paper, all the forests into writing pen, all the seven oceans into ink, they cannot adequately describe his glory. They are blind indeed, who think that the Master is simply a human being.... If you love the Master and worship him, in a moment you will be transported across the three worlds to the higher regions."*

MOTHER -THE EMBODIMENT OF SACRIFICE AND PROTECTION

(Part of this article was presented at Karya Siddhi Hanuman Temple, Frisco TX, USA, in celebration of Mother's Day on May 8, 2016)

"Where women are honored there the gods are pleased; but where they are not honored no sacred rite yields rewards," (Manu Smriti, III.56)

"Youth fades; love droops; the leaves of friendship fall; A mother's secret hope outlives them all." — Oliver Wendell Holmes

First of all, we want to wish all mothers a Happy Mother's Day. We should acknowledge on this Mother's Day, the role of mother in our religion, culture, scriptures, and in many other fields such as science, politics, philosophy, education, music and economy. Her impeccable role in the family is recognized, her unselfish sacrifice to the family is documented, and her indomitable strength is acknowledged. She is considered as the backbone of family, a stabilizing force playing a vital role in the preservation of family.

Hindu religion has accorded a mother the highest position compared to any other religion. **Matru Devo bhava** is the dictum nobody can forget. Mother is divine. It is important to remember that only Hindus worship God in the form of Divine Mother. In Hinduism we have Sri Lakshmi, goddess of wealth; Saraswati, goddess of learning and knowledge; Parvati goddess who bestows women with long married life; and Kali, the Power of time and other goddesses who protected the human race from demonic forces. Women as goddesses are worshipped in all religious festivals. During Navaratri time, different manifestations of Devi are worshipped for ten days. No religious function is complete without the participation of women. The social inconsistencies and injustices in the role of women did not arise from Hindu scriptures, but from the external forces that constrained the movement of women as well as the foreign rule that forced women to take a protective role. Many Hindu scriptures accorded high regard and high status to women.

In fact, the sixth century **Devi-Mahatyam** says: *"By you this universe is borne, by you this world is created. By you it is protected, O Devi: By you it is consumed at the end. You are the Supreme Knowledge, as well as ignorance, intellect and contemplation..."*

Look at what **Manu Smriti** says about the status of women:

"From the point of view of reverence due, a teacher is tenfold superior to a mere lecturer, a father a hundredfold to a teacher, and a mother a thousand-fold to a father." (II.45)

"Women must be honored and adorned by their fathers, brothers, husbands and brothers-in-law, who desire their own welfare." (III, 55)

" Where the female relations live in grief, the family soon wholly perishes; but that family where they are not unhappy ever prospers." (III, 57).

"The houses on which female relations, not being duly honored, pronounce a curse, perish completely as if destroyed by magic." (III, 58)

" Hence men who seek their own welfare, should always honor women on holidays and festivals with gifts of ornaments, clothes, and dainty food." (II, 59)

In an old Shakta hymn it is said - Striyah devah, Striyah pranah "Women are Devas, women are life itself." (Bharata Shakti - By Sir John Woodroffe p. 95).

From the early Vedic times women played vital role in preservation of Hindu heritage. They include such women as Sati, Sita, Anasuya, Arundhatee, Draupadi, Queen Kunti, Shakuntala, Maitreyi, Gargi, Madalasa, Savitri, Ahalya, and others. Many believe that simply reciting their names removes sins and remembering their names gives invincible strength.

Men and women form complement each other, just like heaven and earth, lyric and melody. They are equal partners in married life. Sage Agastya tells his wife Lopamudra – **"In this world, we will overcome all adversities if we two exert ourselves together."** A wife is called Ardhaangini ('half of oneself'), Sahadharaini (a comrade in life), Sahadharmini (an equal participant in performance of and in reaping fruits of good deeds), *Pathni* (the one who leads the husband through life), Dharmapathni (the one who guides the husband in dharma) and *Sahadharmacharini* (one who moves with the husband on the path of dharma--righteousness and duty). We call her better half.

Mother is seen as the cornerstone and foundation of the family. She is considered the upholder of the family traditions and supporter of dharma. She is considered the first Guru to her children as she provides the primary care, love, affection, compassion and moral compass. She is the one who transmits and nurtures the morals, ethics and ideals needed to provide foundation for the off springs. **Stephen Knapp** remarked, *"Women in motherhood, after giving birth to a child that they have carried for nine months, is the first guru and guide of the child and, thus, of humanity. Through this means, before any child learns hatred or aggression, they first know the love of a mother who can instill the ways of forgiveness and kindness in the child. In this way, we can recognize that there is often a strong woman, either as a mother or as a wife, behind most successful men.... In exhibiting the qualities of motherhood, women must be warm and tender, strong and protective, yet also lay the foundation of discipline and the discrimination of right from wrong."*

SRI SWAMI VIVEKANANDA ON THE POSITION OF MOTHER

Swami Vivekananda expressed an abundant appreciation and lavish veneration to the women of Bharat and mother was considered the solid foundation of Hindu philosophy, culture and civilization. He respected her as the symbol of Divine Motherhood. From the childhood until they reach their end of life, Hindus always remember the sacrifices mother has made in shaping their personality. He said, the ideal woman in India is mother, the mother first, and the mother last. The word mother calls up to the mind of the Hindu, motherhood; and God is called Mother.

"The position of the mother is the highest in the world, as it is the one place in which to learn and exercise the greatest unselfishness. The love of God is the only love that is higher than a mother's love; all others are lower. It is the duty of the mother to think of her children first and then of herself. "

He always remembered the love and compassion of mother toward her children. Nothing is comparable to the love of mother toward her progeny. Children may disavow their mother but mother never deserts her children. Her love is color blind and never dissipates. She gladly embraces all the miseries of her children and safeguards them against all the misfortunes. *"Women as mother is marvelous, unselfish, all suffering and ever forgiving."*

In a lecture delivered in Shakespeare Club House, in Pasadena, California, on January 18, 1900, Swami Vivekananda stated, *"The ideal woman in India is the mother, the mother first, and the mother last. The word woman calls up to the mind of the Hindu, motherhood; and God is called Mother... To the ordinary man in India, the whole force of womanhood is concentrated in motherhood. In the Western home, the wife rules. In an Indian home, the mother rules... The name has been called holy once and for ever, for what name is there which no lust can ever approach, no carnality ever come near, then the one-word mother? That is the ideal in India."*

Swami Sivananda: *"The Mother is a mysterious, indescribable power of the Supreme Being. She is the dynamic aspect of the Supreme, Transcendent Being, which is infinity, eternity and ineffable peace, beyond the cognizance of the senses and the mind."*

Francois Gautier *"Thus in India - and it is true that it is often a paradox, as women, because of later Muslim influences, have often been relegated to the background -* **the feminine concept is a symbol of dynamic realization.** *She is the eternal Mother, who is all Wisdom, all Compassion, all Force, Beauty and Perfection. It is in this way that since the dawn of times, Hindus have venerated the feminine element under its different manifestations. Mahalakshmi, Mahakali, Mahasaraswati, Maheshwari - and even India is feminine: "Mother India." "*

BHISHMA GLORIFIED THE MOTHER.

According to Bhishma nothing is superior to serving women. One who respects and serves mother achieves great success in life. Her blessings are ever present and never evaporate, even if her children reach the oldest age possible as long as she is alive.

"The mother is the panacea for all kinds of calamities. The existence of the mother invests one with protection; the reverse deprives one of all protection. The man who, though divested of prosperity enters his house, uttering the words, "O mother!"- has not to indulge in grief. Nor does decrepitude ever assail him. A person whose mother exists, even if he happens to be possessed of sons and grandsons and even he himself is hundred years old, but in the eyes of his mother he looks like a child of two years of age. Whether the mother is able or disabled, lean or robust, the son is always protected by the mother. None else, according to the ordinance, is the son's protector. Then does the son become old, then does he become stricken with grief, then does the world look empty in his eyes, when he becomes deprived of his mother? **There is no shelter like the mother. There is no refuge like the mother. There is no defense like the mother. There is no one so dear as the mother. For having borne him in her womb the mother is the son's Dhatri. For having been the chief cause of his birth, she is his Janani. For having nursed his young limbs, she is called Amva (Amma). For nursing and looking after the son she is called Sura. The mother is one's own body."** (Santi Parva: Mokshadharma Parva; Section CCLXVI)

KUNTI AS MOTHER

After Surya Deva fulfilled her wish to have a son, Kunti became pregnant. He promised her that she would remain a virgin after the delivery. With that promise, a boy came out from her ear; hence he was called Karna. As the promise was fulfilled without any body's knowledge, she decided to leave him in Ashva river. Mother Kunti put him in a box in   much agony, tears rolling down on her cheeks left him in the river. As a mother, she raised her eyes to the scorching Surya Deva requested him by saying: *"Watch over our son, let no evil befall on him."* As the box started floating away from her, she blessed her so: *"May all your paths be auspicious. May the lord of rivers guard you; may the lord of the air watch over you; may all the Gods protect you. And when I see you again one day, let me know you by your golden kavachas and kundala."*

Kunti played a major role as a Mother in influencing her sons to fight the war. She advised her sons to take up arms for the preservation of dharma and to follow the tradition of Kashatriyas whose responsibility it was to protect the people of their land. After the war concluded with Pandavas' victory over Kauravas, she decided to take Vanaprastha Ashrama along with Dhritarashtra and Gandhari. Yudhisthira was shocked and asked her, "you goaded us to wage war and why are you leaving us at this stage." **Bhima** also implored by saying, "why this decision to leave when you should be enjoying the riches your sons have acquired?" Her advice should be taken as a role model for all the mothers across the globe and the children to follow:

*"It is true, son, that I egged you on to fight for your rights when you were roaming about with empty stomachs and grief-laden hearts. Deprived of your rightful patrimony, insulted by your kinsmen, when you were living on the bread of beggary, I did goad you on to fight for your rights. You ask me, why? In order that you may not wait on your inferiors, you who are veterans of war and are as noble as the gods. So that you, **Yudhishthira, righteous and the rightful heir to the throne may not wander about in the woods; so that Bhima, who is far-famed for his prowess, may not suffer humiliation at the hands of his enemies; so that Arjuna, Indra's son, may not drink the cup of misery; so that your dear younger brothers Nakula and Sahadeva may not know the pinch of poverty and hunger.; so that Draupadi, this dear daughter of mine, may not fall prey again to vile molestation. My dear son, it was to arouse you to your own glory that I pushed you into war through the words of Vidura.** I encouraged you to fight in order that the noble line of the great King Pandu may not come to an end with my sons. There is no hope or future for one who brings about the ruin of one's family. My children, I have enjoyed in full all the royal pleasures which my departed husband had earned for me. Charities without number have I performed. And I have sipped the soma juice in solemn sacrifice. I do not crave for any enjoyment earned by my sons. I intend reducing my body through*

penance and service to my elders. May your mind ever remain steadfast in righteousness; may your mind be noble: **Dharme te dhīyatām buddhirmanaste mahadastu ca.** "

GANDHARI AS MOTHER

Before the war between Pandavas and Kauravas commenced, Dhritarashtra and Gandhari counselled their children to make peace with Pandavas. There is a moral lesson to learn from Gandhari and what happens when the children go against the wishes of a mother. It is obvious that the refutation of Gandhari's advice to her sons wiped out the Kaurava family – all her 100 sons killed by Karna.

Gandhari then tried to correct her son, Duryodhana, by saying, **"You are a fool! You never listen to wisdom that is meant for your own interest. All the elders have spoken in favor of peace, but you alone desire war which will destroy our family. You will remember your father's words when struck dead by Bhimasena's mace."**

Gandhari even advised her husband to stop the game of dice twice with no success. She even chided Dhritarashtra for not interfering while the Draupati was being disrobed in the court. She had said that, "This kind of humiliation to Draupati would surely "rekindle a dead fire, topple a bridge re-built" and destroy the Kaurava dynasty. She always advised her sons with words of wisdom and motherly love for them to follow. She pleaded them to eschew the needless war by sharing the kingdom with Pandavas. She argued that they should avoid the greedy ambition to possess the entire kingdom. Even Lord Krishna recognized and appreciated her dharmic counsel by saying that, "You have, in the open court, repeatedly and rightly spoken words of wisdom and justice for the welfare of both the sides thirsting for war."

Before going into the battle on the final day, Duryodhana goes to his Mother Gandhari seeking her blessings before going to the battle. Her blessings have not blinded her motherly affection. She was on the side of dharma, when she remarked, **"Listen to my words, O fool, where there is righteousness there is victory (Srunu mudha vachomyaham yato dharmastato jayah - Salya Parva: 63.62).**

Lord Krishna even lauds Gandhari's wisdom and the passion for her path of dharma by saying, *"O the gracious Lady, there is none comparable to you in the whole world"* (tat samam nasti loke sminnadya simantini shubhe - Salya Parva 63.59).

Mother's love is deep and unconditional. It is profound and unfathomable. When Gandhari realized that the war was immanent, knowing fully well that Duryodhana was not as strong as Bhima, to ensure success in the war, she ask her loving son Duryodhana, **"Before you go into battle, son, come before me without any clothes. When I look upon your body, each part that I see will become hard as a diamond, unyielding to weapons."** Feeling shy and uncomfortable to appear totally naked in front of his mother, he covered his groin and hips with leaves around his waist. First time she removed her blindfold after her marriage to see her son with the leaves around his waist. She was horrified to say, "Oh my son, what have you done? Now, that covered part of your body will be vulnerable to weapons. Your enemies will not fail to strike you there." She bitterly cried and she knew that Duryodhana was destined to be killed by striking at the part that was covered with leaves. During the battle, Bhima struck Duryodhana at his hip ultimately causing his death.

SRI ADI SHANKARA PRAISES MOTHER

Adi Sankara Bhagavatpada's mother, Aryamba, was against his taking up Sanyasa and leave the house. She finally agreed based on the promise he made to his mother that he would be present near her death bed and perform the obsequies also. When he was at Sringeri, with his siddhi (powers), he realized that his mother was nearing death and reached his mother immediately and performed her funeral services. He also said that there is no bad mother, it is only a bad son. At that time, he composed five slokas to reflect the pain they endure and sacrifice mothers make for their children. First sloka gives the emotional appreciation of mother by Adi Shankara.

Oh! mother mine,
With clenched teeth bore thou the excruciating pain,
When I was born to you,
Shared thou the bed made dirty by me for an year,

And thine body became thin and painful,
During those nine months that you bore me,
For all these in return,
Oh mother dearest,
I can never compensate,
Even by my becoming great.

On Mother's Day let us all appreciate, applaud and accolade the role of mother, her importance in rearing the children, instilling everlasting ethical values, sacrificing her life for the sake of children, guiding them through lifelong, and blessing them with incomparable love and compassion.

REMEMBERING MOTHER

O Mother! May the society appreciate your potential. May they seek your blessings from east, west, north, south and everywhere. And may you bless them with prosperity and happiness. (Yajur Veda: 6:36)

As we celebrate Mother's Day as per the traditions in the West on May 12th, let us pay tribute to the role of mother and her contribution in shaping the family as well as a nation. In the Hindu way of life, a Mother is always remembered, reminisced, cherished, respected, honored, glorified and worshipped.

Mother is considered the pillar of Hindu family; a pinnacle of sacrifice; an embodiment of love, affection and compassion; a source of inspiration and encouragement; a personification of peace and harmony; a foundation of strength and courage; an epitome of age-old wisdom and prudence; a hallmark of patience and endurance; a quintessence of solace and comfort; an exemplification of kindness and gentleness; a reservoir of inexhaustible blessings; and as a personification of patience and tolerance.

How can we forget the forbearance of mother who conceived us and carried us for nine months in her womb; suffered months of morning sickness; saw us grow day by day; fed us through the tube; allowed us to take shape as we developed backbone, skin, fingers, nails, eye lids, eye brows, nose, ears, hands, legs, toes, heart, head, brain, and so on for nine months; and carried all the weight all these months; endured all the sounds and kicks; spent countless nights without sleep; withstood all the discomforts; and finally gave birth. How can we forget the mother's endurance and tenacity during those nine months?

How can we forget the anxious mother's first look at the baby in spite of all the pain and suffering during the delivery; her instant motherly instinct to hold and caress; her longing to feed the baby; her excitement to hear the sounds of her infant; her delight in putting him to the bed; her constant vigil of looking at the sleeping baby; her thrill in seeing the baby crawl and walk; her prompting the baby to talk; her enjoyment of feeding the baby; her constant concern for the safety of the child; her passion to narrate bedtime stories; and countless efforts to make the child grow with confidence, trust and love. Who can forget and how can we forget?

Hindu religion has given her an exalted position compared to any other religion. **Matru Devo bhava** is the dictum nobody can forget. Mother is divine. It is important to remember that only Hindus worship God in the form of the Divine Mother. In Hinduism, we have Sri Lakshmi, goddess of wealth; Saraswati, the goddess of learning and knowledge; Parvati, the goddess who bestows women with long married life; and Kali, the power of time and other goddesses who protected the human race from demonic forces. Women as goddesses are worshipped in all religious festivals. During Navaratri time, different manifestations of Devi are worshipped for ten days. And no function is complete without the participation of women as mother. The social inconsistencies and injustices in the role of women did not arise from Hindu scriptures, but from the external forces that constrained the movement of women as well as the foreign rule that forced women to take a protective role.

Hindu scriptures extolled the virtues of a woman starting from her birth as an infant, daughter, kanya, bride, wife, daughter-in-law and a mother. Whether one is young, middle aged or old, he gets immense joy and pleasure thinking and remembering one's mother. There is no one that can be compared to her. Lord Rama addressing his brother Lakshamana said: "Api Swarnamayi Lankaa na me Lakshmana rochate, Janani Janmabhumishcha Swargaadapi Gariyasi" (Lakshmana, even this golden Lanka does not appeal to me; mother and motherland are greater than heaven).

From the early Vedic times, women have played a vital role in the preservation of Hindu heritage. They include women such as Sati, Sita, Anasuya, Arundhati, Draupadi, Kunti, Shakuntala, Maitreyi, Gargi, Madalasa, Savitri, Ahalya, and others. Many believe that simply reciting their names removes sins and remembering their names gives enough strength. The Vedas, Upanishads, Puranas, Manu Sastra, Ramayana, Mahabharata, and other scriptures have eulogized the role of the mother.

Manu Dharma Sastra gave unparalleled respect and honor to the mother. **Friedrich Nietzsche**, a Western philosopher and spiritualist, says: *"I know of no book in which so many tender and kind remarks are addressed to woman as in the Law Book of Manu; these old grey-bearded saints have a way of being polite to women which has perhaps never been surpassed"*

MANU DHARMA SASTRA

Following are some of the examples of the statements found in Manu Dharma Sastra about the status of women:

"Where women are honored there the gods are pleased; but where they are not honored no sacred rite yields rewards," (III.56)

"Women must be honored and adorned by their fathers, brothers, husbands and brothers-in-law, who desire their own welfare." (III, 55)

"Where the female relations live in grief, the family soon wholly perishes; but that family where they are not unhappy ever prospers." (III, 57).

"Wherever women are given their due respect, even the deities like to reside, and where they are not respected, all action remains unfruitful."

VEDAS

Similarly Rig Veda, Yajur Veda, and Atharvana Veda also glorified the status of the mother, beseeched her blessings, sought her advice, obtained her wisdom, reminisced her smile and cherished her unparalleled compassion.

Rigveda 10.17.10: O Mothers! Purify us with your compassion, understanding and enlightenment. The women cleanse us all from all our sins, corruption and defects. We come out firm, pure and noble from their blessed company.

Rigveda 6.61.7: O enlightening Mother! You have the potential to destroy the evil. You have a character as pure as gold. You have the potential to destroy the clouds of frustrations and doubt. You are brave and you only aspire for our well-being and success! We are indeed blessed!

Atharvaveda 7.68.2: O enlightening Mother! May you always shower your blessings in form of peace, happiness and success. May you always be pleased with us and may we never conduct any act that excludes us from your blessing gaze.

Atharvaveda 3.13.7: O pure and blessing Mother! I am your beloved son. O powerful mother, please guide me towards fulfillment of my noble aspirations.

Yajurveda 6.17: O pure and blessing Mothers! Cleanse us all from sins, immorality and pollution. Purge us from falsehood, hatred, jealousy and frustrations.

Yajurveda 6.31: O pure and blessing Mothers! Satisfy our mind, speech, life, eyes, ears, soul and society with nobleness.

SHANKARA BHAGAVADPADA ON MOTHER

Shankara wanted to take up Sanyasa at a tender age, but his mother refused. However, he convinced her that he would be present at her deathbed no matter where he was. Later, when he realized that his mother was indeed on her deathbed, he appeared instantly near his mother with his divine powers, and conducted her funeral ceremony. At that juncture, he was supposed to have written the "Matru Panchakam", a tribute that would bring tears to any son or daughter who reads or listen to it. Nothing surpasses this moving tribute to a mother. Shankara only composed slokas about Gods and Goddesses, with the sole exception being the Matru Panchakam, which contains five verses about a human's mother.

Suffice it to read the last verse about a Mother's constant shower of blessings on her child:

Long live,
Oh, pearl mine,

Oh jewel mine,
Oh my dearest eyes,
Oh mine prince dearest,
And oh my soul of soul,
Sang thou to me,
But in return of that all,
Oh my mother dearest.
I give you but dry rice in your mouth.

BHISHMA'S ACCOLADES TO THE MOTHER

Upon culmination of the Kurukshetra war, Lord Krishna takes the Pandavas to Bhishma who lying on the bed of arrows. Upon the Pandavas' request to impart knowledge about Rajaneeti and various other topics, Bhishma pays a glowing tribute to the place of Mother in the hearts of every human being and the need for her guidance to avert calamities in the society. In the Shanti Parva, Bhishma says that the mother is the panacea for all kinds of evils. Even mention of mother's name would avert the grief and sadness. Even if a mother has a son of hundred-year-old man, in her eyes is like a two-year-old kid to be taken care of. "There is no shelter like the mother. There is no refuge like the mother. There is no defense like the mother. There is no one so dear as the mother. For having borne him in her womb the mother is the son's Dhatri. For having been the chief cause of his birth, she is his Janani. For having nursed his young limbs, she is called Amva (Amma). For nursing and looking after the son she is called Sura. The mother is one's own body."

Devi-Mahatyam goes even farther by saying that she is the source and sustenance of the cosmos: *"By you this universe is borne, by you this world is created. By you it is protected, O Devi: By you it is consumed at the end. You are the Supreme Knowledge, as well as ignorance, intellect and contemplation..."*

A wife and husband are equal partners in married life. Sage Agastya tells his wife Lopamudra, *"In this world, we will overcome all adversities if we two exert ourselves together."* A wife is called Ardhaangini ('half of oneself'), Sahadharmini (a comrade in life, an equal participant in performance of and in reaping fruits of good deeds), Pathni (the one who leads the husband through life), Dharmapathni (the one who guides the husband in dharma) and Sahadharmacharini (one who moves with the husband on the path of dharma--righteousness and duty). Mother is God herself.

To call woman the weaker sex is a libel; it is man's injustice to woman. If by strength is meant brute strength, then, indeed, is woman less brute than man. If by strength is meant moral power, then woman is immeasurably man's superior. Has she not greater intuition, is she not more self-sacrificing, has she not greater powers of endurance, has she not greater courage? Without her, man could not be. If nonviolence is the law of our being, the future is with woman. Who can make a more effective appeal to the heart than woman? -- Mahatma Gandhi.

Let us all remember our MOTHERS, their sacrifices, their compassion, their guidance, their wisdom, their watchful eyes, their smiles, and their bountiful and unconditional blessings.

DHARMA AND DERELICTION OF DHARMA

HINDU INSTITUTIONS MUST SEE THAT HISTORY DOES NOT REPEATS ITSELF

"It is the Hindus, as a nation, who are in danger of extinction, at least in certain parts of India."

This was the forecast of a German lady who adopted Hinduism, changed her name to Savitri Devi, wrote a book entitled, **"A warning to Hindus,"** which was published in 1939. How accurate her warning is! Today we are witnessing the extinction of Hindu population in Kashmir, West Bengal, North Eastern States, Kerala and other parts of India. Her prediction is even more precise when she said: "When one sees Hindudom in its weakness, yielding every day to hostile forces, losing bit by bit its numerical advantages, losing its political rights in India, losing its place as a nation, then one becomes more skeptical." Before her dire forecast of losing India becomes a reality, all Hindus have to shoulder the burden of responsibility of protecting Hinduism; shed the ideology of secularism, atheism, minority appeasement and vote bank politics, abandon the selfishness for fame, name, power and money by mortgaging Bharat; and look at the real possibility of losing freedom and liberty known to Sanatana Dharma. Are we as Hindus ready to lose the identity and lose the nation and experience the horrors our ancestors were subjected to?

WHAT IS DHARMA?

Dharma is defined as duty, responsibility, right living, obligation, expectation, ethics, principle, justice, and/or any act that promoted common good. This is unique concept in Hinduism. Dharma represents moral standing in the society. Ethical, moral and principles life is expected. Dharma is pregnant with different expectations depending on the station of an individual and social order. Adharma, the opposite of dharma, represents evil, chaos, injustice, disunity and discord in the society. If every element in the cosmos performs its duty, there will be order, predictability, stability, and harmony.

Dharma was developed as a solution to the problems confronting human race either through individuals, animals, natural elements, demonic forces or divine powers. When Yudhishtira asked to explain the nature of dharma, Bhishma answered by saying: "It is most difficult to define dharma. Dharma has been explained to be that which helps the upliftment of living beings. Therefore, that which ensures the welfare of living beings is surely Dharma. The learned rishis have declared that which sustains is Dharma." Shanti Parva, 119:9-11)

Source of dharma is traced to as far back as Vedas. Dharma is used as an injunction to perform certain rituals. Dharmas are assigned depending on the varna system, Ashrama system, gender roles, and political system. Different are assigned to different levels based on the stages of life. They are different from celibate bachelor, householder, forest dweller and renouncer. Similarly, dharma is applicable to the rulers of the nation. It is the dharma of king to protect the people, fulfill the needs of the people, enforce the law equally without any bias, maintain social order, and uphold the cosmic order. Irrespective of differences in the performance of dharma by different elements in the society, Hindu scripture identify ten qualities that are the basis of dharma. They are fortitude, forgiveness, self-control, refraining from stealing, purity, control over the senses, intellect, knowledge, truth and absence of anger.

The leaders of the nation or any organization should provide good examples for the subjects. If the leader follow dharma, others follow their examples. **Kautilya** says, "if a king is energetic, his subjects will be equally energetic. If he is reckless, they will only be reckless likewise, but also eat into his works."

Dharma can be identified as any act that upholds, supports, sustains an individual, a family, society, the nation, the eco-system, the world and cosmic order. Anything that inspires, stimulates and fosters unity and growth is Dharma. Dharma also means refraining from slander, deception, envy, pride, egotism, disbelief, dishonesty, praising oneself, hypocrisy, greed, perplexity, anger and jealousy.

Almost all the Hindu scriptures dealt with the concept of dharma extensively and described it in widest possible terms. It is the dharma of air is to blow, fire to burn, water to quench thirst and sustain the earth, ice to melt, father to protect the family, mother to show compassion, plants to give out oxygen, cobra to bite, teacher to impart skills and values, and so on. Every segment of the cosmos has its dharma to sustain the world order. If everybody performs their duties expected of them, harmony, peace and peaceful existence will prevail in the social order.

Thirukkural (verses 31–32) reminds us, *"Dharma yields Heaven's honor and Earth's wealth. What is there then that is more fruitful for a man? There is nothing more rewarding than dharma, nor anything more ruinous than its neglect."*

In the Karna Parva, **Lord Krishna** explains Dharma to Arjuna in the following words: *"Dharma sustains the society. Dharma maintains the social order. Dharma ensures well-being and progress of humanity. Dharma is surely that which fulfills these objectives."*

Madhavacharya, in his commentary on Parashara Smriti, explains the meaning of dharma as, *"Dharma embraces every type of righteous conduct, covering every aspect of life essential for the sustenance and welfare of the individual and society. Further, it includes those rules which guide and enable those who believe in God and heaven to attain moksha."*

Even the corporations should develop broad guidelines consistent with dharmic values. Their dharmic mission is to create wealth, produce quality goods, satisfy the customers, improve the quality of life, establish trust customers, treat people with respect, provide necessary facilities to enhance the skills and talents, introduce activities that promote peace of mind, encourage innovative and creative idea, etc. for the benefit the company, employees, customers and the country itself. **Azim Premji** embraces the concept of dharma to be followed in corporate world. *"Only clear, consistent and unwavering communication and practice of values can create a culture that can withstand and gain from turbulence."*

Hinduism is in critical situation. It is at crossroads. It is crying out loud for her children to intervene and protect. It is waiting for them to rescue from the clutches of anti-Hindu forces. It is being attacked, choked, suffocated, stifled, wounded, and throttled by Muslims, Christians, Marxists, Hindu adversaries, atheists, secularists and the government relentlessly. Hindus are equally, if not more, responsible for the possible collapse of Hindu edifice and negligence and destruction of Hindu Temples. The so-called leftists and secularists are attacking Hinduism ruthlessly without realizing that they are setting fire to their own house, they are losing the precious freedom Hinduism allowed them to exercise freely, and they are joining hands with anti-Hindu governments that are bent on managing, abusing and demolishing the Hindu Temples.

It is also miserable to see that millions of Hindus are becoming witness to the destruction of their own Hindu culture and their places of worship, becoming spectators to the game of the bullfight where Hinduism is being slowly bled to death, becoming silent bystanders watching the government slowly chipping away the fundamental rights of Hindus, and becoming selfish to make a buck. Hindus are becoming strange bedfellows with the enemies of their own religion, and becoming obsessed with making money even to the extent of selling their own motherland and their own mother – Hinduism.

All Hindus who are educated, who have respect for their religion, who manage Hindu Temples and other Hindu organizations, and who are the members of numerous cultural associations, India associations, literary associations, regional associations and performing arts associations should take immediate steps to protect their religion. Being members and the office bearers of these organizations, they have the obligations to know the difference between culture and religion, and make every effort to learn the richness of their culture and religion. Ignorance should not be the criteria to hold offices in these organizations. Once they open up their minds, learn the basics of their culture and religion, they will be the role models for next generations.

Let us learn from Mark Tully, Chief of Bureau BBC in New Delhi, who confessed his mistake in finding faults with one billion Hindus over the years. He used to think and report that Christians and Muslims were discriminated and were denied of their rights and freedom. Over a period of time, he slowly realized the greatness, richness and tolerance of Hinduism.

Mark Tully stated that *"I have repented today: I do profoundly believe that India needs to be able to say with pride, "Yes, our civilization has a Hindu base to it." The genius of Hinduism, the very reason it has survived so long, is that it does not stand up and fight. It changes and adapts and modernizes and absorbs–that is the scientific and proper way of going about it. I believe that Hinduism may actually prove to be the religion of this millennium, because it can adapt itself to change."* He also observed **"Hindus are still slaves to MUSLIMS and CHRISTIANS."**

Swami Vivekananda told the Parliament of Religions in Chicago in 1893 *"Sectarianism, bigotry, and its horrible descendant, fanaticism, have long possessed this beautiful earth. They have filled the earth with violence, drenched it often and often with human blood, destroyed civilization and sent whole nations to despair."*

We urge all Hindus, Hindu institutions, Cultural Organization, Language based organizations, India Associations, and various performing arts organizations to realize the danger they may inherit for not embracing and advocating the principles, ethics, morals, tolerance, spirituality, and universality. It is the sacred duty and full responsibility of all Hindus to learn their own history – how they were massacred by Muslims and Christians, how their Temples were destroyed, how their women were raped, enslaved, and how their resources were looted. Read about the Hindu holocaust, the Muslim onslaught on Hindus, mass killing of Hindus on Hindu Kush mountain, destruction of Somnath Temple, conversion of 2000 Hindu Temples into mosques, the history of Tejo Mahal (now it is called Taj Mahal), demolition of Krishna Janma Sthala and erection of Mosque on top of it, conversion of Ram Temple in Ayodhya into Babri Masjid, the erection of Mosque at the entrance of Kasi Vishwanath Temple, atrocities committed by Christians during Goa inquisition, and deception and deceit of Christian conversion. We cannot negate and neglect the torturous history of Hindus in the hands of Christians and Muslims. We cannot subject our fellow Hindus to the same fate our forefathers experienced. Let us remember the words of Gorge Santayana *"Those that fail to learn from history, are doomed to repeat it."*

DHARMA OF HINDU INSTITUTIONS AND ORGANIZATIONS WITH MAJORITY HINDUS

Hindu organizations such as Hindu Temples, Hindu Foundations, Mattas, Peethams, Ashrams, and other organizations with the mission of upholding the Dharmic values should look beyond and learn the history of Hindus over the last ten centuries if we are realistic to realize the magnitude of the impending danger lurking around the corner. The custodians (office bearers) of these Hindu Institutions cannot ignore the plight of Hindus in India and across the globe, cannot remain indifferent to the atrocities being committed against their own people, cannot negate the centuries of brutality inflicted on Hindus, cannot remain ignorant of their past history sitting in the comforts of their citadels, and cannot build walls around their institutions ignoring the impending danger of losing the freedom and liberty they are enjoying.

Many **Hindu Temples** in USA are doing an excellent job in performing the rituals and festivals, meeting the religious needs of their Hindu attendees, conducting a number of cultural events such as dance programs, Carnatic music programs, Bhajans, discourses, yoga classes, meditation courses, and conducting Sunday schools.

They should make every effort to identify with the roots back in Bharat, nourish these roots, and protect them from being pulled out by selfish Hindus and missionary motivated religions. With few exceptions, many of these institutions are failing in their responsibility to gauge the current happenings affecting our youth here and abroad; failing to witness the dark cloud hovering over their own institutions they manage; failing to impart the knowledge to equip their congregation to deal with the realistic missionary activities of other religions; failing to teach their own youth about other religions are waging a war against Hinduism; failing to address the issues Hindu youth is facing in their schools; failing to guard their own Hindus from the deceptive practices of other faiths; failing to take appropriate action to promote and protect their own religion ignoring the dangers encircling their own institutions; and failing to speak out against the Government of India's assault on Hindu Temples and Hindu culture.

Hindu NRIs in USA, who are managing Hindu Temples have a special obligation to serve their mother country, protect her from being stabbed from all sides, voice their views demanding equality of religions, demand the abolition of minority quotas based on religion, stress the need for the repeal of Endowment Act and oppose any and all efforts to undermine Hindu Temples and Hindu culture by the government and Hindu politicians. They should invite speakers to talk about the policies of the government and politics the government plays to destabilize the Hindu edifice. Hindu Temples cannot operate as separate islands unconnected to the society. They should take active part to protect their edifices.

Whenever a request is made to these Hindu Temples in USA to invite speakers who are experts on such topics as Government control of Hindu Temples, Hajj Subsidy, minority appeasement, conversion menace, Islamic terrorism, Christian and Islamic explosion of their population, and any other burning issues affecting the Hindus, these Temple authorities invariably use the slogans "that is all politics," "we don't invite controversial speakers," "we decided not to invite speakers who talk about other religions," "we are secular," and others , not knowing that the issues the speakers talk about are the ones which are undermining the religion they belong to and the Temples they are managing. It is a pity that they have developed such a closed mind not because of the merits of their arguments but because of their ignorance.

We have another set of organizations in USA called **cultural organizations, language based organizations, India Associations, regional associations and others** who do the same thing as Hindu Temples do. Of course, many of these organizations start their programs with Hindu prayers, light the traditional Hindu lamps, celebrate Hindu festivals, perform Srinivasa Kalyanams, but they refuse to invite "controversial" speakers. They even refuse to give main spot to our revered religious leaders. When a request is made to invite a "controversial" leader they say that they do not want speakers to criticize the government, or other religions. If you ask them to invite Religious Leaders, they also go one step further to say that "they are cultural" to mean that culture and religion have nothing in common as if they are unconnected. Even after numerous discussions and written communication about the inseparable nature of culture and religion, they refuse to open their minds, refuse to learn and refuse to act. They do not want to acknowledge the fact that there is no culture without religion and religion without culture.

Some of the organizations such as **India Associations** also argue that they are "secular" hence they cannot invite any speaker who may talk against the deception and terrorism of other religions. But they celebrate many of Hindu festivals. At the same time, they don't even want to have discussion or a dialogue on a given topic. One wonders how can these secularists keep quiet when one religion is being trampled by other religions. Is it acceptable for the secularists to close their eyes to see the evil and turn their eyes away from it as if nothing happened? They also have another slogan saying, "We have a couple of Christians," in our organization and "we do not want to offend them." These office bearers are willing to sacrifice the interests of 99 percent for the sake of one percent belonging to other religions. We hope one of these days they will address these issues during their celebrations/functions and how they would justify their actions.

Have you ever seen any Pakistan Association, South Arabia Association, Iranian Association, etc with secularists? Do they have any place in these organizations? Why do these 99 percent Hindus in these organizations tolerate this one percent secularists or atheists? Hindus should act like Hindus. Hindus cannot ignore their past, ignore the ten centuries of atrocities their ancestors were subjected, negate their richness and close their eyes to the present intimidation Hindus are experiencing toady in India. We are the people with little knowledge, with little interest in learning, with little appreciation for the richness of our religion and almost no interest in protecting the freedom and liberty we are enjoying today. We are highly opinionated and highly self-centered; we cannot even make a case for our indifference to our own religion. They have very little knowledge about their religion but unfortunately that does not stop criticizing their mother religion.

But let us keep in mind that these **cultural organizations, India Associations, and language based organizations** love to invite all kinds of politicians, all kinds of movie actors, and all kinds of media personnel with questionable backgrounds, and with criminal charges pending. Some of the media people gleefully engage in bashing Hinduism, condemning Hindu Spiritual leaders, and inviting Non-Hindus to their TV stations to talk about Hindu festivals. Can these media people criticize the Muslims and Christians even though mountain of evidence with regard to terrorism and atrocities is documented? Can these media people show any program about the sex scandals of the religious leaders of other faiths, about the methods they use to convert innocent people, about the money trail, about the abuse of nuns in the churches, etc.? Then what is the intent of inviting these kinds of people? These organizations also pay first class tickets for the family members of these "dignitaries", accommodate them in five star hotels and arrange programs across the country. There are some office-bearers who are openly declared themselves as atheists and unhesitatingly express their distaste for Hindu culture. The office bearers of these organizations deny religious leaders proper place on the stage while the politicians and movie actors are given the main stage. Are these organizations supporting political culture, movie culture and media culture while undermining the religion the very basis of culture? In fact, every leader of the organization must make a sincere and constant effort to live the higher values like truth, beauty, goodness or compassion in his thought, feelings, behavior and action to represent the culture and religion they belong to create the universal understanding of the richness of Dharmic values.

For one who is keen on understanding oneself, there is nothing comparable to Hinduism anywhere in the world. While many other religions try to box God and existence in their scriptures or their holy books, **Hinduism gives freedom for everyone to experiment with it and understand the true essence of life. It even allows others to criticize it. Unfortunately, some of these secularists and atheists**

take advantage of this freedom to undermine the religion known for tolerance.

Then there are Hindu institutions, particularly **Hindu Temples** spread across the United States doing little to bring Hindus together. In every other religion, the places of worship bring people together and help defend their religion against external attacks. Many Hindu temples in US have become places of business, the place where management gets engrossed in extending their sphere of influence. There is little thought given to the relevance of these temples when Hinduism itself is under enormous threat.

All Hindus should be proud of their religion; should promote, propagate, preserve, practice and most importantly protect it from "**within**" and "**without**." Silence, neglect and negation from within are as dangerous as from without, that is from other religions such as Islam and Christianity.

"**Within**" refers to the Hindus who are neglecting their religion, criticizing it, passing laws to undermine their religious institutions, supporting political parties that ruin the Hindu Temples, making money off the Hindu Temple properties, remaining silent when their religion is abused and desecrated, failing to practice their religion and neglecting their Temples and failing to protect their religious institutions from the clutches of the government where majority of the office bearers are Hindus..

"**Without**" means the other two major religions whose mission it is to convert the Hindus either through deception, cheating, trickery, bribery, terror, allurement, inducements, and enticements. They want to uproot the Hindu religion from the land of Bharath; erase the very essence of universal values and replace them with parochial exclusive values; wipe out the pagans from the face of the earth; kill all the people who fail to embrace their religion; and destroy the most tolerant culture earth was blessed with for millennia.

WHAT ARE THE RESPONSIBILITIES OF HINDU INSTITUTIONS?

Hindu Institutions is a broad term to include Hindu Temples, Cultural Organizations, Hindu Foundations, VHP, RRS, India Associations,

Language based organization, Music Schools, Dance Schools and host of other organizations are managed by majority Hindus with a mission to practice, promote, encourage and protect the uniqueness of different dimensions of Hinduism. The custodians of these institutions should make every effort to learn about their religion first, and then teach their own children and their fellow Hindus who attend these Hindu institutions. They should invite any and all speakers to discuss about the atrocities committed against Hindus, how Hindus are being denied their basic freedom and liberty, how they may be converted in the near future and how the governments in India is destroying the Hindu culture for their political, selfish and get rich mentality.

LEARN FROM THE PAST

1) Islamic Onslaught

Find out how many millions of Hindus are massacred for refusing to be converted to Islam; how many women were enslaved, raped and killed; how many innocent children were put to death; how many Hindu Temples were ransacked; how many Hind Temples were destroyed; how many deities were defaced or broken into pieces;

Find out about Hindu Kush Mountain, what it means and how many millions of Hindus were massacred and how their blood flowed from the top of the mountain to the streets;

Find out how as many as 2000 Hindu Temples were destroyed and converted them into mosques; hos they used the deities of Hindus were made as steps at the entrances to climb to their mosques;

Find out the day to day accounts of Muslim Historians, Travelers and Ministers of Muslim Kings as to the daily quota of killing the Hindus from their own records; and

Find out what Quran says of non-believers and their fate, how they can be killed, how brutal the methods of killing were sanctioned, and how non-believers should be wiped out.

2) Goa Inquisition

Find out how the Hindu Temples were destroyed, idols were mutilated, how the Temple material is used to build churches, how the children were snatched away and converted, how the priests were banned from doing religious services, how the marriage rites were banned, how the death ceremonies were prohibited, how the Churches forced Hindus to listen to the Christian preaching, and what kind of torturous method were used to convert Hindus;

Find out about the Big House with 200 cells where Hindus were tortured, tormented and killed; how the screams of agony of men, women, and children could be heard in the streets; how they were flogged and dismembered in front of their relatives; how the blood used to gush out of the house to the streets; how the Hindu blood flowed from the house to the streets; and how the skulls of the Hindus were piled up.

FIND OUT HOW THE HINDUS WERE TORTURED:

a) **The torture by rope** consisted of the arms being tied backwards and then raised by a pulley, leaving the victim hanging for some time, and then let the victim drop down to half a foot above the floor, then raised again. These continued up and down movements dislocated the joints and made the prisoner emit horrible cries of pain.

b) **The torture by water** was as follows: the victim was made to lie across an iron bar, and was forced to imbibe water without stopping. The iron bar broke the vertebrae and caused horrible pains, whereas the water treatment provoked vomits and asphyxia.

c) **The torture by fire** was definitely the worst: the victim was hung above a fire, which burnt the soles of the feet, and the jailers rubbed bacon and other combustible materials on the burning feet. The feet were burnt until the victim confessed, "I am Christian."

PRESENT DAY HAPPENINGS AND ATROCITIES

Hindus must wake up from the deep slumber. They have to shoulder the burden of protecting their religion from the shackles of government and revive the richness, grandeur and glory of Sanatana

Dharma. As Swami Vivekananda roared: *"Purity will come, glory will come, goodness will come, purity will come, and everything that is excellent will come when this sleeping is roused to self-conscious activity."*

Find out how and why **Hindu Temples** have been taken over by the government, how the government is abusing and misusing the resources of the Temples, how they are neglecting them to deterioration, how they fail to renovate the Temple and allowing them to collapse; how they are depleting the Hindu lands; how rampant the corruption in the Temple management and how they are making the sacred places into political institutions; how they are insulting Hindu religious leaders.

Find out how in the name of **secularism**, the government is supporting and funding Christian and Muslim institutions depleting the Hindu Temples; how the state treasury is used to send Muslims and Christians to visit their religious places; how many Hajj houses were built across the India to consolidate the political power; and how may special Hajj terminals were built to provide comfortable travel to their pilgrimages while Hindus are "sleeping like beasts on the streets" at their religious places.

Find out how **Kashmiri Pandits** were thrown out from their own land; how they were made to live in filthy tents for decades; how many Hindu Temples were ravaged; how many Hindus were killed and the government is supporting the government by pumping crores of rupees to pacify the Muslims; and how Hindus are denies to buy lands in Kashmir.

Find out how **West Bengal** is becoming a haven for illegal Muslims coming from Bangladesh; how almost all the border districts have become the Muslims majority; how the government is forcing the Hindu festivals to be stopped at the complaints of Muslims; how the religious and pilgrimage centers have become the targets of Islamic terrorism; and how they are destroying the Hindu Temples and defacing the Images of our Deities; and how they are killing the sacred cows and putting them in front Hindu Temples.

Find out how Pakistan has **depleted the Hindu population** from about 27 percent at the time of Independence to near zero Hindu population, how many Hindu Temples were bulldozed and destroyed; how Veer Savarkar fasted until death unable to hear the news about the continued rape of Hindu women; how a your girl pleaded the Supreme Court in Pakistan to kill her in the court instead of sending her back to her village only to be raped and converted; how Hindu women are too afraid to even wear Mangal sutras; and how the Hindu priests wear the half scull Muslim caps to protect their identity.

Find out how Bangladesh is pushing the Muslims to **infiltrate** to destabilize the government in West Bengal, how nearly 32 percent of Hindu population at the independence dwindled to less than 7 percent, how Hindus are facing "government-tolerated murder, rape, abduction, forced conversion, temple attacks, land grabs, and more;" and how Bangladesh and Pakistan plan to break up India into three countries – Mughalistan, Dalitistan, and Dravidistan.

Find out how **Love Jihad** is employed to woo the innocent Hindu girls to get converted to Islam; how much money was paid to Muslim boys to trap Hind, Christian, Sikh, and other non-Muslim girls; how the Hindu girls were drugged and made them compromised; how the Hindu girls were shipped to Islamic countries for prostitution; and how many of Hindu girls committed suicides knowing the real nature of Love Jihad.

Find out how **conversion** is wrecking the Hindu community; how Christian schools, colleges and universities alluring the potential students to get converted to get to their fold; how foreign Christian organizations are pouring billions of dollars to break up India; how the government encouraging and supporting the efforts of conversion for vote bank politics; how the methods of deception, trickery, manipulation, incentives, inducements and dishonesty are employed to woo the innocent and gullible people; and how they target the village heads, Brahmin priests, rich people, popular figures by pumping money.

Also find out about the false claim that all religions are same, the devastating effect of Atrocities Act, the proposed Communal Bill to tarnish Hindu religion, allotment of crores of rupees as salaries for Mullahs but denying the similar salaries to the Hindu priests, the appointment of the most corrupt people as members of the Board of Trustees and Executive Officers to the Hindu Temples, and so on.

BE ACTIVE AND ACT LIKE HINDUS

If the Hindu Institutions do not address these issues affecting the very existence of Hinduism; if they do not invite speakers, who have spent all their life trying to protect the liberty and freedom all Hindus are enjoying today; and if they cannot allow fellow Hindus of their members to have the opportunity to hear, how do they justify their own existence? How do the office bearers of these Institutions explain their role in managing them without discussing the impending dangers affecting their organizations? How do they defend denying the younger generation from learning about their brutalized history? Where do the younger generation learn about the differences between Hinduism and other religions? How do we equip our youngsters to defend their religion if they are not taught in the Institutions that have **Hindu base? How can we deny Hindu base when you are managing the Hindu Institutions?** Let us not become prisoners of preconceived notions and four walls of our institutions. Let us go beyond the four walls and take necessary steps to protect the Hindu base of every Hindu Institution.

It is our mission to encourage all Hindus to take full responsibility of supporting, sustaining, promoting, propagating and protecting the Hindu universal values that are eternal, irrespective of time and place, so that the whole human race will live in peace and harmony. Ahimsa is the basis for all human existence. Any form of violence in the name of religion is the root cause of terror, torment, atrocities, cruelty, destruction, brutality, and massacres. Hindus and Hindu Institutions have a special obligation to protect their religion from being attacked. Ant dereliction of duty on the part of these Institutions will result in untold misery. Some reflection of their responsibility will avoid the catastrophe that may be inflicted on Hindus by other religions whose sole mission is to convert with whatever methods that are available to them.

Let us not hide in the secluded forests of secularism and atheism; let us all remember the Muslim onslaught and Christian atrocities; let us teach our children the untold misery our forefathers were subjected; let us take our children to all those historical Temples that were razed and destroyed as a way lesson; let us be certain that the history of the past is not repeated itself; let us all reflect on the glory of Hinduism; let us all embrace the universal principle of ahimsa where no one is tormented to adopt other faith; let us advocate the inclusive nature of our religion; let us not see other person as prey to be entrapped and converted; and let us deny people of other faiths any attempt to curtail the freedom and liberty, the hallmark of Sanatana Dharma and the human existence itself.

As **Savitri Devi** predicted, we already lost different parts of India to either Christians or Muslims. With our silence and indifference, Hindus are " *yielding every day to hostile forces, losing bit by bit its numerical advantages, losing its political rights in India, losing its place as a nation.* " If Hindus are indifferent to what is taking place in Kashmir, West Bengal, Kerala, Meghalaya, Tripura, Manipura, Andamans and other places, the time may come to our place where we may be isolated and ambushed. There is nobody left to protect us. Since we never protected our own brothers and sisters when they needed the most and since we never went to their rescue to protect them from humiliation and atrocities, there may not be any body left to our rescue when we needed the most. Let all Hindus across the globe wake up before Bharat is fallen to the hostile forces. Let the words of Swami Vivekananda inspire us and make the human race see the light in the wisdom of Hinduism: "Get us and set your shoulder to the wheel – *how long is this life for? As you have come into this world, leave some mark behind. Otherwise where is the difference between you and the trees and stones? They too come into existence, decay and die.*"

Jai Bharath

COWS ARE SACRED:
RESPECT & WORSHIP

SCRIPTURES EXTOL THEM, HINDUS MUST PROTECT THEM

Since Vedic times, cow is considered sacred, treated as mother and hailed as harbinger of auspiciousness. She is a symbol of wealth, health, prosperity, blessing, peace of mind, purity, purification, and success in life. She is identified as **Kamadhenu** - fulfilling all wishes. She is revered, honored, respected as mother – an unselfish giver of bounty without expecting from her children just like a mother. All the scriptures such as Vedas, Upanishads, Puranas, Mahabharata, Manusmriti, and others extoll the virtues of the cow. All the Gods reside in her and killing her is considered the most heinous crime. It is often said *"jivantu avadghnyah ta me vishasya dushanih"* meaning that let cows live without slaughter for their whole life-they remove poison and toxins. Many Sages, many Hindu Temples and numerous Ashrams maintained Goshalas (cow shelters) for centuries recognizing the numerous benefits that accrue from the cows.

It is unfortunate that India has become the largest exporter of beef to other countries, is ignoring the sacredness of the cows, is allowing the people to conduct beef celebration on the university campuses without permission, is tolerating the slaughter houses for political purposes, is failing to take appropriate actions against the minorities and other religious people who are deliberately hurting the sentiments of Hindus, and intentionally failing to take action in implementing constitutional requirements found in the Article 48 of the Constitution: *"The State shall endeavor to organize agriculture and animal husbandry on modern and scientific lines and shall, in particular, take steps for preserving and improving the breeds, and prohibiting the slaughter of cows and calves and other milch and draught cattle."* Knowing the constitutional mandate, and knowing the intentions of minorities and other religions to malign the Hindus, Indian government and Hindu politicians are undermining the rich cultural heritage of Hindus that existed for centuries and selling the country for their selfish and greedy purpose to accumulate wealth for the next few generations for their families.

Hindus have their future cut out for them – either be bulldozed and allow the government, minorities and other religions to root out the very core of Sanatana dharma from the soil of Bharath, or get united and exercise their freedom to restore the glory, grandeur, greatness, and grandness of the richest civilization that has ever surfaced on the planet earth. It is in the hands of Hindus to restore their culture, reestablish the concept of *vasudaika kutumbam*, insist on the welfare of all humanity, root out the sectarian appeasement, wipe out all kinds of terrorist activities, and aspire for peaceful coexistence of the humanity to live in freedom and independence. Hindus must speak and protect their culture, their values and their sentiments. It is in the best interest of the planet earth that Hindus take the lead to protect the mother Cow and stand for virtues of their religion.

ALL GODS RESIDE IN MOTHER COW

As the scriptures proclaim *"Tvam mata sarva devanam"* meaning that you are the mother of all gods. It also means that if we protect the cow, we are honoring all the gods that reside in her. Scriptures have elaborately described the location of gods in the cow. We will examine our scriptures such as Vedas, Upanishads, Puranas, Mahabharata and other scriptures to equip ourselves with enough knowledge to find out the significance, importance and virtues of cows so that we will not only reap the benefits of protecting them but also pass on the richness to our children and grandchildren.

All scriptures agree that four Vedas with their six vedangas (components) reside in the mouth of the cow. Lord Shiva and Lord Vishnu live in her horns forever, Lord Brahma sits in her head, Karthikeya finds his home in her stomach, Sun and Moon live in her eyes, Garuda in her teeth, Ashwini Kumars in her ears, Goddess Saraswati in her tongue, Lord Indra in front of her horns, all pilgrimage centers in her posterior (back), Ganga in her urine, Yamaraj in her mouth, Gandharvas also reside inside her mouth, Goddess Lakshmi in the cow dung, Goddess Parvathi in the urine, Prajapati in the resonant voice, four Oceans in four teats (nipples) and milk, sky in the back portion and Varuna in the joints. In every pore of the body, all thirty-three crore Gods are positioned. In the stomach are the mountains ranges, with the forests, and the entire Earth.

Different kinds of Agni are positioned in different parts of cow. In the liver of the cow Grahpratya-agni, in her liver; dakshina-agni, in her heart; Ahvaniya-agni, in her neck; and Sabhya-agni, in her palette. In the bones of the cows are to be found the Mountains while Rig Veda, Yajur Veda, Sama Veda, and Atharvana Veda in her marrow. Hence many rishis worshipped the cows and also raised them in their ashrams.

Having possessed all Gods in every part of her body, Cow blesses the people and country. Just looking at her enables one to have the fruits of offering salutations to all Gods, visiting all the pilgrimages and acquire health and wealth. Happiness and peace thrive in a house where there is a cow. By circumambulating (pradakshana) around the cow, one gets the Punya (merit) of doing pradakshana to all gods. Padma Purana states. *"The person who touches the cow after having bath daily, frees himself from all kinds of sins. The dust that arises from the cow's hooves is so pure that the person who applies it on his head, is considered to have bathed in the sacred waters of different pilgrim places, and freed from all sins."*

Since all Gods reside and manifest in the cow, she is capable of bestowing her blessings on all creatures. All substances that come from the cow are pure, chaste, and wholesome: they have the potential to purify the entire world. Cow's urine, cow dung, milk, curd, and ghee – by the intake of these five products, the body is absolved of all sin. That is why religious persons consume milk, ghee, and curd every day. Since all gods reside in her, whatever cows consume, her products are the best and purest. Of all the foods we consume, the effect of ghee lasts longest for one month, compared to grains, which lasts for only five days. The effect of milk lasts for seven days and curds till twenty days. Since pre-Vedic period cow is said to bestow dharma, artha, kama, and moksha - the four purusharthas. Hence it is recommended to chant this mantra: **'May cows forever remain in front of me, behind me, may all my limbs be blessed by the touch of the cow.**

May I reside amidst cows.' This chanting will wash away all sins, and one is even worshipped in heaven for the merit of chanting.

KAMADHENU

Kamadhenu is a sacred cow known to fulfill all the wishes and desires. This divine cow, which lives in Swargaloka (heaven), emerged from the ocean of milk (ksheerasagar) during the time of Samudramanthan (the churning of the ocean) by the gods (suras) and demons (asuras). It was presented to the seven sages by the Gods, and in course of time came into the possession of Sage Vasishta.

Kamadhenu is also well known through its other five forms: Nandini, Sunanda, Saurabhi, Susheela and Sumana. According to the legends Lord Brahma created the Brahmins (priests) and the cow at the same time; the Brahmins were to recite the religious scriptures while the cows were to provide ghee for offerings in religious sacrifices. Brahma also declared that Kamadhenu should be the mother of gods, she ought to be worshipped by everybody. Anybody who killed a cow or allowed another to kill would rot in hell.

The cow symbolizes Dharma itself – fulfillment of righteous conduct. Cow represents the mother earth. In Satyayuga dharma stood firmly on four legs of earth (cow), in Tretayuga dharma stood on three legs, in Dwaparyuga dharma stood on two legs while in Kaliyuga it is standing on one leg. Hence dharma is slowly slipping away from the people and the age of deceit, decadence, deception and dishonesty has set in. It is due to the negligence of reverence toward the cows and prevention of abuse and killing them. Consequently, whole world is facing untold misery, turmoil, terrorism, despair, debauchery, stress and natural disasters. A happy cow represents prosperity, peace of mind, blessings, wealth, health and purity. It is time to remember what Nandini cow said to King Dilip after he protected her from the Lion in a forest:

na kevalam payasa prasutim

ve hi man kam dugham prasannam

"Whenever I am pleased and happy I can fulfill all desires. Don't consider me to be just milk supplier."

COWS ARE WELCOMED

In recognition of the virtues of a cow, a special place is accorded to her among Hindus. Cows are associated with prosperity and wealth. A newly purchased cow is welcomed into the home like a new bride. Whenever Pranaprathishta to the deities is performed, cows are brought into the Temples and welcomed as the most revered guests. During certain festivals, the cow's legs are washed, horns are decorated with different colors, hump is smeared with colored powder, body is beautifully decorated with colorful cloth, forehead is anointed with tilak, and it is greeted with a *kula* or winnowing fan on which there is a dab of *sindur* or vermilion. A cow is welcomed into the house or temple with ingredients such as paddy, soft *durva* grass, sesame seeds, and a small brass pot containing a mango twig with leaves. It is like inviting all 33 crore gods into the house.

The Rishis (sages) discovered that the magnetism of a cow is due to the extraordinary virtues she possesses. No other animal equals in her qualities. Even if you give the same kind of food to a cow and a horse, the horse-dung emits an unhealthy stinking smell, while the cow-dung is odorless. In fact, it is an efficacious disinfectant. There can be little doubt that the urine and dung of the cow possess untold virtues. The gods residing in a cow make the difference making the fodder medicinal and sacred by the time it comes out of the cow.

COW IN VEDAS

Cow is referred 723 times in Rig Veda, 87 times in Yajur Veda, 170 times in Sama Veda, 331 times in Atharvana Veda. A total of 1331 times are mentioned in these four Vedas. Similarly, **Aghnya** is referred 20 times in Rig Veda, 5 times in Yajur Veda, 2 times in Sama Veda and 33 times in Atharvana Veda. "**Dhenu**" is referred 76 times in Rig Veda, 22 times in Yajur Veda, 25 times in Sama Veda, 43 times in Atharvana Veda. The meaning of Dhenu is Trupti - meaning contentment and satisfaction.

The three words that are used to identify cow are defined below:

Aghnya the one that ought not to be killed
Ahi the one that must not be slaughtered.

Aditi *the one that ought not to be cut into pieces.*

These three names of cow signify that the animal ought not be killed or tortured. These words appear frequently throughout the Vedas in context of a cow.

The four Vedas considered cow as holy and sacred and commanded that cows be not killed. Severe punishments are recommended for slaughtering the cows. We borrow milk from cow just the way we borrow milk from our own mother. Hence, we can argue that love and affection towards her should be like the one we show towards our own mother.

The word "Aghnya" is referred to the cow in many mantras of Vedas. The meaning of this word means, "not to be killed under any circumstances". In one of the mantras cows were addressed as Aghnya who have been enjoined to keep themselves healthy by use of pure water and green grass so that we, who drink their milk, may be endowed with dharma, knowledge ad wealth.

RIG VEDA

Following are some of the verses you will find in Rig Veda

"She is like the mother of the cosmic Forces, the daughter of the cosmic Matter, the sister of cosmic Energy, the center of the ambrosia. I address to men of wisdom --kill not her, the sinless inviolate cow.

The divine cow, who is skilled in eloquence and gives speech to others, and who helps us for our worship of the divine forces, is abandoned by fools only.

May cows come and bring us good fortune; let them stay in our cowsheds and be content in our company. May many colored cows bring here prolific milk for offerings to the resplendent Lord at many dawns.

Let not the cows run away from us, let no thief carry them away; let no hostile weapon fall upon them. May the master of the cattle be long possessed of them, with the milk products of which he makes offerings and with which he serves the godly men.

Let not the cows fall a victim to the arrogant, dust spurning war-horse. Let them not fall into the hands of a butcher or his shop. Let the cattle of the man, the householder, move about freely and graze without fear.

May the cows be our affluence; may the resplendent Lord grant us cattle; may the cows yield food (milk and butter) of the first libation. These cows, O men, are sacred as the Lord resplendent Himself --the Lord whose blessings we crave for, with head and heart.

O cows, you strengthen even the worn-out and fatigued and make the unlovely beautiful to look on. Your lowing is auspicious, and makes my dwelling prosperous. Great is the abundance that is attributed to you in our religious ceremony.

May you, O cows, have many calves grazing upon good pastures and drinking pure water at accessible ponds. May no thief be your master. May no beast of prey assail you and may the dart of vital Lord never fall on you.

O resplendent Lord, a showerer of virility as you are, may we have by your blessings the sturdy bulls for insemination and let us have plenty of nourishment for the cows.

(Source: Rig Veda viii, 102, 15-16; vi, 28, 1-8 Translation by Swami Satya Prakash Saraswati and Satyakam Vidyalanka)

ATHARVANA VEDA

In the **Atharvana Veda** it is said: "The cow is the mother of Rudras; she is a daughter of the Vasus; she is the sister of Surya. She is a storehouse of ghee that is like the celestial nectar." It further states that cow's milk helps overcome debility and regain lost physical and mental health. It promotes intelligence and improves health. It even goes to the extent that if someone destroys our cows, horses or people, kill him with a bullet of lead. (Atharvana Veda 1.16.4)

The entire Hymn X in Atharvana Veda is dedicated to the glorification of the COW. Selected verses are listed below:

1 Worship to thee springing to life, and worship unto thee when born! Worship, O Cow, to thy tail-hair, and to thy hooves, and to thy form!

2 The man who knows the Seven Floods, who knows the seven distances, Who knows the head of sacrifice, he may receive the holy Cow.

5 Upon her back there are a hundred keepers, a hundred-metal bowls, and a hundred milkers. The Deities who breathe in her all separately know the Cow.

6 Her foot is sacrifice, her milk libation, Svadhā her breath, Mahï-lukā the mighty:
To the God goes with prayer the Cow
who hath Parjanya for her lord.

18 The Kshatriya's mother is the Cow, thy mother, Svadhā! is the Cow. Sacrifice is the weapon of the Cow: the thought arose from, her.

19 From Brahma's summit there went forth a drop that mounted up on high:
From that waist thou produced, O Cow,
from that the Hotar sprang to life.

25 The Cow hath welcomed sacrifice: the Cow hath held the Sun in place. Together with the prayer the mess of rice hath passed into the Cow.

26 They call the Cow immortal life, pay homage to the Cow as Death. She hath become this universe, Fathers, and Rishis, hath become the Gods, and men, and Asuras.

27 The man who hath this knowledge may receive the Cow with welcoming. p. 39

33 He who hath given a Cow unto the Brahmans wined all the worlds. For Right is firmly set in her devotion, and religious zeal.

34 Both Gods and mortal men depend for life and being on the Cow. She hath become this universe: all that the Sun survey is she

YAJUR VEDA

Ghrtam duhaanaamaditim janaayaagne maa himsiheeh (Yajurveda 13.49)

Do not kill cows and bulls who always deserve to be protected.

Antakaaya goghaatam Yajurveda 30.18

Destroy those who kill cows.

The Aghnya cows and bulls bring you prosperity. (12.73)

A verse in *Yajur Veda* abjures all violence: "Protect and rear the animals: do not hit the cow; do not hit the goats; nor the sheep; nor any other creature; nor two-legged animals; nor the one-legged; one should not injure any living being."

SAMA VEDA

Most of the hymns in Sama Veda are taken from Rig Veda. Hence effort is not made to identify any verses dealing with cow to avoid the duplication.

Based on the above selected citations from the Vedas, we can establish the fact that Cow is a highly-revered animal for many, many centuries and thus Hindus are duty bound to protect it. It is our hope that these verses will provide enough knowledge to consider cow as sacred mother that needs to be respected, honored, revered and sheltered. Knowledge is the harbinger of proper action. With this knowledge let us take necessary actions against cruelty to Cows in India and around the world. We should also support all the organizations that are sheltering the cows, support the agencies that are working to prevent the export of beef, advocate the strict passage of anti-slaughter Bill across Bharath. Let us honor our Vedic injunction to stop the animal slaughter and work toward the preservation of sacred cows.

COW SLAUGHTER MAFIA

COWS ARE SLAUGHTERED:
GRAPHIC, HORRIFIC, GRUESOME AND UNBEARABLE

"Cow protection is the gift of Hinduism to the world. And Hinduism will live so long as there are Hindus to protect the cow." Mahatma Gandhi

Few days back, Global Hindu Heritage Foundation received this three-part series videos produced by a Kannada TV Channel on the atrocious, brutal and appalling killings of loads and loads of cows. It is shocking, alarming, and outrageous. It is hard to watch. I am not sure how many people can watch all three of these videos. You wonder as to what kind of country Bharath is? Is this the sacred land that respects, worships, adores and loves Gaumata? Do we call ourselves Hindus, if we keep turning our heads away from the ghastly cow slaughter Mafia who are relentlessly inflicting most heinous, inhuman, merciless, cruel killings on COWS? Do we call ourselves Hindus if we cannot or do not voice our outrage and anger at these grim and gruesome killings? How can we remain silent listening to the cries of Mother Cow? She is the only animal, which gives everything to sustain the whole humanity. Panchagavyas (all five elements – milk, butter, ghee, urine and cow dung) provide health, wealth and brain power. It is divine. All Gods reside in different parts of Cow.

Why we Hindus are silent? Why the government cannot act? Why the government cannot ban cow slaughter? Why they cannot prosecute the culprits? Why police departments are not being held responsible for illegal transportation of cows across the states? Why we cannot enforce Directive Principles dealing with article 48? and why we cannot bring the mafia to justice?

We request all our friends in BJP and the government officials to be aware of the extent of cruelty that is drenching Bharath our country, the land that is always known for ahimsa, tolerance, and compassion for all living creatures. Every Hindu should be briefed or shown these gruesome videos at the earliest. The suffering of Gaumata (Mother Cow) will not be either auspicious or acceptable in the ONLY LAND that considers COW as MOTHER.

IS THIS WHAT WE WANT TO DO TO MOTHER COW?

The cow slaughter mafia from Kerala steal cows during night, treat them in the worst possible way, dumping them in trucks and put green chilies to cut tail of cows and even putting chilies in the anal area making them cry and dump them to river to get them across to Kerala to butcher them. The reporter who did the story to a TV has been threatened for her life by the cattle mafia.

TRANSPORTATION OF COWS TO SLAUGHTER HOUSES

Transportation of cows in the vans and trucks is a horrifying experience to the cows. It is abominable, inhuman and grueling for the cows. They are being abused, injured and maltreated during the transportation. The mafia defies any kind of rules or guidelines to transport the cows. They make cows stand in the trucks to accommodate as many as possible. They apply red and green chilies into the eyes to prevent them to rest and lie down. They are not either fed or allowed to drink in the journey that may take up to a week or so.

Since Independence, the fate of the cows has deteriorated to the extent that the government run by Congress Party publicly denigrated the Hindu scriptures and to appease a certain sections of Muslims for the Vote bank politics, started allowing the construction of slaughter houses. They slowly subsidized the construction of these slaughter houses and failed to take action against the illegal construction of this abattoir. The government has made our country, which respects, honors and worships Cows, to be the top exporter of beef in the world, sidelining Brazil as the second largest beef exporter. To make India the top exporter, the Congress government has given as much as 40 percent subsidy to the beef exporters. To please the Secularists, Communists, Muslims, Christians and greedy business people like

Kapil Sibal, the Congress government failed to take appropriate action to enforce the Article 48 of the Indian Constitution.

Gandhi Snubbed: The Congress government, which considers Mahatma Gandhi as their role model and mentor and follows him as a true believer of Indian legacy, has even refuted and detested his own philosophy and negated his own views on cow. Gandhi venerated and worshipped cow. According to him "The core value of Hinduism is cow protection." He even called cow as "the mother to millions of Indian mankind." Let us remember that Gandhi said the cow is the mother of Indian mankind not just Hindu mankind. The Congress party totally ignored him on many of his views and took advantage of the rural masses' love and affection toward Gandhi and exploited their weakness for political gains.

Gandhi said, *"Mother Cow is in many ways better than the mother who gave us birth. Our mother gives us milk for a couple of years and then expects us to serve her when we grow up. Mother cow expects from us nothing but grass and grain. Our mother often falls ill and expects service from us. Mother cow rarely falls ill. Here is an unbroken record of service which does not end with her death. Our mother, when she dies, means expenses of burial or cremation. Mother cow is as useful dead as when she is alive. We can make use of every part of her body-her flesh, her bones, her intestines, her horns and her skin. Well, I say this is not to disparage the mother who gives us birth, but to show you the substantial reasons for my worshipping the cow.* (H, 15-9-1940, p. 281)

Hindu Scriptures Desecrated: Hinduism is the dominant dharma or way of life. It is called Sanatana dharma meaning the duties of human being, irrespective of religion, such as honesty, tolerance, purity, truth, self-restraint, ahimsa, peace, self-realization, and live let live. This kind of philosophy is exemplified by the views expressed by M C Chagla, former Union Education Minister, "I am a Muslim by religion; but by culture and race I am a Hindu. All Muslims of this country are Hindus."

Why would Gandhiji and Chagla call themselves as Hindus? Would they embrace Hinduism if it epitomizes hatred toward other religions, and exemplify the sectarian ideology? They believed in Hinduism because it never advocated the building of boundaries around the narrow sectarian thinking and never claim its supremacy over other religions.

Many Hindu scriptures extolled the virtues of cow, considered her as sacred and worshipped her as Gomata. She is considered the fulfiller of all desires. She should not be considered as a mere giver of milk. Her welfare is tantamount to the welfare, protection and happiness of the nation. Let us give few examples from the Hindu scriptures on how the Holy Cow was extolled.

VEDAS AND COWS

Not only the Vedas are against animal slaughter but also vehemently oppose and prohibit cow slaughter. Yajurveda forbids killing of cows, for they provide energizing food for human beings.

⚔ Do not kill cows and bulls who always deserve to be protected. (Yajurveda 13.49)

⚔ In Rigveda cow slaughter has been declared a heinous crime equivalent to human murder and it has been said that those who commit this crime should be punished. (Rigveda 7.56.17)

⚔ The Aghnya cows – which are not to be killed under any circumstances - may keep themselves healthy by use of pure water and green grass, so that we may be endowed with virtues, knowledge and wealth. (Rigveda 1.164.40 or Atharv 7.73.11 or Atharv 9.10.20)

Rig Veda says:

She is like the mother of the cosmic Forces, the daughter of the cosmic Matter, the sister of cosmic Energy, the centre of the ambrosia. I address to men of wisdom -- kill not her, the sinless inviolate cow.

May cows come and bring us good fortune; let them stay in our cowsheds and be content in our company. May many colored cows bring here prolific milk for offerings to the resplendent Lord at many dawns?

Let not the cows fall a victim to the arrogant, dust spurning war-horse. Let them not fall into the hands of a butcher or his shop. Let the cattle of the man, the householder, move about freely and graze without fear.

The entire 28th Sukta or Hymn of 6th Mandal of Rigveda sings the glory of cow.

1. Everyone should ensure that cows are free from miseries and kept healthy

2. God blesses those who take care of cows

3. Even the enemies should not use any weapon on cows

4. No one should slaughter the cow

5. Cow brings prosperity and strength

6. If cows are kept healthy and happy, men and women shall be disease free and prosperous.

7. May the cow eat green grass and drink pure water? May they not be killed and bring prosperity to us.

In Ayurveda, the importance of cow and her products are described in great detail. It is said that Cow urine which is one of the Panchagavyas is a great elixir, proper diet, pleasing to heart, giver of mental and physical strength, enhances longevity. It balances bile, mucous and airs. Remover of heart diseases and effect of poison.

Padma Purana says: "Cows are the abode of the Goddess of wealth. Sins don't touch them. There exists a fine relationship between man and cow. A home without a cow is like one without dear ones."

MUSLIM RASHTRIYA MANCH (MRM) SUPPORTS BAN OF COW SLAUGHTER

In March 2014, the Muslim Gaurakshak Sammelan under the auspices of Muslim Rashtriya Manch (MRM) demanded that Cow be declared "National Animal" and commanded complete ban on the slaughter of cows for the betterment of people and environment. The MRM passed a resolution to approach the United Nations urging them to direct their member nations to take steps to ban cow slaughter for the welfare of humanity. *Cow is the mother of the universe*, the resolution said. They also made the following resolutions:

⚘ Government should encourage cow-based small scale industries

⚘ Free all encroached lands for grazing of the grass by cows and safeguard these lands

⚘ Government constitute a Commission to look after cows and its progeny

⚘ Demanded a complete ban on export of beef and closing all abattoirs in the country

⚘ Prophet had ruled against eating beef as it caused diseases, but at the same time encouraged consumption of milk and ghee as they are health tonics

⚘ At the holy Mecca, no cow was sacrificed in the past 1432 years. Therefore, the issue of cow slaughter is more of a political in nature and it should be looked from the point of view of human welfare, environment protection

Based on the scriptures about the sacredness of cow, the benefits of Panchagavyas, the scriptural description of the importance of cows for the betterment of humanity, scriptural sanction to ban the cow slaughter, MRM's resolutions to protect the cow from the slaughter, and political manipulation to appease the certain sections of minorities, the present government should take appropriate actions to ban the cow slaughter forthwith.

REQUEST TO THE PRIME MINISTER

This is a rare opportunity to the Prime Minister to take immediate action and make Bharath the land of peace and prosperity that reveres Mother Cow and maintains high standards of decency, morality, humanity and dignity. Global Hindu Heritage Foundation (GHHF) submits the following recommendations to the Prime Minister for his consideration:

Implement Article 48 in The Constitution of India, 1949: *The State shall endeavour to organise agriculture and animal husbandry on modern and scientific lines and shall, in particular, take steps for preserving and improving the breeds, and prohibiting the slaughter, of cows and calves and other milch and draught cattle. Make sure that the States implement this Directive Principle to spare the lives of cows. Stop the slaughter of COWS.*

On April 5, 2012, as Chief Minister of Gujarat, Sri Narendra Modi expressed his desire to provide country-wide protection to cow progeny and demanded a ban on its slaughter. Speaking at a function at Rajkot on the eve of 'Mahavir Janma Jayanti', organized by Mahavir Janmotsav Samittee, he said Gujarat had enacted a law for the protection of cow progeny and demanded a similar protection to cow progeny across the country and called for a ban on its slaughter.

Irrespective of the animal, the government must adopt certain minimum standards of transportation with respect to the space allotted for each animal in a truck. Food and drinking provisions must be established.

- Subsidy to the beef export must be stopped
- Closedown all the cow slaughter houses
- Subsidize all the farmers who are willing to raise cows
- Allot sufficient land for free roaming and gazing by the cows
- Gaushalas established by private individuals and organizations must be subsidized
- Introduce course material on the virtues, significance and sacredness of cows in school educational curriculum
- Propagate the benefits of Panchagavyas – milk, ghee, curds, urine and cow dung. Each of these elements has abundant benefits that must be taught on a scientific basis.
- Negative effects of eating beef and other meat products must be taught

We should act immediately before more torture is inflicted on these gentle, docile and quiet Cows. There are videos produced in Kannada language. Language is no barrier. The visuals will speak in your language. No language can accurately describe the atrocious killings of such gentle, loving, ever giving and respectful animal, we Hindus call COW. When you see even few minutes of these videos, our hearts get throbbed, our emotions get aroused, our minds get numbed, our eyes shed tears and our feelings get murky.

PLEASE ACT, BAN the COW SLAUGHTER, Closedown all SLUAGHTER HOUSES, be HUMANE. Stop ALLOWING KILLINGS. STOP being Silent.

RAMAYANA SPREADING IMMORTAL VALUES

ACROSS THE GLOBE FOR MANY MILLENNIA

(NOTE: This is an expanded version of the FOREWARD written to a book entitled Srimadramayanam. Global Hindu Heritage Foundation is pleased to acknowledge the extraordinary effort to the book entitled "Srimadramayanam" by Dr. S. R. S. Kolluri and Mrs. K. Padmaja which is aimed at providing thorough, well versed questions with answers to the readers who are thirsting for the knowledge about the entire story of Ramayana. Developing more than 1300 questions extracting from Ramayana is no ordinary task. Determination, patience, thorough knowledge and keen intellect are required to produce this kind of compendium. Congratulations are in order for this exceptional book. We appreciate Dr. Ghazal Srinivas for his futuristic vision to pass on these eternal characteristics in Ramayana to the future generations to inspire, imbibe and absorb in shaping their lives.

This book takes me to my younger years listening to numerous Hai-kathas on Ramayana and different characters good and bad. Vivid description of all the characters in Ramayana such as Rama, Sita, Lakshmana, Bharata, Hanuman, Ravana, Vibhishana, Jatayuvu, Sugriva, etc., imprinted in my evolving mind. Anybody who reads this book will also experience similar impressions that will remain with the readers forever. We encourage people of all generations to read and reap the benefits. The more we read, more we will be enriched. By Prakasarao Velagapudi, PhD)

RAMAYANA ACCLAIMED FOR SPREADING DHARMA

Ramayana is universally acclaimed by many scholars as one of the great treasures challenging the imagination. According to **Jules Michelet, "There lies my great poem, as vast as the Indian Ocean, blessed, gilded with the sun, the book of divine harmony wherein is no dissonance. A serene peace reigns there, and in the midst of**

conflict an infinite sweetness, a boundless fraternity, which spreads over all living things, an ocean (without bottom or bound) of love, of pity, of clemency."

Ramayana was written by Sage Valmiki with utmost passion, eloquence and accuracy. This is considered as an Aadi Kaavya – the first poetic book. Valmiki was searching for a suitable hero to write a story in poetic form. One day he saw a hunter killing one of the bird couple and the agony and the heart-breaking cry of the other bird. That incident touched Valmik's heart and soul. Soon after the incident, het met Narada who suggested him to write a poem that revolves around the marital separation. Then Valmiki inquired about the existence of a personality who is endowed with extraordinary qualities that would serve as the main character in the book. Narada describes the unique, heroic and excellent qualities of Rama to Valmiki by saying that he will describe him as requested although that it is very difficult to find a person endowed with such qualities. He is born in the family of Ikshawaku. He is named Rama; *"who is renowned, fully self-controlled, valorous and illustrious, the Lord of All, wise, conversant with the ethical code, eloquent, fortunate, a slayer of his foes, broad-shouldered, long-armed, possessing a conch-shaped neck and prominent chin, eminent in archery, with a muscular body, arms extending to the knees, and a noble head and brow; of mighty prowess; possessing well- proportioned limbs and skin of bluish tint, one renowned for his virtue; of prominent eyes, deep-chested, bearing auspicious marks; one who protects those who take refuge in him and is ever-mindful of the good of those dependent on him; true to his promises, benevolent to his subjects, omniscient, renowned for his good deeds, pure, and ever responsive to devotion; meditating on his own essence."* These are the rare qualities that form the basis for this eternal Ramayana.

"When Rama is enthroned then the world will be highly regaled and rejoiced, exuberant and abundant, also rightly righteous, trouble-free, disease-free, and free from fear of famine..." Thus Narada is foreseeing the future and telling Valmiki. [1-1-90]

"While Rama is on the throne men will not see the deaths of their children anywhere in their lifetime, and the ladies will remain husband-devout and unwidowed during their lifetime... [1-1-91]

"In the kingdom of Rama there is no fear for subjects from wildfires, gale-storms or from diseases, and there is no fear from hunger or thieves, nor the cattle are drowned in floodwaters, as well... [1-1-92, 93a]

"This Ramayana is holy, sin-eradicating, merit-endowing, and conformable with the teachings of all Vedas... and whoever reads this Legend of Rama, he will be verily liberated of all his sins... [1-1-98]

"Any man who reads this lifespan-enriching narrative of actuality; Ramayana, the peregrination of Rama, he will be enjoying worldly pleasures with his sons and grandsons and with assemblages of kinfolks, servants et al., as long as he is in this mortal world and on his demise, he will be adored in heaven... [1-1-99].

Shankaracharya, Madhvacharya, Swami Vivekananda, Bala Gangadhar Tilak, Mahatma Gandhi, Monier Williams, Arthur M MacDonell, Transcendentalists, and many more scholars recognized the universal appeal of Ramayana. Many people across the globe respected Ramayana as a glorious, timeless and universal work ever written in any language or in any country. Dharma, selfless dedication to serve the people, the purity of thought, purity of love, unflinching devotion to parents, the message of universal brotherhood, spiritual compass, time tested wisdom, unshakable friendship and guidance of Sadgurus have become the hall mark of Ramayana. **Swami Tapasyananda** says, *"Here Rama is not only a great personage, an exemplar of the highest ideals of Dharma, but the very God, the divine incarnate, revealing and fully remembering the spiritual glory and bestowing salvation on all who came into intimate contact with him. Thrilling and evocative hymns, discourses on high spiritual themes, philosophical dissertations and directions for spiritual practice appear in every part of it. Besides the instructions they convey, these sections contribute immensely toward the devotional edification of those who adore Rama as their favorite deity."*

LORD HANUMAN

Hanuman is worshiped by millions around the world for his strength, bravery, dedication, unselfishness, intelligence, knowledge and virtuous nature. His Bhakti to Lord Rama was unflinching, unwavering and untainted. He is an embodiment of bhakti-yoga.

As we all know that rishis pronounced curse on Hanuman for all the mischievous deeds done on them by saying that he would never remember his valor, strength and extraordinary power until somebody reminds him of his strength before he realizes and put it to use.

HANUMAN MEETS RAMA

In Ramayana, Hanuman meets Lord Rama and Lakshmana for the first time in the forests and introduces himself and his master Sugriva. This is the first meeting of Hanuman with Lord Rama.

Impressed with the way Hanuman communicated, Lord Rama admired the communication capabilities of Hanuman. Rama said to Lakshmana, "This student must have studied the entire grammar and composition very carefully many a time. He has spoken so many things with meticulous accuracy. There has not been a single error in his words or pronunciation."

Lord Rama further appreciates the communication skills, precise wording, and non-ambiguity of his speech, moderate voice that is audible only to the listeners, pronunciation of the words, etc., that only person who is learned and knowledgeable in Vedas can speak.

Hanuman's behavior, demeanor, gestures, expression, humility, cleverness, wisdom, determination and strength are unmatched. Rama himself described Hanuman thus, "Heroism, cleverness, strength, firmness, sagacity, prudence, prowess, and power have taken up their abode in Hanuman."

HIDDEN TALENTS SURFACED

Rama, Sugriva, Jambavant and others were discussing about ways to find out about Sita's captivity and where she may have been kidnapped to. Everybody was expressing their inability to cross the ocean to go to Lanka. Jambavan recognizing the hidden talents and strength of Lord Hanuman, addressed him, "O Warrior, foremost among the multitude, thou who art versed in the scriptures, why art thou sitting apart, silent? In courage and strength, thou art the equal of Rama and Lakshmana and of the King of the Monkeys himself, 0 Hanuman!"

Many a time I have seen that all-powerful bird of immense wings and exceeding energy bearing away serpents from the ocean; the strength that is in his wings resemble the might and vigor of thine arms; none can withstand thee. Thine energy, intelligence, courage and loyalty sets thee apart from the rest of beings, therefore prepare thyself to cross the ocean … Only you are capable of reaching Lanka and carry out the task … you are the one who can fly and reach the highest area in the sky more than what anyone else can do … Oh Hanuman, Rise up! Leap across the ocean."

Sugriva also spoke about his extraordinary qualities, "O Hanuman, certainly in you exist strength, intelligence, valor, prudence, and the ability to act properly appropriate to time and place, O Pandita."

As Hanuman became aware of his own powers, being reminded, great enthusiasm welled up in him. He stood up and after glancing at them and began to grow. His companions were astonished. As they went on praising him, his stature grew. He grew so tall that he could jump across the sea. Still he was very modest. He bowed to the elders and said, "I am the son of the Wind God who can move in the skies without touching the earth. If need be, I can throw skyward all the water of this ocean and make the three worlds float on water. I will go like lightning and surely find Sitadevi,"

In Sundara Khanda he is described as the most powerful and intelligent.

Atulita-bala-dhaamam Svarnashailaabha-deham
Danujavana-krushaanum gnaninaam-agraganyam
Sakala-guna-nidhaanam vaanaraanaam-adhisham :
Raghupati-vara dutam vaatajaatam namaami.

Here Hanuman is described as the one who is the seat of immense strength; exalted as the mine of all virtues. The wisest among all. The fire against the forest of demons. He is bearing a shining physique like a golden mountain with immense strength. He is the master of all monkeys and the great messenger of Lord of Raghu's Race Sri Ram. I prostrate before such a son of the wind God.

In Lanka, *Sita Devi* was wailing in Ashoka Vana eagerly waiting for Rama to kill Ravana and take her back to Ayodhya. At one point she was desperate and thought of committing suicide. Then Hanuman realizing the mood of Sita Devi, started narrating the whereabouts of Lord Rama and the plans to bring back her back to the kingdom. Sita was pleased, impressed and convinced of his trustworthiness. She blessed him by saying, "You are intelligent, smart, resourceful, the best among monkeys. You shall remain immortal and a treasure of virtues. You will enjoy the affection of Sri Rama." Hanuman met Sita in Ashoka Vana, appraised her of Ram's efforts to bring her back, and returns to Kishkinda to appraise of his mission to find Sita. Rama was excited and elated and was anxious to hear the whereabouts of Sita. He was overjoyed to hear the words of Hanuman. He said of his efforts as, "A very outstanding work, the most arduous in the world has been done by Hanuman, which could not be carried out even in thought by any other on the surface of this earth." Further she said, "So long as this world will speak about Rama, you will stay in this world to listen to the praise of Rama and the world shall be benefited with your presence… That servant to whom his master entrusts a difficult task and who performs it with zeal is said to be a superior person." Rama said that he was indebted to Hanuman for his marvelous and superhuman deeds.

Hanuman's role in Ramayana is unmatched, irreplaceable, eternally remembered and infinitely recognized. During the war, Indrajeet used Brahmastra rendering Rama, Lakshmana, Jambavan, Sugriva and the army unconscious. When Vibhishana reaches Jambavan to revive him from comatose, Jambavan immediately inquired whether Hanuman was alive. When Vibhishana asked him as to why he is so concerned about Hanuman, Jambavan said, "If the courageous Hanuman is alive, he has the wisdom and valor to bring back to life, the entire army even if dead, but if Hanuman is dead all of us are as good as dead even if alive."

Hanuman was responsible for saving the life of Lakshmana. In a battle against Ravana, Lakshman was severely wounded and was almost on deathbed. There was no hope of reviving. Sushena, who was brought to help revive Lakshman, indicated that he would die if untreated with Sanjivani herb by daybreak. Hanuman was sent to Dronagiri mountain to bring the lifesaving herb. Hanuman frantically searched for the herbs with no success. Then Hanuman ripped off the top of the mountain and flew 1000 yojanas to reach the battlefield in Lanka. Realizing that the herb would save Lakshmana's life, Ravana ordered Surya (Sun) to dawn before its appointed time. Sensing the danger, Hanuman increased his size and kept the Sun from rising. Sushena identified the healing herbs from the mountain brought by Hanuman and administered to Lakshman. All his wounds were immediately healed.

For all his numerous selfless services done to Lord Rama and saving the lives of numerous characters in Ramayana, almost at the end of the great epic, Lord Rama offered him liberation as a reward. Hanuman did not accept it, in fact, he did not want anything in return other than expressing his desire to do more service. "Even though liberation destroys the bondage of material existence," Hanuman told Rama, "I have no desire for liberation, in which I would forget that You are the master and I am Your servant." He wanted to remain in this Bhuloka, to propagate the virtues and the principles of Rama, and remain here as long as the names of Lord Rama area chanted. Then Rama goes on to make Hanuman immortal in the hearts of his devotees: "I bless you and offer a boon that you shall have a permanent seat wherever my story is recited, heard, told, read or written. You will be known as Veer (powerful) Hanuman. O son of wind, whosoever takes your name, seeks your help, prays for assistance, whosoever remembers you in distress or difficulty or calamity, that person with your blessings will become free from the trouble. Therefore, you will also be known as Sankat-Vimochak, waiver of disaster and distress."

By chanting Hanuman Chalisa we all can reap the fruits of Hanuman's strength and courage. It will invoke the dormant talents to surface among all of us and give more strength to carry on our respective duties. There is Hanuman within all of us. We have to awake the

Hanuman within to realize our strengths and achieve great things in life.

DHARMA

Rama is the embodiment of Dharma. Everything he has spoken and every act he has undertaken is worth emulating without any reservation. We can give many examples of his adherence to Dharma in the case of accepting his father's promise for him to exile to the forest, following the prevailing family traditions, rejection of Bharath's request for him to return to Ayodhya, making Sugriva the King of Kishkinda, adhering to his promise to remain as Eekapatnivratha (sticking with one wife), giving shelter to Vibhishana, making him the king of Lanka, following the rules in the battlefield, and respecting the talents of his enemy.

While listening to the pangs of Sugriva and how his wife was abducted by Vali, Rama said, "Dharma is the law of land of civilization, based on duty, not desire, which ensures social stability. He who upholds Dharma is an Arya, or noble and he who does not is a Rakshasa ....If civilization is to be stablished, people like Vali and Ravana need to be destroyed." Dharma is followed by many of the characteristic in Ramayana and a number of statements are sprinkled all over the compendium. Rama abandoned the kingdom along with all the comforts and the health for the sake of Dharma. It is his Dharma to obey the commands of his father and follow the Raja Dharma. "The elder brother, the father and the person who imparts knowledge should be known as the three fathers if Dharma is to be followed." In another instance, it states that, "stability in the Dharma is the highest gain." Sita once stated that "From Dharma rises wealth, from Dharma happiness. Through Dharma one obtains Swarga. This world has the Dharma as its essence. Kausalya lamenting on the departure of Rama to the exile stated, "The fragrance of flowers spreads along the blowing. But that of men possessed of Dharma blow everywhere."

Rama says that it is the responsibility, as a Kshatriya, to rule the kingdom based on Dharma and also redeem the suffering of the people. Rama says: "When the oppressed seeks relief, at the hands of a virtuous and capable person, it is supreme Dharma to protect the surrendered even at the cost of one's own life." He has to act against any efforts to breach Dharmic law. Dharma is the source of all happiness and fulfilment of all desires. In Aranya Kanda, Rama says, "Wealth comes out of Dharma. Happiness comes out of Dharma. Everything is obtainable from Dharma. Dharma is the essence of this universe. The adept attains Dharma by disciplining themselves by the conditions of Dharma, with great effort; one cannot get happiness from happiness."

Dharma is eightfold as: "Sacrifice, Vedic study, Charity, Penance, Truth, Fortitude, Forgiveness, Non-desire."

Bharatha followed the Raja Dharma scrupulously without ever wavering from the tradition. He would have taken the advantage of Rama's exile and become a king. He could have taken the advice of the Council of Ministers to ascend to the throne. Instead he stood fast with Dharma by stating the following:

> How can the rule prescribed for succession he violated? I am outside the range of that code. I have no right to occupy the throne being the younger son of the king Emperor. The rule is that the eldest son alone can succeed to the throne. Oh. Jewel among Men, so long as the eldest son is alive, I can never be the king. Therefore, return with me to Ayodhya.

One of the advisors of King Dasaratha, Jabali, tries to persuade Rama to enjoy the fruits of the kingdom, and asks him not to heed father's promise to send him to live in the forest and go through excruciatingly hard and dangerous life. Rama rejects this atheist argument and enunciates the importance of Dharma. Rama says:

> Truthfulness was one of the fundamental essentials of moral life as pictured in the Ramayana. It was held in almost divine regard by the Hindus. "Kingdom is essentially based upon truth; and this world itself is established in truth. Saints and celestials regard truth alone as all-important. In this world a truthful person attains the regions of Brahma. Untruthful persons harass people as much as serpents. In this world, virtue, which is said to be the root of everything, is itself established in truth. In this world truth is the Lord; in truth

> *is established righteousness. Everything has truth for its basis. No condition is superior to truth. The Veda, which inculcates gift, sacrifice, Homa and asceticism, is based on truth... We have heard that the gods and the Pitris (ancestors) do not accept offerings from one inclined to untruth, or who is unsteady and of volatile faculties. This duty of maintaining truth, whose influence radiates all over one's spirit, I certainly find to be the prime one; and this burden has (ere this) been borne by worthy people........The earth, and fame, and renown, and auspiciousness pay court unto the truthful person. The good follow truth, therefore, truth is to be sought by all." (II: 109; 10-22)*

Ravana was smitten by lust toward Sita. In spite of the advice of the emissaries such as Hanuman and Angadha, he refused to hand over Sita to Rama. He was making preparations to wage war with Rama. Malyavan tried to convince his great-nephew about his weakness that may destroy him. He reminded Ravana that he brought this war on himself because of abduction of Sita. All the Gods are on the side of Rama because he is an embodiment of Dharma. The whole creation is created on the basis of good and evil actions of the those that were to be born. "He who concludes peace even with enemies or wages war at a fitting time strengthens his own party and attains a great power. A treaty of peace should be reached by a king who is weaker or equal to an enemy. The king should never underrate that enemy. If the king is more powerful, he should make war on the enemy." **Malyavan** advices Ravana to make alliance with Rama and avoid enmity with him. Righteous is said to be on the side of Mahatmas (high souled ones) while the unrighteousness is on the side of demons. Even great sages are alarmed at your sensual pleasures. **Malyavan** said, "I deem Rama of firm fortitude as Vishnu dwelling in human form. This Rama is not a mere human being, he by whom that most wonderful bridge was built across the sea. O, Ravana! Conclude peace with Rama, who is the king of men. Having come to know of his acts, let that which is good for the future be done after a mature understanding." Ravana turned his blind eye toward this advice by saying that he would not yield to any one even if he is cut into pieces.

Realizing that Rama in not a mere mortal after failing in his several attempts to kill Rama and Lakshmana, Indrajit pleaded his father to surrender Sita to Rama. He asked Ravana to follow the path of Dharma. Indrajit said, "it appears as if the whole Nature is supporting him or else how could he be still alive? Remember, father, that in your youth, you ruled the world supported by Dharma, but now you rule through Adharma alone… you have made the whole world of creation suffer through your inequities… The day you abducted Sita, you took death on your lap. Dharma is on the side of Rama. Dharma alone rules this world. Those who go against it will have to perish at some time or other."

Mandodari the wife of Ravana appears to be a dharmic person. She advised Ravana not get indulged in the sinful deeds such as abducting Sita and threatening her to accept him as her husband. She reached the battlefield to look at her husband's death body and reminisced about his weakness. She never accused Rama for killing Ravana. In fact, she acknowledged Rama as a non-mortal character. She says, "This Rama is certainly a great ascetic, an eternal person, having no beginning, middle or end, greater than distinguished universal spirits like Brahma, the one beyond ignorance, the nourisher, wielding a conch, a disc and a mace, wearing the 'Srivatsa' mark on his chest, of lasting beauty, incapable of being conquered, a perpetual one, being the constant soul of the universe, truly mighty, the lord of all the worlds, the prosperous one having a great splendor and Vishnu, the lord of maintenance of the world with a wish to benefit the worlds, assuming a human form surrounded by all the gods in the form of monkeys, Rama killed you, surrounded by demons. (111:17)

"In the past, by performing a great penance, you conquered the senses and conquered the three worlds. Now, as if revenging that enmity, those very senses conquered you."(111;18)

"There is no doubt that when the time comes, the doer surely reaps a harsh fruit of his sinful deed."

"The doer of an auspicious act obtains happiness, while the doer of a sinful act reaps misery. While Vibhishana has obtained happiness, you met with such an evil destiny."

SITA - IDEAL WIFE

At the behest of Kaikeyi, Dasaratha could not refuse to disobey the two boons given to Kaikeyi as it was the dharma of a king to implement the righteous acts and considered it as his Dharma to allow Rama to go on exile for a period of 14 years. Sita begged to accompany him to his forest retreat. Rama told about all the hardships she has to go and the innumerable dangers in the forest. As an ideal wife she stated, "As shadow to substance, so wife to husband," she reminded Rama. "Is not the wife's Dharma to be at her husband's side? Let me walk ahead of you so that I may smooth the path for your feet," she pleaded. Then Rama, Sita and Lakshmana all went to the forest.

The primary duty of a wife is to have absolute and unconditional devotion to her husband. Anasuya says to Sita: — "They that love their husband whether living in the city or in the forest, whether well or ill-disposed towards them, attain great status. Wicked, or libidinous, **or indigent**, a husband is a supreme deity unto a wife of noble character. (II. 117. 22-28) Further Anasuya advises by saying, "Listen, O Princess: a mother, father and brother are all kind to us; but they bestow only limited joy. A husband, however, bestows unlimited joy (in the shape of blessedness), O Videha's daughter; vile is the woman who refuses to serve him. Fortitude, piety, a friend and a wife - these four are put to the test only in times of adversity. A woman who treats her husband with disrespect - even though he is old, sick, dull-headed, indigent, blind, deaf, wrathful or most wretched - shall suffer various torments in hell (the abode of Yama). Devotion of body, speech and mind to her lord's feet is the only duty, sacred vow and penance of a woman." (Ramacharita Mansa: 654)

Sita says to Rama at the time of the latter's departure to forest, "O dear husband, father, mother, son, brother, daughter-in-law, all of them abide by the consequences of their own actions; it is the wife alone that shares the fate of husband... Neither father, mother, son, friend, nor her own self is the stay of a woman in this or in after-life, it is the husband alone that is her only support, unto woman is preferable under all circumstances the shade of her husband's feet to the tops of a palace, the celestial car or the excursion in the airy Path...," (R. II

27. 4- 23) In reply to Dasaratha, Sita says: "The Vina (lute) without strings does not sound; and the car without wheels does not move, -so although having a hundred sons, a woman without husband cannot attain happiness. The father gives in measure, the brother and the son give in measure, but who does not worship that bestower of limitless treasure - the husband? ...A husband is a deity unto the wife." (Ramayana - II. 39. 29-31) A woman should unhesitatingly prefer the wishes of a husband.

Despite all the troubles Sita underwent, she never blamed Rama for asking her to enter the fire to prove her chastity. Similarly, when Rama decided to leave her in the forest because of the slanderous judgement by the people about her abduction by Ravana, Sita asked Lakshmana to convey the message to Rama thus: "I grieve not for myself, because I have been abandoned on account of what people say, and not for an evil that I have done. The husband is the god of the wife --- her lord and guide, and what seems good unto him he should do at the cost of her life." Swami **Vivekananda** was so much impressed with the role of Site, his admiration of her evident in his statement, "Sita is unique; the character was depicted once and for all. There may have been several Ramas, perhaps, but never more than one Sita."

Sita's patience, tolerance and compassion is well recognized. It is an acknowledged fact that she was born out of mother earth. Like the earth she had more forbearance, tolerance, patience and also compassion. In spite of all the abuse we cause to mother earth, her compassion never diminishes. After Rama killed Ravana, Hanuman goes to Sita Devi and wanted to kill all the guards who harassed her. Sita calmed him down and said, "Son, these poor wretches were simply carrying out their orders. Just as you follow your master's orders with such zeal, so did they. Is it right to punish servants for the folly of their masters? Forgive them for my sake. They have really shown me great lenience, and only pretended to harass me in front of Ravana. In his absence, they often comforted me and gave me hope of seeing my beloved Lord again." Hanuman was so thrilled and surprised at her loving nature and with tearful eyes, he stated, "Mother, you are more compassionate than Lord Rama. His wrath consumed the entire army of Lanka, where as you will not let me pull a single hair of these wicked women. You are truly kindness personified."

RAMA, THE IDEAL SON

Rama is considered an ideal son, ideal husband, ideal brother, ideal friend and even ideal enemy. As an ideal son, he never disobeyed his father. His respect, deference, honor and love toward her parents were unmatched. He never blamed his father or his stepmother Kaikeyi. Tulasidas himself praised Rama by saying that, "No father nor mother can get a son like Rama." He never identified himself as Rama; he only identifies as Dasharatha's son. After he broke Lord Shiva's bow during Sita Swayamvar ceremony, he told Janaka that, **"I am the son of Dasaratha, king of Ayodhya. I cannot accept her until my parents accepts her and find her suitable for me. So kindly send your messenger to get their approval."** When Dasaratha was trying to stop Rama from going to exile, Rama said, "I cannot break my family tradition of keeping promise … If I have to do whatever action is dearer to my revered father, that action is just done in all respects even by renouncing life. There is indeed nothing greater than performance of duty, doing service to father or doing what he commands." (II:20: 21-22).

Kaushalya laments over the impending decision of Rama going to exile. She argues that mother should also be worthy of worship and should abstain from going to the forest as per her wish. In fact, she says that she would not live if Rama would leave for the forest. It is better for her to starve to death. Rama said that he had to implement the promise Dasaratha made to Kaikeyi. He gave the examples of Parasu Rama who slayed his mother and sage Kandu who killed the sacred cow in order to obey the commands of their fathers respectively. Rama said that there are many others who complied with the commands of their fathers in accordance with the prevailing custom. He said to mother Kaushalya, "I am not able to violate my father's words. I am bowing my head and asking your favor. I shall have to go to the forest (2:21:29)." He also informed that, "I cannot do otherwise than acting in accordance with father's words, the prevalent practice on earth. There is no deprivation indeed for anyone who complies with father's commands." Kausalya, as devoted wife, would not do anything against his promise. She would not allow her husband to be insulted by anybody. Her loyalty to her husband was irrevocable. Even though she became emotional and upset at the prospects of Rama going to forests, she regained her composure by invoking blessing on Rama. Consequently, Rama was able to fulfill the father's command without ever questioning. Rama sacrificed the kingdom and went to 14-year exile in order to keep the family tradition.

Rama never harbored any ill will toward Kaikeyi in spite of her wish to send Rama to forest for 14 years because of the promise she received from King Dasaratha. After Rama killed Ravana, Lord Shiva tells him that he is an incarnation of God. He is born only to remove the thorn that was piercing the earth. Then Lord Shiva took Sita, Rama and Lakshman into a heavenly airplane where they see King Dasaratha, who acknowledged their great achievements and blessed them affectionately. Dasaratha said, "Rama, being pleased with you, you will attain religious merit and extensive glory on earth, as also heaven and excellent power. Oh! Knower of righteousness." When Dasaratha remembered the pain that was imprinted in his heart with the words of Kaikeyi that sent Rama into exile, he said, "Sir, you know all the laws of justice and fair play. When queen Kaikeyi asked for my exile, you were angry with her and her son, Bharath. Please change your mind about them, for Kaikeyi had always loved me and brought me up as a child and now Bharath rules the kingdom as a mere representative of mine." Dasaratha accepted his wisdom and praised his magnanimity.

RAMA, THE IDEAL ENEMY

Rama is an embodiment of dharma. In spite of all the difficulties he encountered in search of Sita, undergoing many discomforts in the forests, and humiliation of Sita being kidnapped, Rama never strayed away from Dharma. After he entered Lanka by crossing the bridge built by Vanara Sena, Rama was gracious in allowing two spies sent by Ravana to even inspect his army and its deployment. Rama then asked the spies to carry the message to Ravana thus: "Ravana, you are a great devotee of Lord Shiva. Still, you committed the unforgivable folly of abducting Sita. It is even now not too late to repent and seek my pardon. I give you time till tomorrow morning. If by then you do not come to me to beg my pardon, you will be the one responsible for the destruction of your city and your people." Ravana was outraged at the assessment of Rama's magnanimity and description of all the prowess of Lakshman, Angadha, Sugriva and others. Ravana misunderstood Rama's forgiveness and dharmic nature as a weakness. He denied the conciliatory message sent by Rama.

During the war, Rama was able to strike the elaborately carved headpiece that shielded all his ten heads and make Ravana defenseless. His head armor was shattered to pieces. Ravana was defenseless without the armor to his ten heads. The arrow that made Ravana defenseless returned to Rama's hands. Lakshmana asked Rama, "Why did you not kill....?" Rama replied, "One does not kill a foe who is disarmed and prostrates oneself on the field of battle, Lakshmana. It would be dishonorable to kill Ravana thus." Lakshmana questioned as to, "Why should we show him any honor when he fights without honor." Rama replied, "Because we are Dasaratha's sons, Shishyas of Brahma rishi Vasishta and Vishwamitra, children of Kausalya and Sumitra, kings in waiting of Ayodhya, mightiest of Arya nations. Because we are Kshatriyas, bound by the code of the warriors. Because we are followers of Dharma." In spite of all the grievous crimes committed by Ravana, Rama asked him to return in the morning at sunrise to complete the war. He spared the life of Ravana even though Rama had every opportunity to kill him.

Finally, when Ravana was attacked and was on deathbed, Rama asked Lakshman, "Go to Ravana quickly before he dies and request him to share whatever knowledge he can. A brute he may be, but he is also a great scholar." Ravana said that the most important lesson of life is that you must avoid engaging in bad action as much as you can and you must do good action without any delay; sooner the better. By following this rule, you can save not only yourself but many other people from being damaged. Always trust and heed the advice of your ministers. Do not think that you are always winner even if you are winning all the time. As a king, you must suppress greed as soon as you realize that you want to do good to the people. Do not be attached and be a slave to your senses. One needs to put them in proper place, otherwise they will lead you to your destruction. He guided him to have always good relations with charioteer, cook, gatekeeper and his brothers, because those are the persons who can harm you most. He advised Lakshmana never to underestimate strength of his enemy, a mistake which he made. He told him to trust a minister who criticizes his actions. He asked Lakshmana to always believe in astrology and movement of stars which can never be wrong.

Similarly, Rama showed his benevolence toward Ravana even after he was killed. It was time to attend the funeral arrangements. Rama spoke to Vibhishana as follows: "Let the obsequies of your brother be performed and let these crews of women be consoled." Vibhishana reacted by saying that he is not obligated to perform the obsequies to his brother because he killed many human beings, kidnapped Sita, relinquished the virtuous nature, became slave to his sexual desires and killed his own kin and kith. Hence, he should not be respected for all his evil acts because people may think of these evil acts as good acts, if any respect is given to his body.

Rama acknowledging the demonic qualities of Ravana said, "Hostilities end with death. Our purpose has been accomplished. Let his funeral rites be performed. According to rule, Ravana is eligible to get the last rites on his dead body from you. You will also become fit for glory." Following the advice of Rama, Vibhishana completed obsequies for Ravana, his dead brother.

LAKSHMANA IS AN IDEAL BROTHER

All major characters in Ramayana are upholders of dharma. All four brothers are the supreme example of the highest values. Valmiki called Lakshmana as the other self of Lord Rama and also described him as "Rama's right hand." They are inseparable and are considered as bimba and pratibimba – they are reflection of each other. Lakshmana was considered the symbol of loyalty, faith, dedication, selfless service, sacrifice and commitment toward his brother Rama. He always served Rama and Sita with reverence, obedience and devotion.

When Rama decided to honor his father's promise, Lakshmana was furious, fuming, fretting and enraged. Addressing his mother,

Lakshman said, "Mother, my brother Rama is not guilty of anything. All this transpired from our father, Dasaratha's, weakness in youth… I will not stand this nonsense. I cannot remain idle when the kingdom that rightfully belongs to Rama is being snatched away from him." He wanted to punish those responsible for this sad state of affairs. Lakshman told Rama that he cannot accept Kaikeya's wish of sending him to forest. He cannot see that Ikshuvaku dynasty is insulted. He was even ready to lay down his life in order to repair the injustice that would be done. He was ready to proceed to take vengeance against Kaikeyi. Rama consoled him by saying that, "Oh, Lakshmana! I know your highest affection towards me, your heroic valor, your strength and your unassailable splendor … Righteousness is the best of all qualities in the world. Truth is established in righteousness. Even these best words of father are enjoined with righteousness. One who follows righteousness, does not waste his promise given to one's father, mother or Brahmana. I cannot transgress my father's command. On the word given by my father only, Kaikeyi instigated me to go to the forest. Hence, leave this mean mentality of military heroism. Observe righteousness and not rudeness, follow my perception." (Ayodhya Kanda 21: 38, 40-42).

Lakshmana decided to follow Rama and spend his life in an exile leaving behind his mother and newly married wife, and forsaking all the luxuries of a kingdom with no hesitation. He considered Rama as his brother, friend and a father. Rama was very fond of him and could count on him to assume the responsibilities accorded to him. When Lakshmana fell unconscious in the battlefield, Rama lamented by saying, "If I were to search in the world, I may get a mother like Kausalya and a wife like Sita, but not a brother as noble as Lakshmana. What is the use of life without Lakshmana?" Rama also said, "Lakshmana is the breath of my life, a brother like him never been available for anyone else on earth." Lakshmana's sacrifice and faithful commitment to his brother Rama are shining examples for mankind of all ages.

His determination to serve Rama was commendable and extraordinary. His loyalty to his brother was exemplary. On the very first night of the exile, when Rama and Sita retired for the night in the forest,

Lakshman kept a watch on them. As expected Goddess Nidra (the Goddess of sleep) approached Lakshman that night. But he begged her to excuse him for next 14 years so that he could carry out his dharma unconditionally in protecting Rama and Sita without any hurdle. Nidra commanded that someone else must sleep to maintain balance on his behalf. Lakshman asked her to consider his wife Urmila to sleep for those 14 years. The goddess was impressed by his devotion. Thus, Lakshmana's unwavering responsibility to safeguard his elder brother for the rest of the exile was very impressive. Nidra went to Ayodhya Palace and asked Urmila if she would take up Lakshmana's sleep, which she gladly did.

BHARATA'S PLEDGE

Bharata was away when Rama decided to leave Ayodhya as per the wish of his stepmother Kaikeyi. Her plan was to make Bharat as the King of Ayodhya since Rama left for the forest for 14 years. When Bharata learned what his mother had done, he was furious at his mother and in fact he even banished his mother from Ayodhya. He went to the forest to meet Rama and requested him to come back. His love for Rama was unshakable, deep and unmatched. Tulasidas described Bharata's unwavering faith in Rama. Bharata said, "I do not want wealth, nor righteousness, nor fulfillment of my desires. I do not even want liberation. The only boon I ask is that in life and after life I have pure love for the lotus feet of Shri Rama." He even reminded Rama that "The eldest must rule. Please come back and claim your rightful place as king." Rama refused to go against his father's command by saying that, "Our father the King gave you kingship after him and he ordained for me life in the forest. What right have we to alter or reject his plans? Far from being wrong, it is your duty to rule the land. And I too shall do my duty … I cannot possibly disobey my father's word. You will please me by not persisting in trying to persuade me. Satrughna is there to help you in ruling, as Lakshmana is here to help me in forest life. With Lakshmana by my side, I lack nothing. Let us all four do our father's will."

Then Bharata took his brother's sandals and said, "I shall place these sandals on the throne as symbols of your authority. I shall rule only as regent in your place, and each day I shall put my offerings at the feet of my Lord. When the fourteen years of banishment are over, I shall joyously return the kingdom to you." Rama was very impressed with Bharata's selflessness. As Bharata left, Rama said to him, "I should have known that you would renounce gladly what most men work lifetime to learn to give up."

RAMAYANA'S GLOBAL APPEAL

There is a universal appeal among many nations across the globe. The eternal values related to the day to day living, relevance of dharma, democratic principles, brotherly obligations, parental obedience, responsibilities of husband and wife, sagely advice, Hanuman's selfless service, patience and tolerance, rules guiding the warfare, and others have become the source of inspiration and are being adopted to enrich respective cultures. Ramayana spread to numerous countries such as Malaysia, Indonesia, Cambodia, Thailand, Vietnam, Laos, Colombia, Burma, Philippines, Fiji, Mauritius, Bali, Mexico, Trinidad, Guyana, Surinam, South Africa, Japan, China, New Zealand, Australia, Britain, Belgium, Holland, USA, Canada and may other countries. What is that message that resonated in the hearts and minds of the people. How can one win the Lord Rama's grace and blessings?

Rama admonishes people to follow the path of dharma with devotion that he himself followed: "I am won by the conduct of a man as depicted below:

He who has no enmity or quarrel with anyone and is devoid of hope and fear - to such a man all the quarters are ever full of joy. Undertaking nothing (with an interested motive), without home, without pride and without sin, free from wrath, clever and wise, ever loving the company of saints and accounting the enjoyments, even of heaven as well as final beatitude as no more than a blade of grass, tenaciously adhering to the cult of Devotion but avoiding bigotry, and giving up all sophistical reasoning." (Ramayana, Uttarakanda:46). This kind of universal message permeated the people of all the countries.

It is time to remember our eternal rich traditions, that answers many questions hidden in the storehouse of Ramayana, refreshes our memory about nature and qualities of many personalities and numerous incidents, rearms our knowledge about the grandeur of our way of life, makes all of us proud of the beauty of the ancient poetic compendium, and teaches us the morals and ethics that are relevant even today. Let us remember the words of Sir Monier Williams (1860-1888):

> *"There is not in the whole range of Sanskrit literature a more charming poem than the Ramayana. The classical purity, clearness and simplicity of its style, the exquisite touches of true poetic feeling with which it abounds, its graphic description of heroic incidents, nature's grandest scenes, the deep acquaintance it displays with the conflicting workings of the mind and most refined emotions of human heart, all entitle it to rank among the most beautiful compositions, that have appeared at any period or in any country."*

YOGA-TRIAD WHO PLOWED THE AMERICAN SOIL

EMERSON, THOREAU AND WHITMAN IN 19TH CENTURY.

India's Prime Minister Narendra Modi during his address to UN General Assembly in September 2014, had asked world leaders to adopt an international Yoga Day, saying "Yoga embodies unity of mind and body; thought and action; restraint and fulfillment; harmony between man and nature; a holistic approach to health and wellbeing." On December 11, 2014, the 193-member UN General Assembly adopted a resolution by consensus, proclaiming June 21 as 'International Day of Yoga'. The resolution was introduced by India's Ambassador to the UN and had 175 UN members, including five permanent members of the UN Security Council, as co-sponsors.

As we celebrate the second International Yoga Day, let us take this opportunity to trace the history of three stalwarts – Emerson, Thoreau and Whitman - who paved the way in 19th century for the present abiding interest, widespread enthusiasm, and uninhibited fascination toward yoga and meditation in USA. Let us start with a quotation from Native Americans who inhabited this country long before the British started the voyage to this land of opportunities.

Native American

"Listen to the wind... It talks.

Listen to the Silence... It Speaks.

Listen to your heart... It Knows."

YOGA AND MEDITATION IN USA

The **2016 Yoga in America Study** Conducted by Yoga Journal and Yoga Alliance is a national study, benchmarking a similar study conducted in 2008 and 2012 by Yoga Journal.

Survey highlights:

⅄ The number of American yoga practitioners has increased to over 36 million in 2016, up from 20.4 million in 2012. 28% of all Americans have participated in a yoga class at some point in their lives

⅄ 34% of Americans say they are somewhat or very likely to practice yoga in the next 12 months equal to more than 80 million Americans. Reasons cited include flexibility, stress relief and fitness.

⅄ 75% of all Americans agree "yoga is good for you."

Why the popularity is increasing year by year? It appears the more stress people experience, more they turn to methods that give them peace of mind. Yoga and meditation are considered the best methods to quiet a busy mind. As one practitioner sated, "But yoga is my medication. I feel good—soul, mind, and spirit in clarity." Josephine P. Briggs, M.D., Director of NCCIH says, "This reaffirms how important it is for NIH to rigorously study complementary health approaches and make that information easily available to consumers."

The roots of Yoga and Meditation can be traced to early 19th century starting around 1840s. Before Swami Vivekananda landed in the US and gave that rousing speech at the Parliament of Religions, the triad of scholars prepared the American soil to experience the benefits of yoga and meditation.

They have sown the Oriental seed in the Occidental soil preparing for others to reap the fruits of the yield. These transcendentalists have shifted the paradigm by preparing the ground for others.

RALPH WALDO EMERSON: 1803-1882

"We do not determine what we will think." Ralph Waldo Emerson

The groundwork for this paradigm shift had been established, however, by those Americans who were attracted to the wisdom that they found in those Hindu sacred texts that had been translated into English, some of which were available to American readers as early as the eighteenth century: **texts such as the Bhagavad Gita, Laws of**

Manu, Bhagavad Purana, Vishnu Purana and some of the major Upanishads. The Transcendentalist movement, consisting of such figures as **Ralph Waldo Emerson, Henry David Thoreau, and Walt Whitman**, was deeply indebted to these texts. The Transcendentalists were, in effect, the first American Vedantists.

Emerson is considered to be the most influential author of the 19th century; his name was known far and wide. In the 1830s, Emerson had copies of the Rig Veda, the Upanishads, the Laws of Manu, the Bhagavata Purana, and his favorite Indian text, the Bhagavad Gita. **"I owed a magnificent day to the Bhagavad-Gita. It was the first of books; it was as if an empire spoke to us, nothing small or unworthy, but large, serene, consistent, the voice of an old intelligence which in another age and climate had pondered and thus disposed of the same questions which exercise us."**

Repelled by the increasing materialism of the West, Emerson turned to India for solace:

"The Indian teaching, through its clouds of legends, has yet a simple and grand religion, like a queenly countenance seen through a rich veil. It teaches to speak truth, love others, and to dispose trifles. The East is grand - and makes Europe appear the land of trifles. ...all is soul and the soul is Vishnu ...cheerful and noble is the genius of this cosmogony. Hari is always gentle and serene - he translates to heaven the hunter who has accidentally shot him in his human form, he pursues his sport with boors and milkmaids at the cow pens; all his games are benevolent and he enters into flesh to relieve the burdens of the world."

Emerson, talking of the **Upanishads and the Vedas**, said that having read them, he could not put them away. **"They haunt me. In them I have found eternal compensation, unfathomable power, unbroken peace."**

His essay on **"Over-Soul"** published in 1841 was considered the greatest article appears to have been influenced by Vedanta and yogic experience. This term denotes the transcendence of duality, or plurality. It emphasizes the unity and oneness. It clearly described the inner experiences of mysticism. Yoga and meditation ideas are amply imbedded in this article on Over-Soul.

> "... that Unity, that Over-Soul, within which every man's particular being is contained and made one with all other... We live in succession, in division, in parts, in particles. Meantime within man is the soul of the whole; the wise silence; the universal beauty, to which every part and particle is equally related; the eternal One. And this deep power in which we exist, and whose beatitude is all accessible to us, is not only self-sufficing and perfect in every hour, but the act of seeing and the thing seen, the seer and the spectacle, the subject and the object, are one. We see the world piece by piece, as the sun, the moon, the animal, the tree; but the whole, of which these are the shining parts, is the soul..... .

> From within or from behind, a light shine through us upon things, and makes us aware that we are nothing, but the light is all. A man is the facade of a temple wherein all wisdom and all good abide. . . When it breathes through his intellect, it is genius; when it breathes through his will, it is virtue; when it flows through his affection, it is love. . ."

The concept Over-Soul is equated with Paramatma – Parama to mean super and *atma* to mean soul. Supreme Soul is nothing but Over-Soul. At that level, Emerson observed "brief moments" that contain "more reality" than "all other experiences."

He finds solace in the spiritual dimension of India over the materialistic West. "The Indian teaching, through its clouds of legends, has yet a simple and grand religion, like a queenly countenance seen through a rich veil. It teaches to speak truth, love others, and to dispose trifles. The East is grand - and makes Europe appear the land of trifles. ...all is soul and the soul is Vishnu ...cheerful and noble is the genius of this cosmogony. Hari is always gentle and serene - he translates to heaven the hunter who has accidentally shot him in his human form, he pursues his sport with boors and milkmaids at the cow pens; all his games are benevolent and he enters into flesh to relieve the burdens of the world."

THOREAU WAS AMERICA'S FIRST PRACTICING YOGI.

Henry David Thoreau (1817-1862) spent plenty of time during his seclusion at Walden Pond in 1847, who was probably the first to practice silence and yoga. Thoreau adopted an ascetic diet and spent hours, from sunrise till noon, "rapt in reverie...in undisturbed solitude and stillness," as he put it. He didn't do yoga poses, but his embrace of meditation, which would have been very odd in his day, is impressive. In those days, no record of any one else practicing Yoga to experience the contemplation. This interest in yoga might have been ignited after reading **Manusmriti.** He said that **"I cannot read a single word of the Hindoos without being elevated."**

Practicing yoga faithfully for about two years at Walden and reading several Hindu scriptures, he wrote: *"In the morning I bathe my intellect in the stupendous and cosmogonal philosophy of the Bhagavat Geeta, since whose composition years of the gods have elapsed, and in comparison, with which our modern world and its literature seem puny and trivial; and I doubt if that philosophy is not to be referred to a previous state of existence, so remote is its sublimity from our conceptions. I lay down the book and go to my well for water, and lo! There I meet the servant of the Brahmin, priest of Brahma, and Vishnu and Indra, who still sits in his temple on the River Ganga reading the Vedas, or dwells at the root of a tree with his crust and water---jug. I meet his servant come to draw water for his master, and our buckets as it were grate together in the same well. The pure Walden water is mingled with the sacred water of the Ganga (Ganges)."*

And *"One sentence of the Gita, is worth the State of Massachusetts many times over"*

The book **Walden** reveals the passion, excitement and inspiration Thoreau derived from the Hindu sacred books. It mentions that he used to keep a copy of Bhagavad Gita on his bedside in his cabin; compared the pond with "Ganges River"; and how retreated to the pond to experience the spirit of the ascetic sages of India. He often mentioned about how Asiatic ideas had transformed him spiritually and intellectually. He even mentioned about how his spiritual ecstasy left him "daily intoxicated" with "*an indescribable, infinite, all-absorbing, divine, heavenly pleasure, a sense of elevation and expansion .... I speak as a witness on the stand, and tell what I have perceived. The morning and the evening were sweet to me, and I led a life aloof from the society of men.*"

Henry David Thoreau "I sat in my sunny doorway from sunrise till noon, rapt in a reverie, amidst the pines and hickory and the sumaches in undisturbed solitude and stillness ... I realize what the Oriental mean by contemplation and the forsaking of work." He says that the man's close relationship with the nature would energize the spirits and heal the natural environment and help stimulate contemplation and meditation. He felt that the peace, silence and solitude of the natural environment are essential to practice meditation. He stated that "by the time the villagers had broken their fast the morning sun had dried my house sufficiently to allow me to move in again, and my meditations were almost uninterrupted." The he goes on to say that, "Now that the cars are gone by and all the restless world with them, and the fishes in the pond no longer feel their rumbling, I am more alone than ever. For the rest of the long afternoon, perhaps, my meditations are interrupted only by the faint rattle of a carriage or team along the distant highway."

Thoreau affirmed to **Harrison Blake** that **"to some extent and at rare intervals even I am a yogi."** How highly *Thoreau cherished the inactive life of the yoga, the contemplative life in solitude, can be illustrated by the fact that he devoted two complete chapters of Walden and parts of several others not only to extol the positive virtues of solitude and the meditative life in general, but to show in particular how he himself was a devotee of the yoga while at Walden Pond.*

Thoreau embarked on his Walden experiment in the spirit of Indian asceticism. He went into seclusion not for Christian repentance but for contemplation on the very nature of himself to be released from the daily drudgery and petty daily routines. He was practicing what was prescribed in the sixth chapter of Bhagavad Gita that explains the ashtanga Yoga and the difficulties of the mind and how to gain mastery over it. In a letter written to H. G. O Blake in 1849, he remarked:

*"Free in this world as the birds in the air, disengaged from every kind of chains, those who have practiced the Yoga gather in Brahmin the certain fruit of their works. Depend upon it, rude and careless as I am, I would fain practice the yoga faithfully. This Yogi, absorbed in contemplation, contributes in his degree to creation; he breathes a divine perfume, he heard wonderful things. Divine forms traverse him without tearing him and he goes, he acts as animating original matter. To some extent, and at rare intervals, even **I am a Yogi.***

Thoreau read every book on Indian Philosophy available to him in those days after 1855. His praise to these books are extracted thus:

What extracts from the Vedas I have read fall on me like the light of a higher and purer luminary, which describes a loftier course through a purer stratum.

Whenever I have read any part of the Vedas, I have felt that some unearthly and unknown light illuminated me. In the great teaching of the Vedas, there is no touch of the sectarianism. It is of all ages, climes, and nationalities, and is the royal road for the attainment of the Great Knowledge.

When my imagination travels eastward and backward to those remote years of the gods, I seem to draw near to the habitation of the morning, and the dawn at length has a place.

Like Emerson, Thoreau had mystical experiences that Vedanta helped him to understand. "The texts were a kind of touchstone for his own.

Alan Hodder said, "He had moments of euphoria and rapture in nature, but he couldn't really explain them until he started reading the Indian material. Then he actually saw references to what he was experiencing, and he thought, 'Aha! I'm not the only one having this. There's a long tradition to it. The sacred books also taught Thoreau the important distinction between philosophical inquiry and spiritual practice. "One may discover the root of an Indian religion in his own private history," Thoreau wrote in his journal, "when, in the silent intervals of the day and night, he does sometimes inflict on himself like austerities with stern satisfaction." He may have been the first American to call himself a yogi. "Depend upon it that, rude and careless as I am, I would fain practice the yoga faithfully," he wrote to a friend in 1849. "To some extent, and at rare intervals, even I am a yogi."

HOW DID HE DESCRIBE THE YOGIC EXPERIENCES IN WALDEN?

Thoreau practiced yoga and speaks of it in Walden in explicit terms. He even styled himself a "Yogi." In Walden, he writes: "I know of no more encouraging fact than the unquestionable ability of man to elevate his life by a conscious endeavor." Yoga, as the Vedantist understands it, is not an esoteric practice but meditative discipline, a focusing of consciousness. It is, in the words of the Gita, a conscious endeavor to "lift the self by the self." Only by such mental discipline can one develop the intuitive faculty, which alone will ultimately take one to the deep-lying essence beneath. Thoreau writes, "By a conscious effort of mind we can stand aloof from actions and their consequences; and all things, good and bad, go by us like a torrent. We are not wholly involved in nature."

He found in the Hindu scriptures the conceptions of human life and human potential to a higher elevation. He says that there is divine within each soul and similar divinity is also found in the nature. He said on "rare intervals" his consciousness becomes unbound and experience it as a shoreless and island less ocean. Let us look at what he experiences during those rare intervals:

⅄ If with closed ears and eyes I consult consciousness for a moment, immediately are all walls and barriers dissipated, earth rolls from under me, and I float . . . in the midst of an unknown and infinite sea, or else heave and swell like a vast ocean of thought, without rock or headland, where are all riddles solved, all straight lines making there their two ends to meet, eternity and space gamboling familiarly through my depths. I am from the beginning, knowing no end, no aim. No sun illumines me, for I dissolve all lesser lights in my own intenser and steadier light. I am a restful kernel in the magazine of the universe. . ..

⅄ Men are constantly dinging in my ears their fair theories and plausible solutions of the universe, but ever there is no help, and I return to my shoreless, island less ocean. (*The Selected Journals of*

Henry David Thoreau, ed. Carl Bode (New York: New American Library, Signet Classics, 1960): 39.)

WALT WHITMAN: DID HE EXPERIENCE KUNDALINI SHAKTI?

"If anything is sacred, the human body is sacred."

Walt Whitman (1819-1892) was a poet, essayist, humanist, journalist, transcendentalist and a yogi. He was influenced by Emerson and Thoreau in his philosophical outlook toward nature, life, his affinity to Vedanta and yogic experience. Whitman was clearly describing an experience of transcendence. He was considered as a poet of mysticism, cosmic consciousness and religion. He describes his experience as follows:

Only in the perfect uncontamination and solitariness of individuality. . .. Only here, and on such terms, the meditation, the devout ecstasy, the soaring flight. Only here, communion with the mysteries. . .. The soul emerges, and all statements, churches, sermons, melt away like vapors. Alone, and silent thought and awe, and aspiration — and then the interior consciousness, like a hitherto unseen inscription, in magic ink, beams out its wondrous lines to the sense. Bibles may convey, and priests expound, but it is exclusively for the noiseless operation of one's isolated self, to enter the pure ether of veneration, reach the divine levels, and commune with the unutterable.

Whitman wrote: "There are divine things well enveloped, I swear to you there are divine things more beautiful than words can tell." In many of his writings one would notice Whitman's evolution to the awakening of the Self within and his glimpse of the One Spirit that pervades the universe. To achieve this kind of spirit he suggested that "re-examine all you have been told at school, or church or in any book, dismiss whatever insults your soul, and your very flesh shall be a great poem and have the richest fluency not only in its word but in the silent lines of its lips and face and between the lashes of your eyes and in every motion and joint of your body. "

Whitman's approach was holistic in the sense of establishing connectivity to everything that exists. Everything has a meaning and ever thing is connected. He wanted to remove all barriers to make visible the connectivity between body, spirit and soul; change the mindset; know yourself through knowing others; focus on the present; and experience the moment. He admonishes his readers:

Whitman never set high value on a successful career or worldly aggrandizement; instead his aspiration had always been for the immortal. Looking back on his past life, he wrote in 1871:

> Walt Whitman is now 52 years old. No worldly aim has engrossed his life. He is still unmarried. None of the usual ardors of business ambition, of the acquisition of money, or the claims of society, pleasure, nor even the attractions of culture or art seemed to have enslaved him. The thought and the making of this work has spanned the whole horizon of his life, almost since boyhood. (*Complete Works VI.I: 38*)

Furthermore, Whitman's realization of the transcendental self-enabled him to overcome his inhibitions and helped the enlargement of his vision; the inversions of his sexual nature were transmuted into a spiritual passion for the mass of humanity.

Whitman has written extensively not only about his capacity to disassociate himself but also detaching himself from all surrounding activities so that he can extract thoughts and experiences of his own mind. V K Chari writes that "Whitman is conscious of a **certain trance-like** state leading to the suspension of the conscious intellect and accompanied by a strange feeling of exaltation and joy and a transformation, as it were, of the whole being; a state in which the mystic experiences a new awakening, the awakening of the spiritual vision, and, like the sage in the Upanishad, understands the being whose essence is joy. (Whitman in the Light of Vedantic Mysticism: An Interpretation; p: 104)

In that condition, the whole body is elevated to a higher state consciousness. At this level, there is more illumination both inside and outside, more serenity and purity. It is only through mental discipline and concentration; one can dive deep into the self. At that level duality is dissolved.

Sorrows and disappointments cease -- there is no more borrowing trouble in advance. A man realizes the venerable myth -- he is a god walking the earth, he sees new eligibilities, powers and beauties everywhere; he himself has a new eyesight and hearing. The play of the body in motion takes a previously unknown grace. Merely to move is then a happiness, a pleasure -- to breathe, to see, is also. . .. All the beforehand gratifications, drink, spirits, coffee grease, stimulants, mixtures, late hours, luxuries, deeds of the night, seem as vexatious dreams, and how the awakening; -- many fall into their natural places, wholesome, conveying diviner joys. (Complete Writings, IV, 26-27.)

Whitman, however, sometimes insists that during this state of meditation the "senses are not lost or counteracted" but maintained intact:

a trance, *yet with all the senses alert* -- only a state of high exalted amusing -- *the tangible and material with all its shows, the objective world suspended or surmounted for a while,* and powers in exaltation, freedom, vision *yet the senses not lost or counteracted.* (Clifton Joseph Furness, Walt Whitman's Workshop (Cambridge: Harvard University Press, 1928), p. 21.

There is some evidence that Whitman underwent certain types of the experiences that are usually accompany the practice of Yoga. He may have used such terms as trance, consciousness, sensation, rapture, contemplation and others. There is no question that he experienced a revolutionary transformation in his life. It may have happened when he was about 29 years old.

In fact, Geeta Khadka described a remarkable insight into the experiences of trance like status and consciousness as described by Whitman. In an article entitled "Song of Myself as Kundalini Yantra" she described as to how Whitman may have experienced the **Kundalini Shakti**. She divided the Song of Myself into different locations in the physical body to represent different chakras; Muladhara, Svadhisthana, Manipura, Anahata, Visuddha, Ajna and Sahasrara Chakra.

Sahasrara Chakra means thousand petalled lotus. Kundalini Shakti moves from the base chakra known as Muladhara to final chakra where one experiences tranquility, peace, joy and wisdom. Arguments become irrelevant and nonsensical. At this stage one is released from the time and space and experience the true nature of oneself. The following passage would resemble that of transcendental illumination he may have experienced:

> Swiftly arose and spread around me the peace and knowledge that pass all the arguments of the earth,
>
> And I know that the hand of God is the promise of my own, and I know that the spirit of God is the brother of my own,
>
> And that all the men ever born are also my brothers, and the women my sisters and lovers,
>
> And that a keelson of creation is love.

This passage should not have been written by anyone who did not experience the kundalini power. Whitman's experience is like that described by Gopi Krishna:

> "Suddenly, with a roar like that of a waterfall, I felt a stream of liquid light entering my brain through the spinal cord . . .. I felt the point of consciousness that was myself growing wider, surrounded by the waves of light." (*Higher Consciousness: The evolutionary thrust of Kundalini*).

At this level all barriers disappear, all duality dissolves, everything appears equally important and everything has relevance. Everything looks beautiful, serene and sacred. Everything pulsates with energy.

> I believe a leaf of grass is no less than the journey-work of the stars,
>
> And the pismire is equally perfect, and a grain of sand, and the egg of wren,
>
> And the tree-toad is a chef-d'oeuvre for the highest,
>
> And the running blackberry would adorn the parlours of heaven.

Whitman recognizes the essential unity of matter and body, which find no opposition between the body and soul

I am the poet of the body and I am the poet of the soul.

I have said that the soul is not more than the body,

And I have said that body is not more than the soul,

And nothing, not God, is greater to one's self is.

Similarly, his poems "**Passage to India**" and "**Leaves of Grass**" reveal how much he could absorb and digest the essence of Vedanta philosophy with his transcendental experiences. He lived his life meaningfully without escaping from it. He thought one should outgrow from all the dilemmas; integrate the body, mind and soul; experience the nature; and dissolve the dualities to enjoy the present moment. Let us appreciate the ground work prepared by Emerson, Thoreau and Whitman to introduce yoga and meditation to America and changing the landscape forever.

INTOLERANT INTELLECTUALS
BELITTLE BHARATH

WHY THIS SUDDEN OUTBURST? SUFFERING FROM SECULAR SYNDROME?

In last part of 2015, the so-called intellectuals who comprise of scientists, liberals, film makers, play writes, actors, writers, novelists, artists, painters, communists and others have been criticizing the government about its growing intolerance toward the minorities. They are angry at the murder of Muhammad Akhlaq in Dadri who was supposed to have eaten beef. Some say they are angry at the killing of Dr. M M Kalburgi, considered a rationalist and a writer. These two incidents have supposedly triggered these intolerant liberals to go to the streets, hold news conferences, return awards, accuse the Modi government, denunciate the RSS, BJP leaders, the VHP and other Hindutva advocates. These deranged liberals are trying their best to thrust Hindutva fears down the throats of minorities and charge them with intolerance. It is a contrived story by the liberals and media to flare up their loyalists to blame the Hindus for these two incidents. Nobody really said whether he was killed because he ate beef, or stole the cow, slaughtered the cow or provoked the meek Hindus to a fight. Do any of these liberals know?

In an unprecedented manner, RSS leaders decided to go head on and challenge these intolerant intellectuals about their sincerity and seriousness of their outbursts. The Joint General Secretary of RSS, Dattatreya Hosabale, decided to declare that they are not going to remain silent and allow liberals to use RSS as a punching bag. It is uplifting to hear that: "The RSS is not a punching bag for any of these so-called liberal, pseudo-secular, intolerant people. Where were they when the Pandits were thrown out of Kashmir Valley and 59 Hindus were killed at Godhra railway station in 2002?" It is time to speak up. It is time to tell it like it is. RSS, VHP, BJP and Hindutva ideologists should not allow Hindus to be the scapegoats for these liberals. Every

Hindu has a right to feel proud of their Hindu dharma and our Hindu leaders should lead the way as strong spokespersons.

LIBERALS' CROCODILE TEARS

Arudhata Roy said she was "so ashamed of what is going on in this country." She returned her award in protest against the growing culture of fear and censorship fostered by the government, who encouraged the "lynching, shooting, burning and mass murder of fellow human beings". It appears that she is one of the paid employees and mouth piece of those who want to demean India. If lynching and killing occurred in India, how are Christian and Muslim populations increasing day by day, while the Hindu population is decreasing? If she is ashamed of what is going on in India, she has every right to go to one of the 56 Islamic countries to savor the freedom that never exists there. She is like a carpet beggar who wants to live off the crumbs of the Hindu land and stab the country at the same time for unknown rewards.

Shah Rukh Khan, spoke out on NPR expressing his concern over what he called "growing intolerance in India." Can he say to Pakistan that what happened to nearly 18 percent of Hindus since the time of Independence? Can he be bold enough to say that the Islamic intolerance towards Hindus was the reason that their number has dwindled to less than one percent?

Salman Rushdie, who was the victim of these so-called liberals and the Congress Party, jumped into this debate, telling a local television network: "What has crept into Indian life now is a degree of thuggish violence which is new. And it seems to be given permission by the silence of official bodies, the silence of the Sahitya Akademi ... by the silence of the prime minister's office." What a sad commentary on the part of Rushdie who decided to sleep with the same enemies who stabbed him when his book was banned in India.

MOTIVES AND TIMING OF THE RETURNED AWARDS

Minority groups, Christians, and Muslims were able to influence their media comrades to give disproportionate attention to the Church attacks just before the Delhi elections without ever reporting the actual data on the attacks on religious institutions. Three church attacks received all the attention nationally and internationally by the crooked media without ever mentioning that nearly 200 Hindu Temples were attacked in the same period. Why was there a hue and cry to this disproportionate reaction to the church attacks? Union Minister V K Singh said the debate over intolerance was politically motivated and artificially created by hatemongers of Hinduism. It was deliberately generated ahead of the Bihar assembly polls by those who are "being paid with a lot of money" in order to influence the Bihar elections.

Similar church attacks hype was also created to affect the Delhi elections. Is it mere coincidence that these liberals raise the Church attack issue and Intolerance concerns just before the elections? They want to affect the elections. After the Delhi elections, there were no further discussions on church attacks. Similarly, the hype about returning awards also disappeared after the Bihar elections. According to the Delhi Police Department, 36 temples and three churches reported thefts in 2012; 69 temples and three churches in 2013; 206 temples and three churches in 2014. Myopic, biased and anti-Hindu media would not even mention how many Temples were desecrated during that time. For these intolerant intellectuals three church attacks are more news worthy than 206 Temple attacks. There is no question of mental derangement, myopic Hindu hatred or allurement of money and fame.

GOVERNMENT POSITION

Indian government officials were quick to respond to these intolerant intellectuals' myopic parade of news conferences to surrender their awards by dismissing the growing protest as a political ploy to discredit Modi and tear down the BJP government.

"The entire purpose of these protests is to derail the development agenda of the Narendra Modi government," the urban development minister, **Venkaiah Naidu**, said on Thursday. "The country is being subjected to damage and unnecessarily wrong information is being given about political intolerance."

Similarly, Finance Minister **Arun Jaitley,** who also holds the Information and Broadcasting portfolio, denounced it as "a manufactured rebellion" by the supporters of the Congress and Leftists "who have opposed Modi long before he became Prime Minister" and their "long-standing intolerance of intellectuals towards the Sangh and Hinduism".

These intellectuals have been accused of double standards and giving support to an "orchestrated campaign" to target the National Democratic Alliance government. Hence, they demand evidence of past history of protestors and where they were "when the country was rocked and looted with huge corruption scandals by the UPA", or the Emergency, the 1984 riots, and Ayodhya controversy and so on. Mr. Jaitley also called the protests "politics by other means" even though it is straightforwardly political. When intellectuals, artists, and writers protest against the government and its inaction in situations of communal conflict, they are making a political statement. But in doing so, they are not acting as proxies for parties — they are speaking for constitutional rights that guarantee the freedom to live, express and think differently.

WHY ARE THEY SILENT?

Secular journalists who are angry at Akhlaq's killing adopted total silence on a number of other murders recently. In August, army Jawan Vedmitra Chaudhury was lynched to death in Hardevnagar, near Meerut, for saving a girl from molesters. In March, a Hindu man was abducted and murdered in Hajipur of Bihar for marrying a Muslim girl. Last June, a man was lynched to death near Eluru in Andhra Pradesh. A Christian teacher's hand was hacked by a handful of Muslims for allegedly insulting Allah in Kerala.

Balbir Punj argued against all the documentation about Muslim boys trapping Hindu and Christian girls, marrying them, and converting them into Islam. "After several instances of young Muslim boys enticing Hindu and Christian girls in Kerala, Karnataka, Andhra and several other parts of the country with the show of wealth and promises of marriage and then, ferrying them to Kashmir and other places, converting them and recruiting them forcibly into Islamist

Jihad came to light, concerns at this Love Jihad were raised." But these intellectuals have nothing to say about it and dismiss these atrocities as myths to promote enmity among the communities.

It has been reported that that the number of lives lost to terrorism around the world increased by 80 per cent in 2014, reaching the highest level ever recorded at 32,658. Do these intolerant intellectual have the stomach to chew this kind of news knowing fully well that almost all the terrorist attacks are done by the Muslims.

In November, Indian investigators revealed to the international Task Force that the Pakistan-based Hizb-ul-Mujahideen (HM) raised over Rs 80 crores over eight years, from several Pakistani sources, to fund terrorist acts in India. Are there any intellectuals who will return the awards for radical Islamic group's plans to terrorize India?

ATTACKS ON HINDUS AROUND THE COUNTRY

If the intolerant intellectuals are suffering from short memory and are unaware of the atrocities committed by Islamic groups, please read and react. Why did these intellectuals not return their awards when thousands of innocent citizens were killed by terrorist acts?

May 30, 2015: A 21-year old woman was raped by two Muslim men

May 10, 2015: Seven-year old Hindu girl sexually assaulted by Muslim school van driver in Usthi

May 4, 2015: Five Hindu SCs killed by Muslim mob, over a hundred injured, women molested in Nadia

April 3, 2015: Blasts at Belur Math

February 2015: Abduction of a 14-year-old girl Tuktuki Mondal by Muslims for human trafficking in West Bengal has gone global with protests worldwide

May 28, 2014: Eleven-year old Hindu girl assaulted at Ramona Village

May 27, 2014: Twenty-six persons including a police official received bullet injuries when Muslims opposed celebration of PM Narendra Modi's swearing-in-ceremony

May 25, 2014: A Hindu youth and four policemen were severely beaten up at Shajahan Sheikh

May 20, 2014: Assault on a newly-wed Hindu woman by Muslims

May 16, 2014: A Hindu housewife kidnapped and assaulted for five days by Muslims

May 10, 2014: Muslims attacked a funeral procession at Hajarpur Village with bomb and firing in Arjunpur Village

April 9, 2014: Muslims attacked the Basanti Pooja festival in Dhalaghat Village and broke the Basanti deity by kicking it

March 30, 2014: Over 200 Muslims attacked Hindus' village Sihipur when a Muslim was caught red handed stealing a cow

March 29, 2014: A popular Hindu leader Kartick Methia was brutally murdered at Sarar Hat Village

Feb. 1, 2014: Hindu Samhati workers were attacked at Sarberia Village

Jan. 1, 2014: Muslim procession on Prophet's birthday forcibly entered Hindu villages, attacked Hindu houses and damaged as well as ransacked four temples. Hindu women were also molested

Dec. 12, 2013: Sarathi Maity was molested by Muslims with sharp weapons at Ukiler Bazar Village

Oct. 17, 2013: Durga Pooja procession was attacked in Kashthagara by armed Muslims after being provoked from the mosque

Oct. 16, 2013: Six Muslim families slaughtered cows in the presence of the BDO and Police at Dholkali

Feb. 21, 2013: More than 200 Hindu houses burnt in Canning, Joynagar, Kultali and Basanti Police Stations displacing 2,000 people

May 14, 2012: To retaliate against the murder of a SUCI Muslim leader in Tara Nagar, about 100 Hindu houses of two villages looted.

Can you imagine anybody who is concerned with the tolerance toward the citizens of the country would remain silent when more than 15 terrorist attacks inflicted the country over a three-year period?" Do they not count in their liberal agenda? They have little respect for the lives of majority population. Since all the above mentioned terrorist activities are done mostly by Muslims, it is acceptable to ignore the fundamental rights of majority population. Since majority of the liberals are afflicted with the disease of secularism and since many of them happened during the time of Congress party, they should not insult their favorite Party. Their goal is only to insult Hindu religion and destroy India. As far as the intellectuals are concerned they have nothing to do with any government other Congress party. It does not matter for them even if people elect the other government. It is not acceptable for them if some other is elected by the party at the central level is not a Congress government.

HINDUTVA VS SECULARISM

"Some pen artists afflicted with the disease of secularism have returned their medals to protest attempts at distorting Hindu religion and destroying India. No matter which government the country wants, nothing but the Nehruvian model is acceptable to them.

"These intellectuals were not hurt when they accepted the honors from those guilty of anti-Sikh riots," an editorial in RSS magazine 'Panchjanya' said.

BHARATH DEFENDED

"No Indian can tolerate when the nation is being insulted on a global level and there are those who are doing that right now. They feel that ever since the new government has come into power, the nation has plunged into a state of intolerance. This is not a fresh atmosphere. What about the Emergency, the Kashmiri pandits' exodus and the riots? What is today's level of intolerance being compared to?" Anupam Kher asked.

"My intentions are not political. I am just proud and thankful of the fact that this nation has given me so much. I was just a small guy from a small town, but look where I am right now. Sometimes you have to give back," Kher said. He also admitted that he was concerned about his acting career as he has waded into murky waters with his stand.

Kamal Hasan "They are talented people. Just one article by them will bring more attention than returning an award. They should keep the awards, make us proud and continue to fight any government that is not tolerant enough," he said.

Awards are given by a jury in recognition of work done by creative people. It has nothing to do with a government," he said.

"Nothing will happen by returning the awards. You will insult the government or the people who gave you the award with love. That will bring attention, but there are many more ways to do it," said the 60-year-old actor.

LIBERALS ARE CLOSED MINDED AND COLOR BLIND

Many of these so-called intellectuals who witnessed the slaughter of more than 4000 Sikhs, allowed Indira Gandhi to declare emergency and deny the birth right to express their views, killed scores of people and imprisoned untold number of citizens. Where were all these intellectuals? Were they promised all these awards for keeping quiet or was it acceptable as long as Muslims and Christians were not impacted? Why did they not speak out when nearly 60 Hindus were burned by Muslims in a railway compartment in Gujarat in 2002? Was it because they were color-blind, Muslim-blind and anti-Hindu?

Why do these intellectuals keep harping on the Gujarat riots and charge Modi as being responsible for killing Muslims even after the Supreme Court absolved him of all charges leveled against him? Do these intellectuals believe that the Supreme Court cannot do any justice to these Muslims? It appears that they do not have any confidence, trust or faith in the justice system. In order to appease the Muslims these intellectuals will do anything to tarnish the image of Bharath, denounce the BJP government, and smudge the Hindu ideals, morals and ethos that have shaped this humanity for thousands of centuries. They seem to be allergic to these ideals and ready to dump them to please the minorities. If they have the power, they would be delighted to see the demise of Hindutva. Pushpa Bhargava wrote a letter to the President of India: "No one would be more aware than you that, de facto, BJP is the political front of Rashtriya Swayamsevak Sangh (RSS), and functions under the leadership of RSS that is fully committed to the ideology of Hindutva, which I find divisive, unreasonable and unscientific."

WHO IS SECULAR?

If these intellectuals are so abhorrent toward Bharath and Hindutva, what do they believe that should guide the country? What do these liberals want to replace Hindutva with? They are fond of using the concept "SECULAR." Intolerant intellectuals, atrocious Abrahamic religions and myopic media would love to talk about secularism, they enjoy talking about it, believe in it, advocate it and they fiercely defend it without ever defining the concept "SECULAR." Can any of these so-called secularists define it? No way. They dance around it, and they are the people whom we call 'beat around the bush types' but cannot pinpoint. The Indian Constitution declares India as secular without ever defining the word. The Supreme Court refused to define it. No politician dares to answer the question. They cannot accept the definition.

Taslima Nasreen said most secular people are anti-Hindu. "Most secular people are pro-Muslims and anti-Hindu. They protest against the acts of Hindu fundamentalists and defend the heinous acts of Muslim fundamentalists. Politicians appease Muslims for votes. This annoys many Hindus. Canning, a Hindu village in West Bengal, was burnt down by Muslim fanatics in 2013. If Muslims were brutally persecuted in India, they would have left India for neighboring Muslim countries like Hindu minorities have been leaving Bangladesh and Pakistan since partition", she further added.

They never question the Islamic countries that deny freedom to their females and would not grant freedom either to change their religion, criticize their religion or renounce their religion. In January, liberal writer Raif Badawi was flogged 50 times after being sentenced to

10 years in prison with 1,000 lashes for blasphemy, prompting an international outcry. Badawi is still in prison, but diplomats say he is unlikely to be flogged again.

Tufail Ahmad rightly described the secularists and their true colors. They are not only color blind, they are in fact half Islamists and half Pakistanis meaning that they would not criticize the Muslims, would not talk about fatwas and sharia law, they would not dare say almost all terrorist acts were committed by Muslims and venture to say that Islam and democracy are incompatible. Why do these intolerant intellectuals not talk about the lack of freedom of expression, freedom of speech and freedom of religion in all those 56 Islamic countries? Can these intellectuals go to any of these Arab countries and criticize Islam the way they are demeaning Hinduism and Hindutva? They know that they may not see the day light if they criticize Quran and Mohammad.

It is paradoxical and mind boggling to read about these so-called intellectuals who surrendered their awards would not come to the rescue of A R Rahman the great internationally famed musician when a fatwa was issued for scoring music for a movie on Prophet Mohammad and forcing him to cancel the music show to be held in New Delhi on September 13. When the concert of Ghulam Ali was cancelled in Mumbai upon Shiva Sena's threat to disrupt it, though not a fatwa, Arvind Kejriwal, Akhilesh Yadav, Mamata Banerjee and others volunteered to organize the concert for Gulam Ali in their respective states but not for A R Rahman.

WOULD THEY HEED THE PRESIDENT'S ADVICE?

President Pranab Mukherjee said that prestigious awards "are a public recognition of talent, merit and hard work, by peers and leaders in the profession" and that "such awards should be cherished and valued by those who receive them."

The President observed, "Sensitive minds sometimes get disturbed by some incidents in society. But, expression of concern over such events should be balanced. Emotions should not overrun reason, and disagreement should be expressed through debate and discussion."

"We must, as proud Indians, have confidence in the idea of India and the values and principles enshrined in our Constitution. India has always been able to self-correct whenever such a need has arisen," he said.

INTOLERANCE ALWAYS EXISTED, NOTHING NEW

Bibek Debroy, the famous economist, argues that intolerance has always existed. Nothing new. He cited the examples of Dr. Jagdish Bhagwati who was essentially made to leave the Delhi School of Economics and go abroad as his life was made very uncomfortable. Similarly, Dr. B.R. Shenoy was the only one who opposed the second five-year plan and got completely ostracized thereafter. He could not get a job in India and ended up in Ceylon. In 2002, Debroy decided to organize a conference by inviting Seshadri Chari who was the editor of the Organiser magazine. Let us read the experience of organizing the conference and observe who is intolerant. *"On the day of the seminar, a paper front-paged a report 'Congress think tank invites editor of Organiser." I get a phone call from 10 Janpath, not Mrs Gandhi. "Madam has asked me to speak to you. Please withdraw this invitation to Seshadri Chari." I said I have issued the invitation and if Madam wants to talk to me, let her talk to me. Ten minutes later the phone rings again. "Will you please ask Seshadri Chari to give in writing what he is going to speak?" I said I am not going to do that. "No, Madam wants to see it." "*

Debroy concluded in an interview conducted by The Times of India on November 5, 2015: *If you tell me intolerance is increasing, it is purely anecdotal and is purely a subjective perception, there is no point in arguing with you because you will say it is increasing and I will say there is no evidence of it increasing. The only way I can measure something is that if I have got some quantitative indicator. If I look at any quantitative indicator, communal violence incidents, internet freedom, these are objective indicators, and I don't think it is increasing. In the intellectual circuit there has always been that intolerance. Let's not pretend otherwise.*

WHY THERE IS DEAD SILENCE TOWARD MUSLIM DENOUNCEMENT OF HINDUS?
WILL THE REAL INTELLECTUALS SPEAK UP?

"Hindus shouldn't make the mistake of considering Indian-Muslims any different from the Pakistan-Muslims. If India may dare to attack Pakistan, then 25 crore Indian Muslims will join Pakistan Forces and fight against India." **Asaduddin Owaisi, Member of Parliament, MIM, Hyderabad.**

Hindus do not have any rights to vote in Arab, Pakistan or any one of the 56 Islamic Nations. I challenge: has even a single Hindu the strength (guts) to impose restrictions on our (Muslims') voting-rights in India? **Maulana Badarrudin Ajmal, Lok Sabha Sansad, AIUDF, Assam.**

In Hyderabad, our Muslim population has crossed 50%, and now we are in majority. Therefore, I demand the Administration to impose restrictions on celebration of Hindu festivals such as Ram-navami, Hanuman Jayanti etc. In the Bhagya-Lakshmi temple, near Char-Minar, we have already shown our strength by stopping the ringing of the Bell/gong. We Muslims will ensure that this temple is also destroyed. **Akbaruddin Owaisi, Sansad, Majlis-e-Ittehadul-Musalmeen, (AIMIM), Hyderabad, India.**

"I regret the continuing of massacre of Hindus & Buddhists in Bangladesh, but Bangladesh is an Islamic Nation and not Secular. Now, the Muslims are in majority here. Under the circumstances, if Hindus & Buddhists want to live safely, they should either convert to Islam or go to India." **Begum Khalida Zia, President, Bangla National Party.**

"Hindu-Leaders may wear a Muslim cap any number of times, but we Muslim-Leaders will never put a Tilak. Let Hindus may give any amount of respect to our Namaz, but we Muslims will surely boycott "Vande Matram", because in Islam both Secularism & Patriotism are haraam(prohibited/unclean)." **Azam Khan, Leader, Samajwadi Party, U.P.**

"Muslims have ruled India for 1100 years. Lakhs of Hindus were beheaded. Crores of Hindus were converted into Islam. We divided India,

and snatched Pak & Bangladesh. Demolished 2000 temples and converted these into mosques. It is out of our fear that Hindus even today chant: "Hindu Muslim Bhai Bhai". This is the strength of Islam." **Maulana Jhakir Nayeek, Mumbai.**

"Let Hindus consider Cow as a Mother, even then we Muslims will surely cut the Cows, because sacrifice is Muslims' Religious right. Allah demands Sacrifice. Muslims don't fight an oral-war, we do everything directly with our might. We are not afraid of any ruler or Government because we the Muslim community have already grown sizably. If any mother's son intervenes, we will deal with him, but we will certainly cut Cows." **Nuroor Rahman Barkati, Shahi Imam, Tipu Sultan Masjid, Kolkata, India.**

"In the face of our strength (might), Hindus are not able to build even a single Ram-Temple in their own country. Do Hindus have the spunk to even stall the construction of a Mosque in Saudi-Arabia, Pak or any one of the 56 Islamic countries?" **Maulana Sayyad Ahmad Bukhari, Shahi Imam, Jama Masjid, Delhi.**

"Hindus don't have the spunk to stop infiltration (illegal) of our Bangladeshi Muslim brothers into Assam; we will continue to come (infiltrate)." **Maulana Badarrudin Ajmal, Lok Sabha Sansad, AIUDF, Assam.**

WILL THE REAL INTELLECTUALS STAND UP AND BE HEARD?

It is time we hear from these so-called intellectuals about what the Muslim leaders are saying and what their response would be. Muslims have been openly challenging, demeaning, denouncing and demanding the Hindus to fight with them. The Muslim leaders have openly declared that they would divide India into three counties – Mughalisthan, Dalitisthan and Dravidisthan. They have been succeeding in sending millions of Bangladesh Muslims to infiltrate into India and create havoc in the hearts of Hindus by burning the village house to drive all the Hindu away from their birth places, kidnapping and converting the Hindu girls to Islam, destroy the Hindu Temples and imposing sharia law in certain parts of West Bengal. These intellectuals cannot fathom the gravity of the Islamic terrorism because they refuse to acknowledge or possibly encourage these types of activities to root out Hindu way of life.

The intellectuals do not give a hoot either to the Muslim boy got killed or the rationalist author who was killed. It is a smokescreen for their contempt for Hindu civilization. Anybody who talks about Hindutva is an enemy of Muslims and Christians. They have not expressed this kind of outrage against Congress government in spite of the large number of killings in Punjab, during emergency, and all the terrorist attacks by Muslims groups on the Indian soil, because Congress Party, Communist Party and other similar parties are doing their dirty work, that is working relentlessly for the annihilation of Hindu civilization by destroying the Hindu Temples, allowing Bangladesh infiltration to change the demographics, throwing out Kashmiri Pandits from their homeland, changing the textbooks to insult the freedom fighters, glorifying the Muslim rulers who killed untold number of Hindus, denouncing the Hindu religious worship practices, passing laws pitting one group against the other, and so on. With new government, things are expected to change. The intolerant intellectuals realized that their dream of annihilating Hindu civilization may not be realized. They must come up with a strategy, rather a contrived plan, a manufactured scheme, and vicious tactics to dismantle the Hindu edifice.

EQUATE TOLERANT HINDUISM WITH INTOLERANT, VIOLENT CHRISTIANITY AND ISLAM?

PRESIDENT OBAMA WAS WRONG

In January 27, President Obama, before he left India, stated, *"Around the world, we've seen intolerance and violence and terror perpetrated by those who profess to be standing up for their faith, but, in fact, are betraying it. No society is immune from the darkest impulses of man. And too often religion has been used to tap into those darker impulses as opposed to the light of God."*

Obama said, *"India will succeed so long as it is not splintered along lines of religious faith, splintered along any lines and it is unified as one nation."*

President Barack Obama at the National Prayer Breakfast in Washington on Thursday (February 5, 2014) again repeated the religious tolerance in India by stating, *"In past years, religious faiths of all types have, on occasion, been targeted by other peoples of faith, simply due to their heritage and their beliefs— acts that would have shocked Gandhiji,"* meaning Mahatma Gandhi.

"Michelle and I returned from India -- an incredible, beautiful country, full of magnificent diversity - but a place where, in past years, religious faiths of all types have, on occasion, been targeted by other peoples of faith, simply due to their heritage and their beliefs - acts of intolerance that would have shocked Gandhiji, the person who helped to liberate that nation." He also said, *"We see faith driving us to do right. But we also see faith being twisted and distorted, used as a wedge — or worse, sometimes used as a weapon."*

COMPARING HINDUISM TO ISLAM AND CHRISTIANITY IS OUTRAGEOUS

It is unfortunate, outrageous, deceptive, prejudiced, unwarranted and totally misleading to imply that Hinduism is involved in acts of intolerance. The President has done a disservice to associate Hinduism with Christianity and Islam. Both Abrahamic religions are exclusive, meaning that if you do not believe in my way of worship and my God, you are condemned to hell. Hinduism is tolerant, accommodative, open minded, pluralistic, and embraces the philosophy of "live, let live." It does not believe in conversions, and does not exploit the poor by offering bribes and inducements. Hindus believe in freedom, discussion, dialogue, debates, and questioning the scriptures. They have not annihilated any civilization, destroyed any places of religion, not massacred other religious people, not engaged in deceptive conversions, and not terrorized the humanity. Hindus only see divinity in all living and nonliving entities and never abhor the individual for their religious beliefs. They have not conquered or subdued any nation for establishing their religion. They never play the role of victim in order to incite the media and turn the public opinion against other religions. Hinduism is the most philosophical, spiritual, and scientific religion. Any person in authority should go beyond one's own religion and take the high road instead of plunging into this quagmire of religious controversy. Small mindedness is not the character of an educated, and intelligent person. Religion should not pull one down into a whirlpool from which one cannot escape without being bruised. Equating such a religion with Christianity and Islam is beyond reason, objectivity, rational and scientific. Ignorance or the ploy to cloak behind the religious faith is not the answer for today's mindless terror, brutality, deception and destruction. This is the discussion that should have taken place in classrooms, but not in the halls of US Congress and Whitehouse. Unfortunately, it is the President of the United States who ruffled the feathers of religion and instigating Muslims and Christians to demean Hindus and humiliate them by playing their traditional victim role.

INDIA REACTS

Indian government officials responded with restraint and decency. India has been failing consistently to give appropriate and fitting response to the clandestine statements made over the years. Finance Minister Arun Jaitley said, "India has a huge cultural history of tolerance. Any aberration doesn't alter the history ... its part of

India's tolerance that even he found it comfortable and India found it comfortable to absorb him in the society." He appropriately said the best example of Indian tolerance was sitting next to President Obama referring to His Holiness the Dalai Lama, who exiled to India in 1959 and set up a government of Tibet in exile in Dharamshala.

Similarly, Rajnath Singh, the Home Minister said, "as far as religious tolerance is concerned, it is embedded in our Indian tradition. India is the only country in the world where all the communities including various divisions of Muslims and all sects of Christians are present ... In India, Parsis and Jewish are also there."

HIS HOLINESS DALAI LAMA ON INDIA

President Obama made these remarks in front of His Holiness Dalai Lama who was given shelter in India. They are most inappropriate, disturbing, surreal and stealthy considering what Dalai Lama said about India. "India is a model. Different religious traditions live peacefully and harmoniously. Please keep this tradition," Dalai Lama said at the valedictory of the year-long celebration of the 1,960-year-old Malankara Orthodox Syrian church in Kochi in 2012. "India has great heritage. There is harmony among different religious traditions. India is a land where people of different religious faiths can live peacefully and harmoniously here. India's tradition is very relevant in today's world."

FORMER PRESIDENT OF INDIA, ABDUL KALAM

It is worth remembering the words of the former President of India about the rich heritage if India.

"In 3000 years of our history, people from all over the world have come and invaded us, captured our lands conquered our minds. From Alexander onwards the Greeks, the Portuguese, the British, the Mughals, the French, the Dutch, all of them came and looted us, took over what was ours. Yet we have not done this to any other nation. We have not conquered anyone. We have not grabbed their land, their culture, their history and tried to enforce our way of life on them. Why? Because we respect the freedom of others."
--President Dr. Abdul Kalam

US PRESS REACTS TO PRESIDENT OBAMA

Reacting to President Obamas remarks, Charles Krauthammer appearing on Hugh Hewitt's Radio program said that he is insulting India. *"What the hell is he doing bringing India into this? I mean, it's the first time I've heard India drawn into this discussion. Here he is essentially insulting, and it's because it's a Hindu country. It's not Muslim. I mean, he'll say in the name of Christ. He won't say in the name of Muhammad and in the name of Allah. He won't use those words. And then he goes after India, which is probably our strongest, most stable, most remarkable, democratically on the planet, considering all the languages and religions that it harbors. It has the second-largest Muslim population on Earth. And yet he goes after it as a way of saying hey, everybody here is at fault. They are not at fault."*

President Obama is failing in his responsibility to clearly look at the horrific history of the Abrahamic religions and to equate them with Hinduism, the most tolerant religion the humanity has ever seen or experienced. He is distorting history, misguiding his shepherds, pleasing the Muslims, and trying to be in the good books of people who were successful in banning the US Visa to Narendra Modi in 2005. Both Abrahamic religions have been professing from their inception that anybody who would not embrace their faith would be condemned to hell, death and torture. They can be destroyed, sacrificed and killed. Both Quran and Bible have hundreds of verses that allow the nonbelievers to be slaughtered and their places of would be destroyed. In return what do Hindus do? As Swami Vivekananda said, *"The difference is this. They had not the fanfaronade of the reformers of today; they had no curses on their lips as modern reformers have; their lips pronounced only blessings. They never condemned."*

LOOK HOW INDIA BLESSED THE ABRAHAMIC RELIGIONS

The Presidents of India: The country that has elected four Muslims and one Sikh as Presidents should not be the target for President Obama's insensitive remarks about acts of intolerance. India had five Presidents who belong to other religions. Dr. Zakir Hussain, Mohammad Hidayatullah, Fakhruddin Ali Ahmed, Dr. A. P. J. Abdul Kalam were Muslim and Giani Zail Singh was a Sikh.

Chief Ministers in Five States: Although Christians are only about 3 percent of the population, Hindu dominant voters elected five Chief Minister in India. Hindus have elected them in Nagaland, Mizoram, Meghalaya, Kerala and Andhra Pradesh.

CHRISTIANS AND MUSLIMS OCCUPIED IMPORTANT POSITIONS

Chairperson of the country's ruling political alliance UPA is Sonia Gandhi and her son Rahul Gandhi were practicing Catholic Christians.
Country's Defense Minister - A.K. Antony, (Christian)
The Foreign Secretary - Ranjan Mathai, (Christian)
Head of the Air Wing of military - Anil Kumar Browne, (Christian)
Deputy Chairman, Rajya Sabha - P.J. Kurien –, (Christian)
Newly appointed Congress Spokesperson - P.C. Chacko, (Christian)
The country's Foreign Minister - Mr Salman Khurshid, (Muslim)
Minister of State for External Affairs - Mr E. Ahmed, (Muslim)
Chief Justice of India - Mr Altmas Kabir, (Muslim)
The nation's Vice President and Chairman of Rajya Sabha - Mr Hamid Ansari, (Muslim)
Chief Election Commissioner - Mr S.Y. Qureshi, (Muslim)
Attorney General of India - Mr Goolam Essaji Vahanvati, (Muslim)
Minister for Minorities Affairs - K. Rahman Khan, (Muslim)
The Congress Spokesperson - Rashid Alvi (Muslim).

PRESIDENT OBAMA VS HIS ADMINISTRATION

President is failing to name the names. He is abrogating his responsibility to call a spade a spade. He is refusing to identify Islam as the source of violence, extremism, torture, beheading and radicalism. He is hiding behind the words such as radical terrorists, and Islamic terrorists. You cannot defeat the enemy if you cannot identify the source. **Thomas Friedman** says that, "When you don't call things by their real name, you always get in trouble. And this administration, so fearful of being accused of Islamophobia, is refusing to make any link to radical Islam from the recent explosions of violence against civilians." The administration officials acknowledge that they have list of individuals who cited Islam as the source of their violence. "But it is not good for us or the Muslim world to pretend that this spreading jihadist violence isn't coming out of their faith community." And **Josh Earnest** continues to say that "purposeless violent extremists rummage through the scriptures of great faiths, looking for some verses to cite to support their mayhem and often happen to settle on the holy texts of Islam." But Obama refuses to acknowledge that almost all terrorists are Muslims and cite Quran as the source of their terrorist acts.

RELIGIOUS TOLERANCE IN INDIA

For centuries Hindu have welcomed almost all religions with open hands, respected them and allowed them to practice their religion. Jewish people openly declared that India is the only country that has not discriminated. Likewise, Parsees, the descendants of Zoroastrians, were thrown out from their homeland, Persia, only to be welcomed by India. Jains, Sikhs, Buddhists, and many others religions lived peacefully. Hindus have no history of killing, raping, rampaging, terrorizing, decimating and destroying other religions and annihilating the civilizations. It is worth remembering the former President's words quoted earlier.

BUDDHISTS: In fact, on December 1, 2011 HH Dalai Lama proudly announced that "I consider myself as a son of India" and carried the message of ahimsa across the globe and says that the country's spiritual leaders should promote love and harmony in India and outside. Further he observed "that India has so many languages and dialects, yet remains strongly united because there is the freedom of speech and rule of law."

JEWS: Jewish people lived in peace in India without any discrimination for more than 2000 years. Gary Weiss observed that in India the ethnic diversity "is a historical fact. Much as we in the West may resent it, India has a lot to teach us when it comes to *religious tolerance*. India may be the only country in the world that has been free of anti-Semitic prejudice throughout its history.

That's really a bit astonishing, if not ridiculous, when you think about it. Compare that with any Western nation, be it France or Russia or even the U.S., where discrimination against Jews in housing was a fact of life as recently as the 1950s. But in "backward" India, from the beginning, the Jewish communities have not only been free of discrimination but have dominated the commercial life of every place where they have settled–something that has fed traditional European anti-Semitism.

Why has India remained free of this scourge? Various reasons have been advanced for that–such as, the **Hindu religion does not seek to convert** those from other faiths. What we do know is that anti-Semitism seems alien to the Indian character."

MUSLIMS: Shah Rukh Khan, the Muslim movie actor said, "that we in India are extremely safe and happy. We have an amazing democratic, free and secular way of life. In the environs that we live here in my country India, we have no safety issues regarding life or material. As a matter of fact it is irksome for me to clarify this non-existent issue."

PARSEES: Chief Justice of India, **S H Kapadia,** observed, "I am proud to be an Indian. India is the only country where a member of the minority Parsi community with a population of 167,000, like myself, can aspire to attain the post of the Chief Justice of India. These things do not happen in our neighboring countries.

Maria Wirth brings up the question, "Are Indians good natured?" They generally are, and probably more than other people. There are few countries where the attitude of "live and let live" is as pronounced as in India. "All are one family" is the traditional attitude.

It is worth remembering the words of A L Basham about Indian humility, gentleness and kindness: 'To us the most striking thing feature of ancient Indian civilization is its humanity….Our second general impression of ancient India is that her people enjoyed life, passionately delighting both in the things of the senses and the things of the spirit….India was a cheerful land, whose people, each finding a niche in a complex and slowly evolving social system , reached a higher level of kindliness and gentleness in their mutual relationships than any other nation of antiquity. For this, as well as for her great achievements in religion, literature, art and mathematics, one European student at least would record his admiration of India's ancient culture'.

CHRISTIANITY

That is absolutely correct if Christians and Muslims have lived with few principles of respecting other religion, if they have not claimed as the exclusive religions where nonbelievers in their religion are dammed to hell, where torture, terror, bombings, killings, explosions, rape, jihad, deceptions, hatred toward 'idol' worshippers, allurement are used to create fear and convert the Hindus into their intolerant, dishonest and brutal religions. Both religions should stop cheating, deceiving, forcing and coercing Hindus to get converted to their respective religions.

Comparing Hinduism with other faiths, **Josh Shrei** stated that "**Hinduism**" is Open Source; and most other faiths are Closed Source ... "Open source is an approach to the design, development, and distribution of software, offering practical accessibility to a software's source code.... India has been the place where the doors have been thrown wide open and the coders have been given free rein to craft, invent, reinvent, refine, imagine, and re-imagine to the point that literally every variety of the spiritual and cognitive experience has been explored, celebrated, and documented." He goes on to say, "The results of India's God Project -- as I like to refer to Hinduism -- have been absolutely **staggering.** The body of knowledge -- scientific, faith-based, and experience-based -- that has been accrued on the nature of mind, consciousness, and human behavior, and the number of practical methods that have been specifically identified to work with one's own mind are without compare."

In comparison, aces to God in Christianity is considered a trade mark that means it is considered most closed system. Josh Shrei observed that, "*The ability to reinterpret the bible, or the teachings of Christ, or the Old Testament, or to challenge the basic fundamental authority of the church has been nonexistent for most of the church's history. **Those who dared to do so were quite often killed.**"*

Dithering any longer identify the culprit for all the atrocities will be result in more bombings, massacres, beheadings, decimation and untold brutality.

> *"Perhaps in return for conquest,*
> *arrogance and spoliation, India will teach us*
> *the tolerance and gentleness of the mature mind,*
> *the quiet content of the unacquisitive soul,*
> *the calm of the understanding spirit,*
> *and a unifying, a pacifying love for all*
> *living things."Will Durant*

Avigdor Liberman, Foreign Minister of Israel said on February 15, 2015 that "The chain of terrorism incidents in Copenhagen at the synagogue and at the freedom of expression conference, proves what we have said throughout the years - Israel and Jews have been made to absorb terror attacks first and foremost because we are the front line in the war of terrorism being waged against the West and the entire free world."

"The international community should not settle for declarations and rallies against this, but shake up the rules of "political correctness", and **wage total war against Islamic terrorism and its roots,**" Liberman said.

Thomas Jefferson, *"Millions of innocent men, women, and children, since the introduction of Christianity, have been burnt, tortured, fined, and imprisoned; yet we have not advanced one inch toward uniformity. What has been the effect of coercion? To make one-half the world fools and the other half hypocrites."*

GOA INQUISITION

According to Dr. T. R. De Souza at least from 1540 onwards that all the Hindu idols disappeared because all the temples were destroyed, their sites and building materials were used erect new Christian Churches and chapels. Church council banished the Hindu priests from the Portuguese territories; practices of Hindu rites including marriage rites, were banned; Hindu orphan children were to raise as Christians; the Hindus were denied many types of employment; they were forced to assemble in Churches to listen to preaching or to the refutation of their religion.

THE BIG HOUSE WITH 200 CELLS

Inquisitions were conducted in what was known as the Big House where the screams of agony of men, women, and children could be heard in the streets, in the stillness of the night, as they were brutally interrogated, flogged, and slowly dismembered in front of their relatives. Eyelids were sliced off and extremities were amputated so carefully that a person could remain conscious, even though the only thing that remained was his torso and a head.

Three kinds of torture were practiced against the Hindus

- The torture by rope consisted of the arms being tied backwards and then raised by a pulley, leaving the victim hanging for some time, and then let the victim drop down to half a foot above the floor, then rose again. These continued up and down movements dislocated the joints and made the prisoner emit horrible cries of pain.

- The torture by water made the victim to lie across an iron bar, and was forced to imbibe water without stopping. The iron bar broke the vertebrae and caused horrible pains, whereas the water treatment provoked vomits and asphyxia.

- The torture by fire was definitely the worst: the victim was hung above a fire, which burnt the soles of the feet, and the jailers rubbed bacon and other combustible materials on the burning feet. The feet were burnt until the victim confessed, "I am Christian."

SWAMI LAKSHMANANANDA WAS KILLED

In 2008, Swami Lakshmanananda was killed at his Kanya Ashram (a residential girl's school) in Tumudibandh, about 100 km from Phulbani, the district headquarters of Kandhamal district along with four others because Swamiji was considered as the main reason for the failure of Christian organizations to make inroads in converting the locals.

CHRISTIANS BAN HINDU FESTIVALS AND RESORT TO TERRORISM

Genevieve Bhat, who is a practicing Christian from Kerala, worried about the deception of Christian missionaries and how they are supporting terrorists to root out Hindus. Once all the traditional deceptive practices have failed, the Christians resort to open intimidation and violence. To convert tribal area people, the terrorists are substantially funded and controlled by Christian churches, sometimes even openly. Bhat explains the tactics the Christians play to drive out Hindus from Tripura. She says, *"the Tripura Tigers and other groups have officially put a ban on the celebration of all religious festivals except the Christian ones, and on the traditional decorations of Hindu women - bangles and bindis. The houses of those who refuse to convert are torched, and people are routinely kidnapped, raped, maimed and killed until the rest flee away, leaving the "Indian Promised Land" in the hands of the Christian converts. And after all, these methods are not much different than those described in The Bible of the historical conquest of the "Promised Land" of Israel."*

NEW BIBLE IS WRITTEN FOR INDIA

A team of 30 biblical scholars spent 15 years to write *The New Community Bible* for Indians only to **allure the poor, gullible Hindus by comparing the Bible with many of Hindus scriptures** such as Bhagavad Gita, Upanishads, Mahabharata, and the Gandhi's statement about turning the other cheek.

You see many pictures that resemble the pictures of Hindus Deities to fool the villagers. Mary is shown with barefoot wearing a simple sari with head covered, and applying Bindi on her forehead alongside Joseph in a turban and loincloth carrying a basket on his head to resemble the images of Vasudeva & Devaki carrying Lord Krishna across the Yamuna River. There is also a full-page portrait of Mother Teresa, the nun who served the destitute on the streets of Kolkata, above the words *"pure and blameless religion lies in coming to help orphans and widows".*

DIGESTION OF HINDU CUSTOMS

On Christmas Day, many churches conduct Masses in Indian style, using Aarti, breaking coconuts, offering camphor, lighting incense sticks, singing kirtans and even offer Prasadam to Jesus. So much for Idol worship! It is done only to trap the Hindus by making the m comfortable with worship services. Mother Karen observed, "*The Indian style Mass is being celebrated in many Christian ashrams in India.*" There are hundreds of Christian ashrams in India where Christianity is presented to show that it is an Eastern faith. B R Haran in his article stated in article on "*Christian missionaries target every single component of Hindu society*" that, "The Church uses the process of enculturation with an aim to adopt the well-established Hindu cultural practices to confuse, corrupt and change the minds of the gullible masses."

Christ is dressed to look like an Indian sadhu. Jesus was shown in Radham (chariot) giving message similar to Lord Krishna's images. They celebrate Hindu festivals like Pongal and Diwali. They will conduct shodashopachara Puja (16 steps of doing any regular Hindu puja) to Jesus. Churches are being built in a Hindu Temple style with similar architecture, intricate artisan work and several steeples. They will have OM and Cross on the Temples. They also have developed Sahasranamavali (Thousand names) for Jesus in Sanskrit with meaning for each Nama. Since many Hindus are used to listening to Ashtottara Nama and Sahasranamavali for many Hindu Gods and Goddesses, the Christians have gone to the extent of composing them to lure and attract Hindus.

POPE CALLED FOR ESTABLISHING CROSS-OVER INDIA

On November 7, 1999, the Pope John Paul II addressing the missionaries gave a call to convert Asia to Christianity as follows: –

"Just as the first millennium saw the cross firmly planted in the soil of Europe, and the second in that of America and Africa, so may the Third Christian Millennium witness a great harvest of faith on this vast and vital continent." **Pope Benedict XVI** also reiterated conversion agenda with the words, "The church is by its very nature missionary; its first task is evangelization."

DECEPTION IS THE GAME THEY PLAY

What method do the Christians use to propagate and convert innocent and gullible Hindus into Christianity? Father Joseph Menengis, priest of St James Church in Mariyannapalya, Bangalore, confessed before the Justice B K Somashekara Commission of Inquiry on Wednesday (March 11, 2009) "The duty of every Christian is to convert non-Christians to Christianity **by any means.**" When he says "by any means" what does it mean? They can use any means such as deception, deceit, force, manipulation, allurement, tricks, treachery, exploitation, violence, killings, educational indoctrination, defamation od other religions, demeaning our gods, denouncing our scriptures, sexual exploitation and so on to convert Hindus.

CRITICS OF CHRISTIANITY WERE TORTURED AND/OR KILLED

History of Christianity is loaded with cruelty, torture, imprisonment, excommunication, and death. **Anybody who refuses to obey the orders of church officials are put to untold torture and death.**

Origen was an ardent believer in reincarnation. He was cast into prison, tortured, and condemned to the stake. The death of the emperor prevented his execution, but He died in prison

Leo Tolstoy was excommunicated for criticizing the Church practices and Christianity.

Pelagius was excommunicated from the Church for believing in the theory of Karma and deny only God's grace as the cause for salvation

Galileo published a book entitled "Dialogue" on the two chief Systems of the world, which said that the Earth was not flat and not the center of the universe. He was imprisoned for life for failing to withdraw his views.

Hypatia was a female mathematician, philosopher and astronomer in 4th century AD Roman Egypt. Due to religious objections against heliocentrism, the Christians have now forbidden Hypatia from teaching at the school. Cyril, the leader of the Christians, views Hypatia as having too much influence over her pupils, he convinces a mob of Christians that Hypatia is a witch and they vow to kill her.

Before killing her, the mob strip Hypatia naked and beat her until Davus, Hypatia's slave, tells the mob to stone her. When everyone was busy collecting the stones, Davus secretly suffocates Hypatia to death.

WHAT THE BIBLE SAYS

What do scriptures say about Tolerance and respecting other faiths?

President Obama should have known what is written in the major religious scriptures to realize that he should not compare other religions with Hinduism and treat all religions as same and treat them as peace loving. All religions are not same. Both major Abrahamic religions are brutal, barbaric, ruthless, deceptive, disrespecting, insulting, offensive, threatening, undemocratic, and intolerant and freedom less. Let us give few verses from Bible. Look what Bible says:

Deuteronomy 12:3 **Break down their altars**, smash their sacred stones and burn their Asherah poles in the fire; cut down the idols of their gods and wipe out their names from those places.

Deuteronomy 7:25 The images of their gods **you are to burn in the fire**. Do not covet the silver and gold on them, and do not take it for yourselves, or you will be ensnared by it, for it is detestable to the LORD your God.

Jeremiah 25:6 Do not follow other gods to serve and worship them; **do not provoke me to anger** with what your hands have made. Then I will not harm you."

Exodus 23:24 Do not bow down before their gods or worship them or follow their practices. You must **demolish them and break their sacred stones to pieces.**

God who is supposed to be compassionate, loving and caring acting and thinking like a small kid, who wants to possess his toys and do not want to share with others, is not Godly. Anybody, who is envious, bitter and resentful, cannot be called God. Thinking that the worship belongs to him only but nobody else is antichrist.

GANDHI ON CONVERSION.

There is no question that Gandhiji would have been shocked or fasted to death if he had seen the poison that is being fed to the innocent people. The fraudulent missionary activities would have made him sick. The kind of enculturation taking place to allure the innocent Hindus is nothing but a shameful, shocking and scandalous deceptive act. If Mahatma Gandhi was alive, he would have lead the second freedom movement to make India free of this scourge of conversion and terrorism. If he was alive, he would have walked the length and breadth of India to rid this menace. **Gandhi** himself said:

> *If I had the power and could legislate, I should stop all proselytizing. In Hindu households the advent of a missionary has meant the disruption of the family coming in the wake of change of dress, manners, language, food and drink. (November 5, 1935).*

> *"It is impossible for me to reconcile myself to the idea of conversion after the style that goes on in India and elsewhere today. It is an error which is perhaps the greatest impediment to the world's progress toward peace. Why should a Christian want to convert a Hindu to Christianity? Why should he not be satisfied if the Hindu is a good or godly man?" (Harijan: January 30, 1937).*

VIDEOS SHOWING HOW CHRISTIANS ARE CONVERTING HINDUS WITH DECEPTION

Hindus have never denied the freedom of speech, freedom of expression, and freedom to practice one's own faith. A lady from Scandinavia produces the following videos. She came to India to visit enjoy the diversity, richness, greatness, lushness, and glory of the ancient Sanatana Dharma culture. Soon she was aghast at the intensity of conversions through allurement. She was appalled at the way the Christian missionaries were demeaning the Hindu way of life, with the aim to destroy the Hindu culture. She was horrified at the dissension the new converts have caused in their families, kith and kin. She was shocked to see, on the commands of the pastors, the new converts stepping on the idols of Hindu Gods, breaking them and tearing up the pictures of the Hindu Gods. She was stunned to hear the stories of the Hindu who got converted as to how they were deceived by the missionaries and the kind tricks played on them.

Please watch the videos in Youtube.com. These are the stories that should have received the uproar in the Parliament.

Hindus must remember that the Christians have an open mission to convert the whole of India. In fact, they are doing openly under our noses. They are very aggressively pursuing the mission. If we are not careful, these termites will crumble the Hindu edifice in front our own eyes. History of the last two millennia of Christian dominance in Europe, Africa and America; and the Pope Paul's command to put a Cross on Indian soil should not be taken lightly. It is a serious matter and due attention must be paid without wasting even one minutes of time. Let us remember the words of **Thomas Jefferson who said that the Christian God and their followers are cruel, revengeful and capricious. History cannot be hidden. Equating Hinduism with Christianity and Islam is not genuine, sincere, honest, and truthful. Can Hindus sleep in peace knowing their cunning, deceptive nature?**

It is time to read the verses from the Bible and ask the Christians to explain.

President Obama has willingly dirtied his hands by meddling in the religious matters of India. He has deliberately associated Hinduism with deception, terror and torture by equating with Christianity and Islam. Would he dare to make these remarks in Southie Arabia?

ISLAM

Will Durant said, "The Islamic conquest of India is probably the bloodiest story in history. It is a discouraging tale, for its evident moral is that civilization is a precious good, whose delicate complex of order and freedom, culture and peace, can at any moment be overthrown by barbarians invading from without or multiplying within."

President Obama failed to identify the root of Terrorism

Not to identify the root of terrorism, beheadings, torture, deception, luring, allurement, tricking, tracking, targeting, etc., is an indication of an empty talk, sign of escapism, failing to call spade a spade, dismissing the real conflict between Islam and the humanity, and hiding behind the ideologies of the two major Abrahamic religions.

On February 18, 2015 President Obama delivered a major speech on combating violent extremism —while refusing to use the words "Muslim terrorists." "No religion is responsible for terrorism — people are responsible for violence and terrorism." President Obama continued by stating that "**We are not at war with Islam. We are at war with people who have perverted Islam.**"

Two questions can be raised based on his statement.

⚔ If religion is not responsible and only people are responsible, then why did he say that "India will succeed so long as **it is not splintered along lines of religious faith**, splintered along any lines and it is unified as one nation?" If he believes that **religion is not responsible for terrorism**, then **why did he not say that India will succeed as long as it is not splintered along lines of people who are responsible for violence and terror?**"

⚔ The second question is why would anybody resort to terrorism and violence without cause? They must have read or somewhere, or they must have been taught somewhere. Since Muslims go to mosques and listen to the Mullahs about what is written in their HOLY QURAN, it is only logical to assume that whatever is written in Quran is the source of their belief that translated into action – violence, terror, torture, beheading and killing.

Roger Cohen in The Opinion Pages of The New York Times, detailing the atrocities of Islam in the West, observed, "*The Islamists' war is against freedom of expression, freedom of conscience, freedom of the press, freedom of blasphemy, sexual freedom — in short, core characteristics of democracies seen by the would-be rebuilders of the Caliphate as signs of Western debasement.*" (Feb 16, 2015).

Unfortunately, President Obama is failing to ranslate his own statement to identify the religions that have crucified and terrorized the humanity. He said, "We see faith driving us to do right. But we also see faith being twisted and distorted, used as a wedge — or worse, sometimes used as a weapon." It is time to name the names and call the spade a spade. Both Abrahamic religions have drenched humanity with blood with their conversion tactics and intolerance toward other religions.

HINDU GENOCIDE

The genocide suffered by the Hindus of India at the hands of Arab, Turkish, Mughal and Afghan rulers for a period of 800 years is not yet discussed, addressed and assessed. For fear of consequences, the whole Muslim history in India is not only formally unrecognized by the World, but Indian government for nearly seven decades has distorted the history of Islamic atrocities and put the matter under the rug so to speak.

Dr. Keonraad Elst also writes in his book "**Negationism in India**": "The Muslim conquests, down to the 16th century, were for the Hindus a pure struggle of life and death. Entire cities were burnt down and the populations massacred, with hundreds of thousands killed in every campaign, and similar numbers deported as slaves. Every new invader made (often literally) his hills of Hindus skulls. Thus, the conquest of Afghanistan in the year 1000 was followed by the annihilation of the Hindu population; the region is still called the Hindu Kush, i.e. Hindu slaughter."

Francois Gautier in his book 'Rewriting Indian History' (1996) wrote: "The massacres perpetuated by Muslims in India are unparalleled in history, bigger than the Holocaust of the Jews by the Nazis; or the massacre of the Armenians by the Turks; more extensive even than the slaughter of the South American native populations by the invading Spanish and Portuguese."

"Breaking India" is a groundbreaking work written by Rajiv Malhotra who spent seven years to gather information about the external forces that are planning to break up India. Muslims have vowed to break up India through terror and infiltration into three countries – Mughalisthan, Dalitisthan and Dravidisthan. They are working relentlessly to complete what they call "unfinished business" of converting India into Islamic States. Muslims are inflicting untold misery, terror, and killings on Indian soil to go to paradise as promised in the Quran to enjoy waiting sensate objects. He also mentions that Christians and Maoists e equally waging a war to break up India.

It is worth remembering the agony of **Robert D. Blackwill,** the former US Ambassador to India from 2001 to 2003. Before he came to India, he kept a count of deaths that Muslims were causing in Kashmir. *"India's death toll from terrorism mounted as the snow fell and melted in Cambridge ... Innocent human beings murdered as a systemic instrument of twisted political purpose. Terror against India that rose and fell with the seasons, year after year after year... All snuffed out by the killing hand of terror.* ***On September 11 in America. Nearly every day in India****....No respectable religion could excuse these merciless acts. No moral framework could sanction these abominations. No political cause could justify these murders of innocents. And yet, they go on."*

Anybody who is familiar with 1400 years of Islamic expansion, anybody who is willing to read about Islamic terrorism with open, objective, and academic mind or anybody willing to visit India and see the destruction of as many as 2000 Hindu Temples would realize the mission of Islam is to subjugate the entire human race and conquer the world. The Muslims deny their roots and their heritage because the fanatic Muslims consider India as "unfinished business" and Jihadists are busy terrorizing the populace in the name of Islam.

Quran and many Islamic leaders openly declared war on infidels. As **Ayatollah Khomeini** stated: "Those who know nothing of Islam pretend that Islam counsels against war. Those [who say this] are witless. Islam says: Kill all the unbelievers just as they would kill you all!   . . . **Islam says: Kill in the service of Allah those who may want to kill you!** . . . Islam says: Whatever good there is exists thanks to the sword and in the shadow of the sword! People cannot be made obedient except with the sword! . . . There are hundreds of other psalms [from the Koran] and Hadiths [sayings and acts of

Muhammad] urging **Muslims to value war and to fight**. Does all that mean that Islam is a religion that prevents men from waging war? I spit upon those foolish souls who make such a claim."

It means Islam urges to kill all nonbelievers such as Christians, Jews, Hindus, Buddhists, Jains, Parsees, Shinto and others. For centuries, the Hindus were converted through coercion with the idea of spreading Islam and it continues to date. Few examples of Muslim atrocities and slaughters committed on Hindus.

⚔ As many as 80 million Hindus in India were murdered for refusing to be converted to Islam.

⚔ In 1947, Pakistan has 24% Hindus, today there are less than 1 percent Hindus.

⚔ In Bangladesh, the Hindu population is dwindled from nearly 30 percent to less than 7 percent.

⚔ India, Lo and behold, the Muslim population is multiplying day by day to make India a Muslim nation. The percentage of Muslims in India has risen from about 8% in 1951 to 13.6% in 2001 and 14.6 % in 2010.

⚔ Hindu Kush Mountains, where Hindus were slaughtered for refusing to get converted to Islam. Blood used to flow all the way from the mountain top to the streets below.

⚔ In Afghanistan, the two largest standing Buddha's were blown up Taliban by a lorry load of dynamites.

EIGHT CENTURIES OF ATROCITIES ON HINDUS BY MUSLIM RULERS

Dr. Younis Shaik observed atrocities of Muslims by saying that "eighty million were slaughtered and millions of women were raped….. it was standard practice for Islamic warlords like Ghori and Ghazni to unleash the mass rape and enslavement of hundreds of thousands of women after the slaughter of all males ….. A large percentage of Muslims in South Asia today are the progeny of forcible conversions and systematic rape campaigns by marauding Muslim invaders."

HINDU TEMPLES – WHAT HAPPENED TO THEM?

This is a two-volume book written by **Sita Ram Goel, Arun Shourie, Harsh Narain, Jay Dubashi and Ram Swarup**. The first volume was published in spring 1990. The first volume includes a list of 2000 mosques that were built on Hindu temples. It includes the names of the original Hindu Temples and the Mosque names – district-by-district and state-by-state. This list is based primarily on the books of Muslim historians of the period or the inscriptions of the mosques and also personal investigation. Muslims have always targeted the most sacred religious places and Temples by destroying them in order to humiliate, annihilate and mutilate Hindus.

SRI RAMA TEMPLE AT AYODHYA

On the site of the birth of Lord Rama, a magnificent temple devoted to Him was erected. However, Babur, a fifteenth century Mogul invader, brutalized India and also destroyed this Rama Temple. He raised a structure in its place, which he called Babri Masjid. The temple complex comprised of the Janmasthan of Sri Rama at Kot Ram Chander, the private apartments (mahal sarai) of King Dashrath and Sri Rama, and a temple and a kitchen popularly known as Sita Ki Rasoi, where tradition held that Sita (wife of Sri Rama) lived. All three were demolished and a mosque constructed thereupon in 1528 A.D. For centuries Hindus tried to recover this auspicious site. In 2010, a somewhat confusing verdict was issued by Allahabad High court accepting Ayodhya as a birth of Rama.

KRISHNA JANMASTHALA IN MATHURA

The Keshava Rai Temple at Mathura was built by Bir Singh Deo Bundela during Jahangir's time at a cost of thirty-three lakhs of rupees. The Dehra of Keshava Rai was one of the most magnificent temples ever built in India and enjoyed veneration of the Hindus throughout the land. Alberuni observed that this temple was approximately 20 times larger than the largest mosque he ever saw in his life.

⚔ The next big temple was constructed here during the time of the Gupta Emperor Chandragupta Vikramaditya around 400 AD. This temple was so grand that it was said that neither painting nor description could describe it. Mahmud of Ghazni destroyed the temple in 1017 AD.

⚐ Another temple was built here in 1150. It was destroyed in the 16th century during the reign of Sikander Lodi.

⚐ The Dehra of Keshava Rai was demolished in the month of Ramzan (13 January – 11 February 1670) by Aurangzeb's order. "In a short time, by the great exertion of the officers, the destruction of this strong foundation of infidelity was accomplished and on its site a lofty mosque was built at the expenditure of a large sum".

Thus, the barbarian Islamic rulers Mohamud Ghazni, Sikander Lodi and Aurangzeb destroyed the Krishna Janmasthala. In fact, Aurangzeb not only destroyed the Mandir in 1669-1670 but he built Idgah Qila (mosque) over it. Even today, visitors can still see the mosque on top of the Krishna Janmasthala to prove that the Hindus can be crushed, and made gutless and spineless.

VISHWANATH TEMPLE IN BENARES WAS THE TARGET OF ISLAMIC TERROR:

Kashi Vishwanath Temple, Varanasi Kashi Vishwanath temple is dedicated to Lord Shiva. It is popularly known as the 'Golden Temple' due to the gold plating done on its 15.5-meter high spire. One tonnes of gold donated by Maharaja Ranjit Singh has been used in the gold plating of the spire. The temple was destroyed by various invaders and was rebuilt in 1776 by Rani Ahilyabai of Indore. Due to security reasons, metal detectors are placed throughout the temple. The Mughal Emperor Aurangzeb who built the Gaynvapi Mosque in its place destroyed the Vishwanath temple. Even today the western wall of the mosque show the remnants of a temple, which had very intricate and fine artwork on it.

The original Shiva temple of Kashi finds mention in the scriptures. The current temple is believed to have been built in the eleventh century, which was destroyed by Muhammad Ghori in the twelfth century. The temple was rebuilt by devotees but then demolished by the slave king QutubuddinAibak. After Aibak's death, the temple was rebuilt with the permission of his successor, the slave king Altutmish, better known as the father of the first woman ruler of Delhi, Razia Sultana.

The temple of Kashi Vishwanath was again destroyed by Feroze Shah Tughlaq in the fourteenth century. The temple was rebuilt by Raja Todarmal, the revenue minister in the court of the Mughal king Akbar. Aurangzeb, Akbar's great grandson demolished the temple, built a mosque known as the Gyanvapi mosque in its place, and even renamed the city Mohammedabad from Kashi. In the eighteenth century, the queen Ahilyabai Holkar rebuilt the temple, and in the nineteenth century, Maharaja Ranjit Singh donated 1000 kilos of gold to gold plate the temple spire and the dome.

It is believed that the Gyanvapi well is the place where the original Shiva lingam was buried. It is said that the priests of the temple saved the lingam when Aurangzeb attacked the temple, by throwing it in a well. Visible from here, is the Gyanvapi mosque that Aurangzeb had built, the living proof from history of the destructive nature and the uselessness of narrow-mindedness and hatred.

WHAT THE HISTORIANS AND ISLAMIC TRAVELERS SAID ABOUT THE BRUTALITY

Irfan Husain (Pakistani Writer) in his article "Demons from the Past" observes: "Their temples were razed, their idols smashed, their women raped, their men killed or taken slaves. When Mahmud of Ghazni entered Somnath on one of his annual raids, he slaughtered all 50,000 inhabitants. Aibak killed and enslaved hundreds of thousands. **The list of horrors is long and painful.** These conquerors justified their deeds by claiming it was their **religious duty** to smite non-believers. Cloaking themselves in the banner of Islam, they claimed they were fighting for their faith when, in reality, they were indulging in straightforward slaughter and pillage…"

Fernand Braudel wrote in A History of Civilizations (1995), that Islamic rule in India was "**extremely violent**", and "**the Muslims could not rule the country except by systematic terror. Cruelty was the norm – burnings, summary executions, crucifixions or impalements, inventive tortures.** Hindu temples were destroyed to make way for mosques. On occasion there were forced conversions. If ever there were an uprising, it was instantly and savagely repressed:

houses were burned, the countryside was laid waste, men were slaughtered and women were taken as slaves."

V S Naipaul has written extensively on the brutality of Muslims and how it wounded the richest, lone surviving cultures, that is Hinduism. Islam is born only to both enslaved and attempted to wipe out other cultures. *"It has had a calamitous effect on converted peoples. To be converted you have to destroy your past, destroy your history. You have to stamp on it, you have to say 'my ancestral culture does not exist, it doesn't matter'."*

FATWAS ISSUED TO SLAUGHTER HINDUS

The Muslims who issue Fatwas against Hindu Deities and Hindus are never prosecuted and brought to justice, thereby encouraging them to repeat their activities with more blasts and multiple bombs killing thousands of people. They have even issued Fatwa against National song, yoga, Bhagavad Gita, Surya Namaskar, etc. The Indian Mujahedeen had circulated an e-mail on July 8, 2008, in which they unequivocally threatened the Hindus thus:

"(O Disbelievers). We are guiltless of you and whatever worship beside Allah, we have rejected you and there has arisen between us and you, enmity and hatred for ever – unless you believe in Allah and Him alone" (Quran 60.4). After quoting verse from Quran the e-mail commanded the Hindus to convert to Islam in English in the following words:

"O Hindus! O' disbelieving faithless Indians! Haven't you still realized that the falsehood of your 33 crore dirty mud idols and the blasphemy of your deaf, dumb, mute and naked idols of Ram, Krishna and Hanuman are not at all going to save your neck, Insha-Allah, from being slaughtered by our hands"?

What action the government has taken against the IM who issued this Fatwa? Nothing. By not taking action against terrorists, Muslims who make hate speeches, Muslims who attack Hindus and Hindu Temples and stop the Temple activities, the central government is encouraging Muslims to openly express their hatred toward Hindu.

ISLAM MEANS TERROR ACROSS GLOBE

History cannot be ignored, hidden, negated and whitewashed. Nearly 14 centuries of brutality, terror, bombings, killings, rapes, destruction of Hindu Temples, kidnapping Hindu women, enslaving Hindu women should teach us about the brutality of Islam and believers of Quran. Anybody equating the this violent, brutal, vicious, and intolerant with Hindus must be either a Hindu hater, hiding behind his religion, fearful of consequences of his actions, promoting the exclusive religion, encouraging Hindu holocaust, or failing to name the names. Let us look at what Muslims have done over the last two-three decades and some of the incidents they have engaged in and some of the incidents that have resulted in numerous deaths:

The Shoe Bomber was a Muslim; The Beltway Snipers were Muslims; The Fort Hood Shooter was a Muslim; The Underwear Bomber was a Muslim; The U-S.S. Cole Bombers were Muslims; The Madrid Train Bombers were Muslims, The Bali Nightclub Bombers were Muslims; The London Subway Bombers were Muslims; The Moscow Theatre Attackers were Muslims; The Boston Marathon Bombers were Muslims; The Pan-Am flight #93 Bombers were Muslims; The Air France Entebbe Hijackers were Muslims; The Iranian Embassy Takeover, was by Muslims; The Beirut U.S. Embassy Bombers were Muslims; The Libyan U.S. Embassy Attack was by Muslims; The Buenos Aires Suicide Bombers were Muslims; The Israeli Olympic Team Attackers were Muslims; The Kenyan U.S, Embassy Bombers were Muslims; The Saudi, Khobar Towers Bombers were Muslims; The Beirut Marine Barracks Bombers were Muslims; The Besian Russian School Attackers were Muslims; The First World Trade Center Bombers were Muslims; The Bombay, Mumbai, India Attackers were Muslims; The Achille Lauro Cruise Ship Hijackers were Muslims; The Nairobi, Kenya Shopping Mall Killers were Muslims; The September 11th 2001 Airline Hijackers were Muslims; The Sydney, Australia Lindt Cafe Kidnapper was a Muslim; The Peshawar, Pakistani School Children Killers were Muslims; Charlie Hebdo killers; Copenhagen attackers; Yezidi killers; Boko Haram killers and numerous other such attacks and bombings were all MUSLIMS. Ignorance or denial of history is not the answer to deal with terrorism and in fact, failure to identify and take appropriate action only encourages the Muslim terrorist to continue their mission to subdue the humanity to untold misery. (Source:http://en.wikipedia.org/wiki/List_of_Islamic_ terrorist_attacks)

MAJOR TERROR ATTACKS IN INDIA

Muslims have terrorized, bombed, destroyed sacred places, attacked the Parliament and High Court, torched the hotels, exploded bombs in the train, bombed market places, killed foreigners, targeted Jews, and terrorized the innocent people and sacrificed the lives of these people in the name of Allah. These terrorist attacks spread all over India in such places as New Delhi, Bombay, Pune, Hyderabad, Varanasi, Mumbai, Malegaon, Jaipur, Bangalore, Ahmedabad, Guwahati, Kanpur, Mathura and other places. It is in the name of Allah. It is all according the verses found in Quran and Hadiths.

List of Major Terrorist Activities in India:

http://www.savetemples.org/2015/02/24/time-line-of-maor-terrorist-attacks-in-india/

VERSES FROM QURAN

Now let us look at some of the verses in Quran that might have influenced their violent behavior. For brevity sake only very few verses from Quran are listed.

"And as for those who disbelieved, I will punish them with a severe punishment in this world and the Hereafter, and they will have no helpers". Quran 3:56.

Allah will throw fear into the hearts of the disbelievers, and smite their necks and fingers. The Quran, Sura 8:12

The fires of hell will be fueled with the bodies of idolaters and unbelievers. They will experience an ever-greater torment. The Quran, Sura 72:15-17

Smite the necks of the disbelievers whenever you fight against them. Those who die fighting for Allah will be rewarded. The Quran, Sura 47:4

"So when the sacred months have passed away, then slay the idolaters wherever you find them, and take them captives and besiege them and lie in wait for them in every ambush, then if they repent and keep up prayer and pay the poor-rate, leave their way free to them." Quran, Sura 9:5.

"Fight those who believe not in Allah nor the Last Day, nor hold that forbidden which hath been forbidden by Allah and His Messenger, nor acknowledge the religion of Truth, (even if they are) of the People of the Book, until they pay the Jizya with willing submission, and feel themselves subdued." Quran (9:29)

"And if any fail to judge by the light of what Allah has revealed, they are no better than unbelievers." (Q 5:47) "Sovereignty in Islam is the prerogative of Almighty Allah alone. He is the absolute arbiter of values and it is His will that determines good and evil, right and wrong." (Mohammed Hashim Kamali, Principles of Islamic Jurisprudence, 3d rev. ed., (Cambridge, UK: The Islamic Text Society, 2003), 8.).

These and other similar verses in Quran are used by many radical Muslims to justify their brutal, violent, torturous, and treacherous actions against nonbelievers and declare jihad (struggle). There are many verses in the Qur'an that call for the destruction of Jews and Christians in addition to nonbelievers.

DEMOCRACY IS ILLEGITIMATE AS PER ISLAM

That means any constitution or any law passed by anybody or any country is considered illicit under Islamic law. If any country fail to the test of Sharia law, they are considered unbelievers. The only law that is accepted by adherents of Allah is Shariah. A democratic society or any other society that would not adhere to Islamic law should be overthrown. That is the reason that the Muslims have massacred nearly billion people in India, destroyed the Temples, ruthlessly converted people with the sword, overthrew many kingdoms, converted thousands of Hindu Temples into mosques, looted wealth, and raped countless Hindu women. Sharia law guides all aspects of Muslim law such as marriage, abortion, divorce, dress, inheritance, custody, women's rights, punishments for the crime, and others.

If we fail to identify the roots of the evil, terrorism, beheading, and killings as Quran, we are delaying the agony and torture of people by Islamic terrorists and most likely give more impetus for the ISIS and other Terrorists more time to occupy more and more countries and slowly reach the shores of Western societies and United States, if they have not already in a position strike at will.

BLASPHEMY AGAINST ISLAM ARGUMENT MAY BAN QURAN ITSELF

Raymond Ibrahim observed that Organization of Islamic Cooperation (OIC) with membership of 57 Muslim countries called on United Nations to criminalize "blasphemy" against Islam. Blasphemy is defined as any act of insulting or showing contempt or lack of reverence for God or irreverence toward something that is considered sacred. As per OIC request if UN criminalize blasphemy of Islam, that means if somebody defames, or insults Islam, Allah or Mohammad by publishing books critical of Quran like Satanic Verses; criticizes Islam like Geert Wilders and Hyaan Hirsi Ali; and draws controversial cartoons of Muhammad, they will be treated as criminals.

If UN agrees to their request, it would ban cartoons, books, films, and critical speeches because they defame, demean, insult and slander Islam. By the same token, **the Quran would be banned as it contains hundreds of verses defaming other religions, their belief system, and their worship places**. A number of verses are listed in the article about kafirs (non-believers). There are some verses condemning Christians and Jews by name. Since these statements are hateful, insulting and slander other religions, is it logical that the UN resolution would ban the Quran itself?

PRESIDENT OBAMA FALSELY LINKS POVERTY TO TERRORISM

Based on the statement made by **Marie Harf,** State Department spokesperson, who appeared on the **Hardball** program, it is clear that the Obama administration is operating under the patently false belief that Muslims are joining the Islamic State and engaged in beheading, terrorizing, immolating, crucifying, enslaving, intimidating, and raping "infidels" because they are economically impoverished. These Islamic terrorists lack job opportunities. According to the President, they resort to terrorism because they lack educational opportunities, are trapped in impoverished condition, and do not see any path for advancement. "So if we're serious about countering violent extremism, we have to get serious about confronting these economic grievances." It is preposterous, unfortunate and ridiculous to even imply that Islam is the root cause of all the terrorism even since Islam came in to existence.

A number of studies have shown that that poverty, economic condition, or job opportunities have nothing to do with extremism, terrorism and torture. **Claude Berreb**i, Princeton trained economist concluded: "If there is a link between income level, education and participation in terrorist activities, it is either very weak or in the opposite direction of what one intuitively might have expected." Similarly, **Marc Sageman** could not find any correlation between poverty and terrorism and in his book, Understanding Terror Networks, he stated that overwhelming majority of jihadis "were generally middle-class, educated young men from caring and religious families, who grew up with strong positive values of religion, spirituality and concern for their communities." Egyptian sociologist **Saad E Ibrahim** also conclude that the Islamist radicals he analyzed "were significantly above the average of their generation" in education, financial background, and motivation. Other studies further buttress these conclusions. **Nasra Hassan**, based on her interviews with nearly 250 Palestinians, concluded that "None of [the bombers] were uneducated, desperately poor, simple-minded, or depressed. Many were middle class and, unless they were fugitives, held paying jobs…Two were the sons of millionaires."

If poverty, lack of educational opportunities and economic grievances are the root cause of Islamic terrorism, then why do we not see similar terrorism, bombings, beheading, and intimidation in most of the Asian countries, South American countries and some African counties? In the history of India where Hindus are majority, can we imagine Hindu radicalism to the level of Islamic radicalism? Can we imagine Hindus using poverty for justifying the untold torture, brutality, and radicalism on the humanity? Sooner we identify Islam as the root cause of terrorism, sooner we find the solution and better we will be equipped to deal with the enemy. As **Ira Straus** mentioned that, *"Islam is the bottom-floor root cause of Islamic terrorism."*

HINDUISM

The main thrust of this paper is that President Obama is mistaken to equate tolerant, peaceful, respectful and nonviolent Hinduism with deceptive, violent, intolerant, disrespectful, and terrorist Christianity and Islam. Let us remember the words of **Arnold Toynbee**, who has written 18 volumes describing all great civilizations, about the survival of humanity, *"It is already becoming clear that a chapter which had a Western beginning will have to have an Indian ending if it is not to end in self-destruction of the human race. At this supremely dangerous moment in human history, the only way of salvation is the ancient Hindu way."* What is this Hindu way? *PEACE ON EARTH.*

Mutual Respect is utmost important among all religions and to remain in peace and harmony without being splintered on religious lines. **Rajiv Malhotra** argued that being respectful is to acknowledge that all religions are legitimate and equally valid paths to God as long as one religion claims to be exclusive and demean the practices of other religions. He argued that tolerance should be replaced by mutual respect. Tolerance implies inferiority while mutual respect implies equality. President Obama should advocate mutual respect among all religions so that they would not splinter on the exclusivity and superiority. In 2013, **Pope Francis** wrote to Muslims following the end of Ramadan that there should be mutual respect between the two religions. By respect, he meant "an attitude of kindness towards people for whom we have consideration and esteem' and goes on to say that mutuality is something shared by both sides and this is not a one-way process. Hindus have always displayed the symbols of all religions at homes, Ashrama, Mutts and other places to imply that we respect other religions for what they are. Similar approach to other religions is lacking by Christians and Muslims. One wonders as to why Pope did not address the issue referring to all the religions instead of talking about mutual respect only between Christians and Muslims.

PEACE ON EARTH FOR EVERYBODY

Hindus only talk about peace, mutual respect, kindness, and nonviolence. Hindu literature is replete with peace mantra that are chanted in every home, every temple and on every occasion. This is one of the Peace Mantras that passes the lips of millions of Hindus every day to bless the entire cosmos. *"May peace radiate there in the whole sky as well as in the vast ethereal space everywhere? May peace reign all over this earth, in water and in all herbs, trees and creepers? May peace flow over the whole universe? May peace be in the Supreme Being Brahman? And May there always exist in all peace and peace alone."*

Arnold Toynbee was so much convinced about the richness and peacefulness of India, he was asking India to be save the world with its message of tolerance, peace and tranquility. *"So now we turn to India. This spiritual gift, that makes a man human, is still alive in Indian souls. Go on giving the world Indian examples of it. Nothing else can do so much to help mankind to save itself from destruction."*

Om peace, peace and peace to us and all beings!

SPIRITUALITY

ONLY KEY FOR HUMAN SURVIVAL

'It is already becoming clear that a chapter which had a Western beginning will have to have an Indian ending if it is not to end in self-destruction of the human race. At this supremely dangerous moment in human history, the only way of salvation is the ancient Hindu way. Here we have the attitude and spirit that can make it possible for the human race to grow together into a single family. Now we turn towards India.

This spiritual gift, that makes a man human, is still alive in Indian souls. One can go on giving the world examples from India. Nothing else can do so much to help mankind to save itself from destruction.... in the 21st century. "India will conquer her conquerors," as mentioned by **Arnold Toynbee**, a British historian (1889-1975).

Both Abrahamic religions have caused untold misery by killing the nonbelievers, destroying property, enslaving the subjects, raping the women, occupying the lands forcefully, converting the nations to their respective religions either with force or with deception. In India and elsewhere, Christian authorities have used every trick, deceit and deception to convert gullible and innocent Hindus to Christianity. Their goal is to dismantle the Hindu edifice and erect Christianity. They do not even mind going against their own religious scripture, Bible. Why do they use so many deceptive techniques to convert people?

Billions of dollars are pouring into India from many foreign countries. The Christian preachers must show that they are converting in order to get more and more funds from these countries. The Christian Preachers' remuneration depends on the number's game. The more they show the number of converts, the more money they get. Many of these Christian missionaries are deluded into thinking that they go to heaven by converting non-Christians to Christianity. This erroneous thinking and greed for money makes the Preachers smack and slap their own Bible and the teachings of their only savior Jesus. They use such method as deception, deceit, force, manipulation, allurement, tricks, treachery, exploitation, violence, killings, educational indoctrination, defamation of other religions, demean other gods, denounce other scriptures, sexual exploitation and the list goes on. **Thomas Jefferson**, the third President of the United States stated, "Millions of innocent men, women and children, since the introduction of Christianity, have been burnt, tortured, fined, imprisoned; yet we have not advanced one inch towards humanity. What has been the effect of coercion? To make one half of the world fools, and the other half hypocrites. To support error and roguery all over the earth."

Islamic brutality on Hindus was unmatched in the annals of human history. It is bigger than the holocaust of Jews by the Nazis and also much bigger than the massacre of the Armenians by the Turks. According to the estimates, as many as 60 million Hindus were massacred by Islamic rulers. Actual numbers could be very well be approximately one billion.

Every Islamic ruler made hills of Hindu skulls to outnumber the previous rulers. In Afghanistan, Hindu Kush mountain has seen more blood and brutality. Will Durant has argued in his 1935 book, **"The Story of Civilization: Our Oriental Heritage"** that *"The Mohammedan conquest of India is probably the bloodiest story in history. The Islamic historians and scholars have recorded with great glee and pride the slaughters of Hindus, forced conversions, abduction of Hindu women and children to provide for slave markets and the destruction of temples carried out by the warriors of Islam during 800 AD to 1700 AD. Millions of Hindus were converted to Islam by sword during this period"* (P:459).

Even after Independence, the atrocities have not declined as the Hindu population was reduced to almost nil in Pakistan from nearly 18 percent to approximately 6 percent; and in Bangladesh to nearly 24 percent. Muslim population is increasing day by day in India and with the sole purpose of converting India into an Islamic Country.

ISIS is formed to establish a new Islamic caliphate across the Middle East. ISIS' desire (and apparent strategy) is to overthrow the existing governments of unstable, heavily Muslim populated nations and establish their own theocratic state in its place. They have spread across the globe to establish Islam through force and terror. The German writer and journalist **Jurgen Todenhofer,** who actually did the unthinkable and spent 10 days in the Islamic State as the Caliph's guest, says that the ISIS wants to kill "*all non-believers and apostates and enslave their women and children. All Shiites, Yazidi, Hindus, atheists and polytheists should be killed . . . Hundreds of millions of people are to be eliminated during this religious cleansing. All moderate Muslims who promote democracy should be killed [as well]. From ISIS perspective, moderates promote human laws over the laws of God.*"

The only solution to this mentality of conquering the humanity by terror and deception to submit to their respective religion is follow the advice of Toynbee who suggested that all the nations turn to India and embrace the spiritual path couched in the principle of ahimsa. Patanjali Yoga Sutras enumerates five yamas that are considered the codes: restraints, truthfulness, abstaining from immoral acts, thinking of highest reality and non-acquisitiveness. The five Niyamas prescribing the virtues, such as purity, contentment, control of the senses, surrender and self-study. By practicing one will be elevated to the path of spirituality allowing one to know the true nature of human existence and find the truth (Atman) and even higher truth (Paramatma). Patanjali says "*Ahimsa pratishtayam tat sannidhau vairatyagaha,*" that is, "*When a person is established in non-violence, then violence is dropped in his or her presence.*" (2:35). Dropping off these violent behaviors is the need of the hour if the humanity must prevent itself from self-destruction. As Toynbee stated that the only salvation for the humanity is to turn to India for her spiritual legacy that can prevent the holocausts.

WHAT IS SPIRITUALITY

Spirituality is an inward journey that enables us to go beneath the surface of Atma, true Self and allows one to examine who we are, what we think and we are. It leads each one of us home to our Truest Self. Spirituality is a broad concept with room for many perspectives. **In general, it includes a sense of connection to something bigger than ourselves, and it typically involves a search for meaning in life. As such, it is a universal human experience—something that touches us all.**

Christina Puchalski, MD, Director of the George Washington Institute for Spirituality and Health contends that "spirituality is the aspect of humanity that refers to the way **individuals seek and express meaning and purpose and the way they experience their connectedness to the moment, to self, to others, to nature, and to the significant or sacred.**"

According to **Mario Beauregard and Denyse O'Leary**, authors of "The Spiritual Brain", "spirituality means any experience that is thought to bring the experiencer into contact with the divine (in other words, not just any experience that feels meaningful)."

Ruth Beckmann Murray and Judith Proctor Zenter write that spirituality is "a quality that goes beyond religious affiliation, that strives for inspiration, reverence, awe, meaning and purpose, even in those who do not believe in God. The spiritual dimension tries to be in harmony with the universe, strives for answers about the infinite, and comes essentially into focus in times of emotional stress, physical (and mental) illness, loss, bereavement and death" (1989:259).

L Kaiser "... refers to a broad set of principles that transcend all religions. Spirituality is about the relationship between ourselves and something larger. That something can be the good of the community or the people who are served by your agency or school or with energies greater than ourselves. Spirituality means being in the right relationship with all that is. It is a stance of harmlessness toward all living beings and an understanding of their mutual interdependence." (L. Kaiser 2000)

Spirituality is perceived in the context of integrating every segment in the universe to bring about unity – nothing is excluded and everything that brings happiness and harmony is included. Spirituality involves the integration of three dimensions— knowledge base and belief systems, interior life and inner self, and exterior life and institutional activity. These three domains overlap and interact with each other – one dealing with individual experience, search for inner life and the external world. Spirituality is the experience of connection to something higher level that transcends our ordinary lives. **The most prominent feature of spirituality in Indian culture is the ideal of oneness of all beings in the universe (Radhakrishnan 1929).**

The oneness of the knowledge of the self, the internal self and external life is exemplified in the story of Lord Dattatreya. Nature guided to acquire the needed wisdom and knowledge. He also learned and developed his spiritual equanimity that provided him with requisite arsenal to have a different perspective. This is the best example for the saying that true knowledge of the nature will provide true knowledge of self and God.

Lord Dattatreya as He was wanderer, observed 24 elements in nature that became His Gurus. They provided Him with the necessary ammunition to lead a spiritual life thereby resulting in His salvation. **Earth, Air, Sky, Water, Fire, Moon, Sun, Pigeon, Boa constrictor, Sea, Moth, Bee, Elephant, Honey-thief, Deer, Fish, A Harlot named Pingala, Osprey, Boy, Maiden, Arrow-maker, Snake, Spider and Insect were his twenty-four gurus who provided the wisdom to realize that all things follow the universal natural divine law.** He learned from **earth** two virtues of forgiveness and being good to others. From **air**, he learned the quality of nonattachment and stainlessness. From the **sea**, he learned that although the sea is very large, it does not even allow a small dry leaf landing on its surface to stay there. Instead, the sea drives it away to the shore. If the sea had not always done so, it would have dried up like a tank by now. In the same way, however great a tapasvin or yogi might be, he should not allow even the smallest desire or agitation to enter his mind. He learned from **honeybee** to collect little bit of nectar going from one flower to another without causing any flower to shrivel. He realized that he should study all the scriptures, grasp the knowledge skillfully and use it in his search for the Self.

Swami Prabhavananda argued based on the Upanishads, which comprise the foundations of Indian culture, that the ultimate reality in this world is the universal spirit, which lies deep within us. Often it remains so deep within us that we are unaware of its existence. Hence, we falsely imagine that we are individuals composed only of body, senses and mind. We imagine further that this individual being has a separate and independent existence, whereas in fact, it is only an appearance—a light upon a screen, the source of which is the spirit that we do not see. **"The little space within the heart is as great as the vast universe. The heavens and the earth are there, and the sun and the moon and the stars. Fire and lightening and winds are there, and all that now is and all that is not."**

The process of realizing the spirit for what it is (the reality) and our individual being for what it is (a mere appearance) is the process of spiritual growth (Prabhavananda 1960). When a person is aware of this reality, he or she begins to feel that, for instance, backbiting a colleague is a denigration of himself or herself. Cheating, lying or concealing for selfish gain at someone else's expense is really harm done to oneself. Hating someone else is hating oneself (Chakraborty 1995: 25).

Those who are high on spirituality or those who perceive their oneness with others can be characterized by certain qualities. **Spirituality or oneness makes individuals friendly and compassionate, and love all living beings**. When people see no difference between themselves and others, they cannot be prejudiced or biased with respect to one person and will, thus, be fair to all. Oneness involves sympathy, empathy and identification not only with the feelings of others, but also with their goals and objectives. Spirituality is characterized by sensitivity, such that the person can identify with the feelings, needs, demands and aspirations of people around.

WHY SPIRITUALITY IS IMPORTANT

Whenever we talk about spirituality, we describe our perception, attitude and desire to know God through the inner journey to awaken the light within the self. **In this process one would be discerning the godlike qualities such as love, compassion, forgiveness, gratitude,**

kindness, Ananda (bliss), and truth. According to Wayne Teasdale, in his book, The Mystic Heart, "The divine calls us all into being out of itself. We are meant for it: That is the point of the spiritual journey. The journey puts us on the road to realizing and actualizing who we really are in our ultimate being. Enlightenment is the awakening to our identity as boundless awareness, but it is incomplete unless our compassion, sensitivity, and love are similarly awakened and actualized in our lives and relationships … **Awakening and developing compassion, sensitivity, and love is thus also part of the spiritual journey."**

Scriptures clearly stated that one can embark on the spiritual journey provided he understands the permanence of the self and renounce the path of violence. "The wise who knows the Self as bodiless within the bodies, as unchanging among changing things, as great and omnipresent, does never grieve. That self cannot be gained by the Veda, nor by understanding, nor by much learning. He whom the Self chooses, by him the Self can be gained. The Self chooses him (his body) as his own. But he who has not first turned away from his wickedness, who is not tranquil, and subdued, or whose mind is not at rest, he can never obtain the Self (even) by knowledge." **Katha Upanishad 1.2.22-24**

Spiritual approach is the key to avert human tragedy, mitigate terror and violence across the world, alleviate the natural disasters, ease the tensions across the nations, bridge the gap between religions, and establish world peace. There is going to be a long journey to convince all the religions to pursue the virtue of universal peace and harmony without resorting to the ideology of dominance, religious conversion, demeaning other faiths, and tarnishing the universal freedom and liberty. There is a lesson to learn from **Bhagavad Gita** (6:26-28) which says: "And whenever the mind unsteady and restless strays away from the Spirit, let him ever and forever lead it again to the Spirit. **Thus, supreme joy comes to the Yogi whose heart is still, whose passions are peace, who is pure from sin, who is one with Brahman, with God**. The Yogi, pure from sin ever prays in this harmony of soul soon feels the joy of Eternity, the infinite joy of union with God."

Spirituality is associated with **love, compassion, Ahimsa (non-violence)**, kindness and consideration for others. Based on the review of the responses to over 30 surveys, **Ryan Howell** listed five unique characteristics of spiritual people. **Being gracious, compassionate, optimistic, pursuing of self-actualization and building of lasting memories**, as the unique characteristics of spiritual people. In the book, The Art of Happiness, His Holiness Dalai Lama defines compassion in this way: **"Compassion can be roughly defined in terms of a state of mind that is nonviolent, non-harming, and nonaggressive. It is a mental attitude based on the wish for others to be free of their suffering and is associated with a sense of commitment, responsibility, and respect towards the other"** (114). He further spells out, -In developing compassion, perhaps one could begin with the wish that oneself be free of suffering, and then take that natural feeling towards oneself and cultivate it, enhance it, and extend it out to include and embrace others" (114).

Dr. Steven Southwick's book, **Resilience: The Science of Mastering Life's Greatest Challenges**, describes how some people overcome trauma—such as abduction, war, and imprisonment—by seeking comfort in spirituality or religion. He gives examples where spiritual people find ways to **"meet the challenge and continue with purposeful lives...they bounce back and carry on."** Having a strong spiritual outlook may help you find meaning in life's difficult circumstances. Southwick describes the story of a woman who overcame the post-traumatic stress following an abduction and rape by believing that her trauma "served as a platform for her personal development, forcing her to evaluate her life and gradually change it for the better. She credits her ability to move forward with her life...to her dedication to spirituality."

Over the decades, spirituality is enjoying positive evaluation with increased number of people embracing the ideals while the numbers of people believing in religion is declining. **David John Tracy** states, "If religion is in serious trouble, spirituality is in the ascendancy and the irony of this situation evokes puzzlement and anxiety in the religious establishments, scrutiny among theologians, and justification among those who have traded religion of their past for the spirituality of present." There is more talk about spirituality and how to relate oneself and one's self development. **The spiritual quest is slowly but definitely establishing firm roots in all the societies with the decline of Church attendance in Europe and USA.**

Spiritual revolution is taking place across the globe and spreading without any support or propagation from any organizational structure. Spirituality is transforming all sections of the population whether they are religious or secular, theists or atheists, educated or uneducated, young or old, men or women, and married or unmarried. There is an increased realization among people, especially younger generation, that the society needs rejuvenation and spirituality is the key that can unlock the vacuum for the development of personal, professional, social, cultural and educational growth for future survival.

Majority of the scholars in the Western societies were concerned with religion, worldly matters and pragmatism. They had taken an objective and critical attitude toward spirituality that may have included the concepts of reincarnation, karma theory and the true nature of human existence. But the result is disappointing. In his lecture, ***Origin of the Vedanta***, Max Muller quotes the remarks of the German philosopher, Frederick Schlegel:

". . . It cannot be denied that the early Indians possessed a knowledge of the true God; all their writings are replete with sentiments and expressions, noble, clear, and severely grand, as deeply conceived and reverentially expressed as in any human language in which men have spoken of their God. . . Even the loftiest philosophy of the Europeans, the idealism of reason, as it is set forth by the Greek philosophers, appears, in comparison with the abundant light and vigour of Oriental idealism, like a feeble Promethean spark in the full flood of heavenly glory of the noon day sun-faltering and feeble, and ever ready to be extinguished." With regard to the Vedanta Philosophy especially, he says: 'The divine origin of man is continually inculcated to stimulate his efforts to return, to animate him in the struggle, and incite him to consider a reunion and reincorporation with divinity as the one primary object of every action and exertion" (Three Lectures on the Vedanta Philosophy, pp. 10-11).

The impact of this spiritual revolution is far reaching as it shakes the very foundation of Christianity that believed in the supremacy of the teachings of Jesus and the dominance of the clergy who controlled the mind of their congregation.

As far back as 1875, Henry Steel Olcott, one of the founders of Theosophical Society was looking toward East to find answers for the modern ills by tapping into the well of Ancient Wisdom. He was looking for alternatives to the Christian dogma and fundamentalism and the liberal skeptical scientific minds and find answers in the profound scientific attainments of ancient India. He stated that, **"Society has reached a point where something must be done; it is for us to indicate where that something may be found."**

WHAT IS SPIRIT?

A Hindu believes that an individual is a spirit more than a matter or a body. But somehow or other it has got itself bound down by matter, and thinks of itself as matter. Many Hindu scriptures explain the myth that matter is the solution for modern ills.

The soul is eternal and immortal, perfect, infinite, ever blissful, and transcends time and space. Death means change of the center to another body. It never dies. It moves to another center. Lord Krishna describes that eternal essence or permanent nature of soul as follows:

Whosoever knows this (eternal essence) to be imperishable, eternal, birthless and changeless, how can that individual, O Paartha, slay or cause anyone to be slain? (2:21)

Weapons cannot pierce this (the eternal essence), fire cannot burn this, water cannot wet this, and wind cannot dry this. (2:23)

This is uncleavable, incombustible, and cannot be wetted or dried. It is eternal, all-pervading, stable, immovable and everlasting. (2:24)

This (eternal essence) is imperceptible, this is incomprehensible, this is unchanging. Therefore, having known this, it is not worthy of grief. (2:25)

Atman is the inmost Self or Spirit of man. **Atman is the fundamental, ultimate, eternal, immutable pure consciousness.** Thus, it appears that *Brahman* is the ultimate reality behind all world-objects and *Atman* is pure spirit in all beings. **Truly speaking, both Brahman and Atman are not different realities.** They are identical. Only for our basic understanding, they are referred to separately. They are the eternal, all-pervading realities underlying all existence. They are two different 'labels' for one and the same reality behind all the objects, all matter, all beings of the universe.

> "The Self pervades. Bright, without body, free from harm, unmuscular, pure, exempt from evil, wise, equipped with Mind, encompassing, Self-existent, appropriately he assigned values throughout eternity" (Īśā-upanishad, 8).

WHERE CAN WE FIND THIS SOUL/ATMA?

Katha Upanishad states that the Atma is "smaller than the atom and (at the same time) greater than the greatest (which is the universe)" and dwells in the hrudaya guha (heart's cave)" (1.2.20). It says that the soul is a particle that is the size of a thumb while some other scriptures talk of varying sizes. Irrespective of the size, it is located in the heart chakra. But the individual Atma reflects the same qualities as Paramatma. They are one and the same. They are not separate entities. **But, Swami Vivekananda says, "It is impossible to find God outside of ourselves. Our own souls contribute all of the divinity that is outside of us. We are the greatest temple. The objectification is only a faint limitation of what we see within ourselves."**

Alain Danielou studied extensively the relationship between Atma (Self) and Brahman (Supersoul). **It is through yoga he was able to connect the mind, body and soul. In fact, he says, one can understand the whole universe by understanding one's own self.** "It is by studying the microcosm that we can understand macrocosm; it is through our own impermanent being that we can reach the Universal Being. It is in the cavern of our heart that we can realize the immensity of spaces, and by controlling our own vital rhythms that we can escape the power of time. It is by reaching the source of life that we can escape the power of death. It is by exploring the unknown spheres within ourselves that we can visit the celestial and infernal worlds."

RELIGION AND VIOLENCE

Many people heard that "Religion is the cause of wars," "Religion caused holocaust," "Religion caused bloodshed," and so on, and in fact religion caused all kinds of violence. To quote just one contemporary author, Matteo Ricci Professor of Theology at Georgetown University and Leo D. Lefebure, a scholar who dedicated his academic career to interreligious understanding and the pursuit of peace:

"The brutal facts of the history of religions impose the stark realization of the intertwining of religion and violence: violence, clothed in religious garb, has repeatedly cast a spell over religion and culture, luring countless 'decent' people —from unlettered peasants to learned priests, preachers and professors — into its destructive dance." *(Revelation, the Religions, and Violence; Maryknoll: Orbis, 2000).* Religion continues to be used as a deadly weapon to dominate the counties by ruthless and used to motivate and justify horrific acts of unspeakable brutality.

Valerie Tarico in her article, **"God as the Original Terrorist"** says, "By one count, the Quran has only 532 cruel or violent passages, while the Bible has 1,321. Christians respond that the Bible is longer, so the cruel, violent passages make up a smaller percent of the whole." ISIS terrorists find enough passages in Quran to justify for jihad, executions, sex slavery, and forced conversions. Similarly, Christians find in Bible enough passages to endorse terrorism, savagery, crusade, inquisitions, slavery and executions.

Islam caused more bloodshed in India than any other religion anywhere. According to historian **Will Durant**, *"The Islamic conquest of India is probably the bloodiest story in history".* By the estimate of **Koenraad Els**t the population of Indian subcontinent reduced by almost 80 million between 1000 and 1525. During their conquests and rule in India, the number of Muslims in India increased through Immigration and Conversion. The Ancient Indian Kingdoms in Afghanistan and Pakistan became Muslim majority areas, as did the

Eastern Part of Bengal. This ultimately lead to the Partition of India in 1947 after the end of British rule.

His Holiness the **Dalai Lama** appeals to our common humanity, advocating spirituality rather than religion and an ethic based on compassion and the realization of our profound interrelatedness, in a move to go beyond exclusive understandings of religion and conflicting metaphysics, dogma, etc. He goes so far as to say, "*We can do without religion but not without spirituality.*" **Archbishop Tutu** in his book **God is Not a Christian**, says "*Some of the ghastliest atrocities have happened in the name of religion. It need not be so, if we can learn the obvious: that no religion can hope to have a monopoly on God, on goodness and virtue and truth.*"

WHY EUROPEAN AND AMERICAN CHRISTIANS ARE LEAVING CHURCH?

Disappointed with the message of the Bible coupled with their inability to quench their thirst for spiritual needs and scientific explanations, percentage of Christians who are members of a Church or synagogue is steadily declining from 70 percent in 1992 and 63 percent in to 2009 to 59 percent in 2014, as per Gallup poll. "Christianity in the United States hasn't done a good job of engaging serious Christian reflection with young people, in ways that would be relevant to their lives." Church is unable to address the spiritual needs of the members of their congregation. It is insulated from the reality and isolated from the members. Church is more interested in controlling the mind -set of their members rather than addressing the "nothingness" they experience in their heart. Bible teachings look hallow and unable to justify the absurdities, inconsistencies and inaccuracies; Church authorities and the Christian ministers do not reflect the true message of the Bible. For their own hegemony, they distort the Bible to exercise their authority over the congregation. Church is narrow minded and unbending on their moral standings. Salvation to heaven is only for those who follow the Bible and the ministers, and who are fearful of the God. This kind of approach limited the number of people who can enter the gate of heaven. The church goers feel that Christianity is not about self-fulfillment and self-realization but it is only about sinners and how they can be saved. Any infraction from the Bible can lead one to hell.

Ryan Sheehan reports that, "There is an ongoing silent migration away from the church of an estimated 3,500 individuals each and every day. A 2014 study indicated that over 1.2 million people will leave the church in the next year." It was estimated that over 10,000 churches would have been closed in 2015. That means an average of 100 church goers would be left without any place of worship to go. In fact, about 80 percent of 14-33 year olds reported that church was not important in their life. (The Christian Post, May 27, 2015).

Pew Research Center asked respondents to explain in their own words, why they no longer identify with a religious group. Some of the responses include "learning about evolution when I went to college," "Too many Christians doing unchristian things," Rational thought makes religion go out the window," "Lack of any sort scientific or specific evidence of a creator," "I see organizes religious groups are more divisive than uniting," "Because I think religion is no longer a religion anymore. It is a business … It's all about money." Further they also mentioned the higher studies, clergy sexual abuse, church teachings of homosexuality, and lack of time as the reasons for not attending the church. Some said their belief in higher power, which does not require one to go to church, inspired them to lean toward spirituality. (**Michael Lipka 2016**)

ORGANIZED RELIGION DENIES SPIRITUALITY

Organized religions are partly responsible for the many Christians to flee their churches. **Religion and spirituality are two related yet distinct entities associated with faith**. Religion denotes "a set of beliefs concerning the cause, nature, and purpose of the universe, usually involving devotional and ritual observances and a moral code," (www.dictionary.com). Many things that are attributed to religion are true to organized religions such as Islam and Christianity. They exert considerable influence on their followers in instilling morality, condemning other religions, waging wars, killing non-believers, and converting them forcefully. Religion develops dogmatic and unquestionable rules for follower to adhere to; threatens and terrorizes; speaks of sinners; creates divisions, talks of eternal hell, makes one dependent, and feeds fear and insecurity. **On the other hand, spirituality instills confidence, embraces freedom, promotes individuality, infuses consciousness, recognizes divine nature, inspires inner peace, allows exploration, creates independence, encourages discussion, and stimulates questioning. In general, religion controls while spirituality frees. Religion is given and spirituality is chosen. Religion is external; spirituality is internal.**

Deepak Chopra says that the "the custodians of organized religion have frequently ended up with destructive behaviors — power mongering, cronyism, control, corruption, and influence peddling. As a result, organized religion has frequently become quarrelsome, divisive, leading to conflict. No organized religion has been immune to this unfortunate tendency. So, we have had crusades and witch-hunts of Christianity, the Jihads of Islam, violent communal riots instigated by fundamentalist Hindus and the persecution of minorities and ethnic cleansing, all in the name of God."

According to **Austin Cline**, "Religion is an institution established by man for various reasons: exert control, instill morality, stroke egos, or whatever it does. Organized, structured religions do all but remove god from the equation. You confess your sins to a clergy member, go to elaborate churches to worship, advise what to pray and when to pray. All those factors remove you from god. Spirituality is born in a person and develops in the person. It may be kick started by a religion, or it may be kick started by a revelation. Spirituality extends to all facets of a person's life. **Spirituality is chosen while religion is often times forced. Being spiritual to me is more important and better than being religious.**"

On the other hand, spirituality allows you to reach higher conscious level as to who you are, why you are here and how you are connected to the Super soul; leading one to develop moral and ethical compass. It is through the engagement of meditation, personal prayers, self-inquiry, selfless service, full devotion and practice of Yamas and Niyamas. Spirituality is allowed to flower.

INDIA TO CONQUER THE WORLD SPIRITUALLY

Sri Aurobindo:

August 15th is the birthday of free India. It is also Sri Aurobindo's birthday. On this day in 1947 Sri Aurobindo gave a message to the nation on the All India Radio. He outlined in the message his prophetic vision for India, for the globe and for humanity.

> *"August 15th is the birthday of free India. It marks for her the end of an old era, the beginning of a new age.* ***But it has significance not only for us, but for Asia and the whole world, for it signifies the entry into the community of nations of a new power with untold potentialities which has a great part to play in determining the political, social, cultural and spiritual future of humanity".*** . . .
> **He foresaw that India's spiritual teaching will enter the West in an ever-increasing measure.**

> *"The spiritual gift of India to the world has already begun. India's spirituality is entering Europe and America in an ever-increasing measure. That movement will grow. With the disasters of the time more and more eyes are turning towards India with a hope. There is an increase in the number of people turning not only toward her teachings, but to her psychic and spiritual practice."*

Swami Vivekananda: *"Up, India, and conquer the world with your spirituality! Aye, as has been declared on this soil first, love must conquer hatred, hatred cannot conquer itself. Materialism and all its miseries can never be conquered by materialism. Armies, when they attempt to conquer armies only multiply and make brutes of humanity. Spirituality must conquer the West. Slowly they are finding out that what they want is spirituality to preserve them as nations. They are waiting for it; they are eager for it. Where is the supply to come from? Where are the men ready to go out to every country in the world with the message of the great sages of India? Where are the men who are ready to sacrifice everything, so that this message shall reach every corner of the world? Such heroic souls are wanted to help the spread of truth."*

He further stated that India's greatness did not come from the military conquest of other countries but spiritual conquest. *"We must conquer the world or die. There is no alternative. The sign of life is expansion; we must go out and expand, show life or degrade, fester and die. There is no other alternative. Take either of these, either live or die… India must conquer the world and nothing less than that is my idea. You must expand or perish. That is the law of life.*" He also said that it was his dream to tell the story of the noble Emperor Ashoka who used religion and spirituality as the central theme of his Kingdom. *"We must go out, we must conquer the world through our spirituality and philosophy. The only condition of our national life, of awakened and vigorous national life, is the conquest of the world by Indian thought."*

APPROACHES TO AROUSE SPIRITUALITY

1) Advaita and Spirituality

Advaita Vedanta, states **Eliot Deutsch, "has been and continues to be the most widely accepted system of thought among philosophers in India, and it is, we believe, one of the greatest philosophical achievements to be found in the East or the West"**

The Vedantic explanation is that **man's ultimate nature is divine and it is Spiritua**l: eternal existence, eternal knowledge, and eternal bliss. It is through yoga and meditation, the soul is purified, and mind is put to rest. Through it, all the obstacles within me are removed until no thought remaining in the mind. Then the true nature and eternal bliss of the Atman, the true self, manifests itself.

Happiness, satisfaction, peace of mind, and gratification are the essential nature of human beings. All the material acquisitions and limitless desires are the cause of human misery, dissatisfaction and turmoil. One may get temporary satisfaction in acquisition of certain material objects, they are not the cause of internal and immanent peace of mind. Peace of mind comes from within not from outside to mean through the material objects or preconceived notions. **Romain Rolland**, French Nobel Laureate, observed, **"The true Vedantic spirit does not start out with a system of preconceived ideas…. each man has been entirely free to search wherever he pleased for the spiritual explanation of the spectacle of the universe."**

According to Advaita philosophy, individual soul is nothing but Brahman. Realization of him being Supreme Soul is clouded by ignorance. Individual soul is the source of all experience and wisdom. Ancient Rishis experienced the Brahman that is innate divinity, infinitude, luminosity and blissfulness of the soul as they dusted off the mirror layer by layer. Advaita philosophy declares that there is absolute reality beyond material world, individual consciousness and all the world. That is called Brahman. It is the root cause of spirituality – connecting individual consciousness and collective consciousness. Spirituality is imbued in Advaita philosophy, the belief that one is Brahman that can be experienced through yoga and meditation. "Brahman or Oneness is not something to be looked for outside. It is within me, or rather it is me myself. That part of me which is not Brahman, my individual ego, my thoughts and sensations, etc. have only an ambiguous, half formed reality. It rests on my true identity, that is Brahman. I need only to realize this and I will know the Truth of this universe." The essence of Advaita philosophy is the realization that individual soul is not different from Supreme soul which is achieved by asking the question 'Who Am I" that leads to the practice of yoga and meditation. **V. Ravi** summarized the process as thus: "Therefore, the initial stages of spirituality, one is bound to feel the difference between God and self. This happens because of ignorance. You have to transcend several stages and cross several impediments to ultimately realise, that God and you are one. For this, practice is essential. Practice is called sadhana. Sadhana can be explained as the practice that ultimately leads you to your goal."

2) Guru and Spiritual Awakening.

Guru Gita talks about the great importance and significant role a Guru can play in directing the disciple into the path of spiritual journey through his enlightened state. Guru has already attained the self-illumination and self-mastery over the sense objects. **A Sadguru has seen the God and is soaked in the divine consciousness. As Guru Gita states that guru can dispel the ignorance and show the path to undertake inward journey to attain the perfection and truth; and the real nature of human existence.**

As human beings, we are all roaming in the darkness, swimming in the ocean of samsara, stumbling in the day to day hurdles, chasing the mirage of material objects, and failing to experience the real happiness. **We are unable to realize who we are and what we are and what this journey is all about. The awakened Guru is the only one that can awaken the divinity in his disciples. It is through his touch, speech and looks he can awaken the God hidden within his disciple. He knows his disciple better than disciple himself.** A guru is described as a father, mother teacher, friend, and son all in one. He knows what is good for his disciple. The relationship between a Guru and a disciple is unlike any other relationship. His love, compassion and mercy are unmatched. There is no selfish motive in awakening the divine within. He can be gentle, soft, tender, merciless and hard to cop off the layers to chop off the ignorance layer by layer to realize the true nature of man.

Sadhguru Sri Ganapathy Sachchidananda Swamiji stated that a real guru has reached competence and who has reached perfection. He is the beacon light of the suffering humanity. He comes to the level of the disciple recognizing that he is merged in ignorance and he preaches him the knowledge to find the light within and to experience the eternal bliss by winning over the worldly entanglement and by taming the ego. Guru encourages his disciples to dive deep into the chamber of heart to find light that removes the ignorance. *"The inner light is shining constantly. It reveals through the mirror called the mind. The defects in the mind blurs the light within, but that light remains ever unaffected by the modifications of the mind. Man should ignore the limitations of the mind and should get fixed on the inner light. The inner light is God. To seek Him should be the aim of man."*

3) Yoga and Spirituality

The modern world is pushing the interests of the people to chase for material accumulation, strive for ruthless capitalistic enterprise to satisfy the ego, compete with the fellow human beings to exceed in the display of conspicuous consumption and get trapped in the vicious circle of "more is better." With all the stresses of the modern world, constant mental agony, restlessness, egoism, helplessness, mental strain, anxiety, excessive pressures in the work force, and agitation, society is experiencing severe health problems, family problems and problems in the world of work. It is taxing the mind to the extend where people rely on medications to suppress the mental problems.

Over the years that people have been looking for alternative to experience relative peace of mind, happiness and harmony. Yoga and meditation are providing the needed help in pursuing spiritual path to calm the restive mind. **Many movie actors, directors, singers, football players, basketball players, golfers, politicians, university faculty and students, artists, TV personalities, musician and ordinary people are practicing yoga and meditation to experience the Vedantic concept Sachidananda.** Realization that material wealth, fame and ego would not bring happiness, many people across the globe turn to yoga to embark on a spiritual journey to find peace of mind and to strike a balance between the material and spiritual paths.

Yoga tradition was started by a spiritual teacher by the name Patanjali more than 2000 years ago culling all the experiences of great ages of India into a book called *The Yoga Sutras.* **Patanjali's Yoga Sutras have become a roadmap for the journey into self-discovery.** Just one phrase "yoagas chitta vritti nirodaha" revolutionized the spiritual journey across the globe. It says that the essential teaching of yoga is to retrain the mind. **Yoga means to "to join". There is a realization that the individual soul is a facet of Super soul. Yoga is a means to join the Jivatma with Paramatma.**

Yoga is the only method that can unite the body, mind, soul and breath. Mind is like a monkey jumping back and forth constantly, oscillates between past and present, causing worry, restlessness, fear, aversion and dissatisfaction. To restore to the very nature of human nature that is peace and happiness, mind must be brought back to the present leaving all the baggage behind. Mind should be transported to the concept "be here now. "**Yoga cleanses the body and purifies the mind. Yoga directs one to look for truth about ourselves as to who we are, why we are here and what is the purpose of life.**

Meditation connects us to our deeper spiritual nature allowing us to tap our senses, feelings, beliefs and inner most thoughts. Meditation peels off our negative tendencies, erratic behaviors, violent tendencies and restlessness. In "The Places That Scare You," Pema Chodron describes the basis of Buddhist sitting meditation in this way: "Sitting meditation cultivates loving-kindness and compassion. . .. It gives us a way to move closer to our thoughts and emotions and to get in touch with our bodies. It is a method of cultivating unconditional friendliness toward ourselves and for parting the curtain of indifference that distances us from the suffering of others. It is our vehicle for learning to be a truly loving person."

4) Third Eye and Spirituality

Lord Shiva's the third eye (also known as the inner eye) is a mystical and esoteric concept referring to a speculative invisible eye which provides perception beyond ordinary sight. In certain dharmic spiritual traditions such as Hinduism, the third eye refers to the ajna, or brow, chakra. The third eye is referred to as the gate that leads within to inner realms and spaces of higher consciousness. In New Age spirituality, the third eye often symbolizes a state of enlightenment or the evocation of mental images having deeply personal spiritual or psychological significance. **The third eye is often associated with religious visions, clairvoyance, the ability to observe chakras and auras, precognition, and out-of-body experiences. People who are claimed to have the capacity to utilize their third eyes are sometimes known as seers.**

The third eye is considered inner eye and also known as Ajna Chakra, which is located between the eye brows. It is also referred to eye of knowledge. It is a commanding center for all decision-making process. It will enable a man to get connected to inner world. It is though meditation the third eye can be activated to see inside yourself and its connection to beyond. At certain stage of mediation, one can establish connection with pineal gland and pituitary gland enabling one to experience peace of mind and happiness. As long as one cannot tap this inner eye, he is said to be in spiritual darkness.

The third eye is the eye of vision to see the light inside. It is by opening the third eye, you can achieve deeper penetration. The third eye means your perception has gone beyond the dualities of life. You are able to see the true nature of self, the potential for enlightenment and its connectivity with the Super Soul. All the dualities disappear at that level.

5) Transcendentalists and Spirituality

Ralph Waldo Emerson, Henry David Thoreau, Margaret Fuller, Theodore Parker, and dozens of others, mostly young Unitarian ministers have left us a great legacy of spiritualism. Most Unitarian Universalists (UUs) know vaguely of the Transcendentalists, their alleged pantheism, their love of Nature, their intellectual and literary power. But what is the "spiritual achievement" the Transcendentalists have bequeathed to us? During early 19th century, many writers were preaching about outward things and not enough about inward pious life.

Many transcendentalists in those days practiced several activities to practice spirituality. They concentrated on the stillness of the nature; contemplation, prayer and meditation; reading sacred books; writing and journal keeping; conversations/discussions; setting aside sacred space and sacred time; and expressed their ideas through art. In nature, the Transcendentalists saw the presence of the divine. In his journal, Henry David Thoreau wrote, "My profession is always to be on the alert to find God in nature, to know his lurking places, to attend all the oratories, the operas in nature. To watch for, describe, all the divine features which I detect in Nature."

For many transcendentalists, Meditation and Contemplation was a vehicle for mindfully and thoughtfully experiencing our own divinity. Emerson preached on prayer: "It is not only when we audibly and in form, address our petitions to the Deity, that we pray. We pray without ceasing. Every secret wish is a prayer. Every desire of the human mind is a prayer uttered to God and registered in heaven." **For Emerson, "true prayers are the daily, hourly, momentary desires, which come without impediment, without fear, into the soul."**

They showed great interest in reading different books not just for the sake information but for inspiration and for new ideas. They read widely other worldly religions such as Hinduism and Buddhism. **Ralph Waldo Emerson**, following the death of his wife, resigned as a Minister of Church claiming that he was unable to preach the gospel he no longer believed. His inquiring mind was not satiated. He found refuge in the spiritual and idealism of Hinduism. He read extensively the Indian scriptures such as Bhagavad Gita, Upanishads and others. He said this about the **Bhagavad Gita: "I owed a magnificent day to the Bhagavad-Gita. It was as if an empire spoke to us, nothing small or unworthy, but large, serene, consistent, the voice of an old intelligence which in another age and climate had pondered and thus disposed of the same questions which exercise us."**

Disgusted by the increasing materialism of the West, Emerson turned to India for solace:

"The Indian teaching, through its clouds of legends, has yet a simple and grand religion, like a queenly countenance seen through a rich veil. It teaches to speak truth, love others, and to dispose trifles. The East is grand - and makes Europe appear the land of trifles. ...all is soul and the soul is Vishnu.

They realized that everybody should find some sacred time and sacred space for themselves in solitude to grow spiritually. **Henry Thoreau** wrote: "This world is a place of business. What an infinite bustle! I am awaked almost every night by the panting of the locomotive. It interrupts my dreams. There is no Sabbath. It would be glorious to see mankind at leisure for once. It is nothing but work, work, work." Rather than observing the Sabbath as an obligation, they believed that it was important to take time away from the regularity of our daily lives.

Ralph Emerson also recognized the importance of **sacred space** for meditation, prayer and reflection. He advised all his listeners to set aside a sacred place in their houses. "In your arrangements for your residence see that you have a chamber to yourself, though you sell your coat and wear a blanket." It was important for the Transcendentalists to consecrate time and space for the mindful practice of spirituality.

HEALTH AND SPIRITUAL BENEFITS

Mayo Clinic asks a question, "is yoga right for you?" It says, "It is if you want to fight stress, get fit and stay healthy". Numerous studies have well documented the wealth of information on the health and spiritual benefits of yoga. Yoga is credited with the reduction of stress and anxiety while at the same time it enhances the mood and overall well-being. It helped reduce risk factors for chronic diseases, such as heart diseases and high blood pressure, alleviated chronic conditions such as depression, pain and insomnia. It is attributed to improving balance, flexibility in mind and body, range of emotions and strength. Benefits also include muscle strength and tone, improved respiration, energy and vitality, weight reduction, improved athletic performance and increased blood flow.

The study conducted by Richard Davidson at the University of Wisconsin revealed that consistent yoga practice led to a significant increase in the serotonin levels and a decrease in the levels of monoamine oxidase (an enzyme that breaks down neurotransmitters) and cortisol. He also reported that the left prefrontal cortex showed heightened activity in meditators, a finding that has been correlated with greater levels of happiness and better immune function. More dramatic left-sided activation was found in dedicated, long-term practitioners.

Yoga helps one to find who you are and how to achieve of control over mind by concentrating on the divine within. It will help you to understand the world around you better and appreciate your own life. It will help you find stillness and silence within you and it enables you to enjoy life with more contentment and happiness as you develop discriminatory wisdom to tap what is essential in life and the true nature of human existence. The things that were stressful, frustrating and nerve wrecking lose their importance as you keep practicing yoga that allows one to focus on the divinity. Many yoga practitioners feel the connection between mind, body and spirit and finally they are able to feel the "oneness" within themselves.

According to 2016 study conducted by Yoga Journal and Yoga Alliance, the number of yoga practitioners has increased to more than

36 million, up from 20.4 million in 2012. Also, thirty-four percent of Americans or 80 million people say they are likely to try yoga for the first time in the next 12 months. "What's fascinating is the data shows that those who practice and teach yoga have measurably better perceptions of their individual strength, balance, dexterity, and mental clarity versus non-practitioners," said Yoga Alliance Executive Director and COO, **Barbara Dobberthien**.

HOW SANYASI DEFEATED ALEXANDER THE GREAT

When Alexander, the Great, visited India after conquering all the other countries in the world that were known to him, he wanted to see the strange Indians of whom he had been hearing so much. He was just led to a monk/sanyasi or priest on the bank of the Indus river. The monk lay there on the sands, bare-footed, naked, wearing no clothes and not knowing where from his tomorrow's food was to come, just lying there and basking in the sun, meditating for the enhancement of the self and for the well-being of the Universe.

Alexander, the Great, with his crown shining, dazzling with the brilliant diamonds and gems that he had got from Persia, stood beside him in all his glory. Beside him was the monk with no clothes on -what a contrast! The riches of the whole world represented by the body of Alexander on one side, and all the outward poverty represented by the saint on the other side! But you have simply to look at their faces to be convinced of the poverty or riches of their true souls. The Fakir was seating fearlessly in front of the world conqueror.

Look at the beaming countenance of the saint, the happy, joyful face of the saint. Alexander, the Great was struck by his appearance. He fell in love with him, and just asked the saint to come with him to Athence (Greece). The saint laughed, and his answer was: "The world is in Me (Soham...!!!!)." The world cannot contain Me. The universe is in Me. I cannot be confined in the Universe. Greece, Rome and Persia are in Me. The suns and stars rise and set in Me." Alexander, the Great, not being used to this kind of language, was surprised. He said, *"I will give you riches and wealth. I will just flood you with worldly pleasures and amenities. All sort of things that people desire, all sorts of things which captivate and charm people will be in wild profusion at your service. Please accompany me to Greece."*

The saint laughed, laughed at his reply and said, "There is not a diamond, there is not a sun or star which shines, but to Me is due its luster. To Me is, due the glory of all the heavenly bodies. To Me is due all the attractive nature, all the charms of the things desired. It would be beneath my dignity, it would be degrading on my part, first, to lend the glory and charm to these objects, and then go about seeking them, to go begging at the door of worldly riches, to go begging at the door of flesh and animal desires to receive pleasure, happiness. It is below my dignity. I can never stoop to that level. No, I can never go begging for them.

This astonished Alexander, the Great. He just drew his sword and was going to strike off the head of that saint. And again, the saint laughed a hearty laugh and said, "Oh! Alexander! never in your life did you speak such a falsehood, such an abominable lie. Kill Me, kill Me! Where is the sword that can kill Me? Where is the weapon that can wound Me? Where is the calamity that can mar my cheerfulness? Where is the sorrow that can tamper with my Happiness? Everlasting, the same yesterday, today and forever, pure and holy of holies, the Master of the Universe, that I am.

Even in your hands I am the power that makes them move, Oh! Alexander! If this body dies, there I remain, the power that makes your hand move. I am the power that makes your muscles move." The sword fell from the hands of Alexander. He totally surrendered at the feet of the Master. The Great conqueror of the world was lying near the feet of the Sanyasi(Monk). The sword, which has claimed thousands life, was kissing the dust of the Sanyasi feet. Sanyasi said to Alexander the Great, Oh! King, awake, arise and leave this violence, embrace love and affection. You will become universe conqueror!!!!!!! leave aside the mirage of the world Conqueror. Alexander, touched the feet of Sanyasi and ordered the retreat of his army from the Indus.

CONCLUSION

With so much violence, terror and deception reigning the entire globe, it is absolutely essential to adopt the way of spirituality if humanity has to be spared from continuous terror, bloodshed, brutality and incessant killing. As Arnold Toynbee said that we need to adopt the India way, that is, Ahimsa if we have to stop self-destruction. Strive and drive toward spiritual experience whereby self can shed the state of alienation, anxiety, egoism and dominance. With constant bombings and killings by ISIS and other terrorist organizations, the mankind is yearning for global peace and international brotherhood and love. Spirituality may not totally shield us from these dangers but it will have impact on the environment and the mind-set of the people. It will give courage and fearlessness to influence the negative elements. It may even transform the ruthless leaders and blood thirsty organizations allowing spirituality to flourish and peace to flower.

Hindus scriptures talk about **Vasudaiva kutumbam** – the whole world is a family. Oneness is emphasized. Every being reflects divinity and Ananda which is the essential nature of human beings. In all prayers, Hindus talk about peace and prosperity which is reflected in this invocation:

Om sarve bhavantu sukhinah. Sarve santu niraamayaah.
Sarve bhadraani pashyantu. Maa kaschid dukhbhaag bhavet.

May all beings be happy. May all beings be healthy.
May all beings experience prosperity. May none in the world suffer.

Its aim is global peace irrespective of religion, nationality, sex or age.

Dr Zakir Husain, the third President of India expressed his anguish at the communal violence preceding the Partition: **"The raging fire of our mutual hatred has vitiated the atmosphere which makes work of garden-tending seem a mad pursuit. This fire will scorch the earth and wipe out humanity and civility ... "For God's sake, unite to introspect to extinguish the fire. Fire is on, put it down. It is not the question of survival of this or that other community, it is the time to choose between civilized way of life or of a jungle rule."**

The only solution to avoid the human catastrophe is the Hindu way because of its pluralism, tolerance, accommodation, peaceful existence, open dialogue, respect for life, and human dignity. **Dinesh Chandra** captured the essence of Hindu ethos when he stated, "Hinduism, thus, is the only progressive religion, nay the only way of life that has to be adopted by the world if it has to survive the tumultuous chaos it has landed itself in. Sanity demands that people need to be granted freedom of thought and to live the way they desire as long as they do not interfere with others. That is the crux of Hinduism" (Hinduism: Dawn of Civilization; 2008).

For centuries India is known for both material plane and spiritual plane, It excelled in almost every conceivable field of study. They have not left out any subject unexplored. But India is primarily known as a spiritual leader of the world. It emphasized the churning of the soul rather than waging war that lead to the human destruction. It believes that once the country is strong spiritually it would reflect in all other areas such as political, economic, social, religious, scientific and cultural dimensions. Hence every Indian should take up the challenge to recognize the potential of spirituality, study it, digest it, and disseminate to the rest of the world. **Let us heed the words of Arnold Toynbee and give humanity a chance to live in peaceful coexistence through the spiritual plane. "So now we turn to India. This spiritual gift, that makes a man human, is still alive in Indian souls. Go on giving the world Indian examples of it. Nothing else can do so much to help mankind to save itself from destruction."**

Swami Vivekananda summed up the role of India in promoting the world peace, harmony and love to conquer the world. *"India will be raised, not with the power of the flesh, but with the power of the spirit; not with the flag of destruction, but with the flag of peace and love ... One vision I see clear as life before me: that the ancient Mother has awakened once more, sitting on Her throne rejuvenated, more glorious than ever. Proclaim Her to all the world with the voice of peace and benediction."* (CW IV 352-353).

CHRISTIAN DECEPTIVE CONVERSION

HOW TO STOP CONVERSIONS AND START RECONVERSIONS

"The divinity of Jesus is made a convenient cover for absurdity. Nowhere in the Gospels do we find a precept for Creeds, Confessions, Oaths, Doctrines, and whole cartloads of other foolish trumpery that we find in Christianity." **John Adams**

Christian church authorities are using every trick, deceit and deception to convert gullible and innocent Hindus into Christianity. Their goal is to dismantle the Hindu edifice and erect a Christian one, for which they do not even mind going against their own religious scripture, the Bible. Why do they use so many deceptive techniques to convert people? Billions of dollars are pouring into India from many foreign countries. Christian preachers have to show that they are converting in order to get more and more money from these countries. The Christian Preachers remuneration is a numbers game, the more they show the number of converts, the more money they get. Many of these Christians are delusional to think that they go to heaven if they can convert non-Christians to Christianity. This delusional thinking and greed to make more money would make the Preachers to smack and slap their own Bible and the teachings of their only savior Jesus.

They believe that Jesus gave them the right to deceive, convert, subjugate, conquer, and proselytize any nation or religion, by any and all possible means. They are entitled to such methods as allurement, fraud, coercion and violence in converting but they criticize Hindus even if they to talk about their atrocities of conversion. They do not even accept our right to convert.

In 1999, the Southern Baptist Mission released a pamphlet asking its 40,000 churches to head to India to convert Hindus from the darkness and embrace Christianity. The very first sentence of the pamphlet states that, *"More than 900 million people are lost in the hopeless darkness of Hinduism......Pray that Hindus who celebrate the festival of lights would become aware of the darkness in their hearts that no lamp can dispel."* The shepherds followed the instructions on a war footing and converted many Hindus into Christianity. This is more evident in Southern States and especially in Andhra Pradesh. They convert Hindus and make them their foot soldiers to destroy Hindu deities, step on them, and also tear up the pictures of Hindu Gods and Goddesses. According to unofficial statistics, as many as 30 percent of Hindus in villages have got converted.

DENIGRATION OF HINDUS

Many Christians complain that Hindus are attacking them and not allowing them to practice their faith. In 2012, retired Judge of Karnataka High Court, M. F. Saldana stated that Christians in Karnataka State are under an unprecedented wave of persecution. He has also termed Karnataka as "the Rogue State No.1". At the same time, he himself admits that the State has not recorded any killing in this season of "persecution". He even alleged that there were 1,000 attacks against Christians without any evidence or producing the names of the victims. Unfortunately, these Christians make derogatory statements about Hinduism, insult Hindu Gods, mock Hindu rituals and adopt Hindu practices to entice gullible Hindus into their fold. They blame RSS, Sangh Parivar, and other Hindu organizations for the so-called persecution of Christians. P N Benjamin, a Christian who investigated the alleged attacks of Christians by Hindus, did not find any evidence to prove their claims. "India and its tolerance for the diversity of its religious communities were built up over thousands of years. But, it looks like if individuals like Saldanha and his like-minded friends are not checked and their false propaganda countered, your children and the children of India's minorities will have no future anywhere near the equity and fairness that they have so far enjoyed despite India being a predominantly Hindu nation." He further goes on to say that Christians should be thankful to the Hindu majority who are tolerant despite the aggressive postures of Christians. Christians need not worry about violent acts against them. Instead the Christians should worry about "internal cancer it carries with its body." They should engage in serious reflections and identify the causes for the growing antagonism of people of other faiths against certain Christian groups in India.

DECEPTIVE PRACTICES

Father Joseph Menengis, priest of St James Church in Mariyannapalya, Bangalore, confessed before the Justice B K Somashekara Commission of Inquiry on Wednesday (March 11, 2009). "The duty of every Christian is to convert non-Christians to Christianity **by any means.**" When he says "**by any means**" what does it mean? That means Christians can go against their own Bible teachings, ignore their own Bible, and insult their own God for their selfish monetary motives. They use such method as deception, deceit, force, manipulation, allurement, tricks, treachery, exploitation, violence, killings, educational indoctrination, defame other religions, demean other gods, denounce other scriptures, sexual exploitation and the list goes on.

One may ask why they use these different means to convert Hindus into Christianity. Honestly speaking Hindus are more knowledgeable, have more wisdom, are equipped with reservoir of tolerance toward other religions, do not see other religious people as prey for conversion and do not see other religious people as commodities to be exploited. They just treat humans as humans with no ulterior motive. They are happy with their religion. Their religion has all the answers for their day to day living. Hence the Preachers cannot convert Hindus into Christianity by using legitimate, honest, truthful and open methods. They know that they cannot convert them truthfully. Their teachings are not based on logic, reasoning, rationale and cross examination. Hence the Preachers rely on deceptive, secretive methods to conversion. They recognize that the Hindus will not accept, support the teachings of deception, violence, and intolerance. Therefore, it is important for them to use any trick in the book. That is the reason Father Joseph Menengis said that they convert Hindus by any means to Christianity.

Over jealous preachers addicted to deception, violence, and wealth do not mind even abusing their own teachings and throw mud on their own scriptures. Then the question may be asked what are they doing that is so contradictory to the teachings in the Bible.

Father Joseph Menengis also said "Hindus believe in idol worship. So, to attract them to Christianity, idol worship is performed in churches." During cross-examination, the priest said that "despite idol worship being prohibited in Bible, we have idol worship in churches." Most of the churches have adopted the policy of what is called "inculturation" in order to attract Hindus to these churches. In fact, some churches are using Hindu methods of worshiping such as offering arthi, performing abhishekam, reciting Ashtottaranama and Sahasranaarchanas to Jesus, singing bhajans, etc. only to convert and modifying the churches to look like Hindu Temples. Some Preachers are dressed like a Hindu saint with long saffron robes to mislead Hindus. The Outlook magazine observed that "Om Namah Jesus could well reverberate inside hundreds of Catholic churches in India very soon, if the changing physical face of these places of worship is anything to go by." A number of shrines for Mary Mata, different saints are springing up. How can that reconcile to the injunctions of Bible condemning the idol worship? For example in Vijayawada thousands of pilgrims queued up to visit Mary Matha shrine at Gunadala on the second day of the three-day Gunadala Matha festival on Tuesday.... Many pilgrims had their heads tonsured on the hillock before offering something. (The Hindu Feb 11, 2009).

Majority of Christian Churches advocate proselytization with a plan to harvest of souls, devising new strategies. Terms such as "evangelistic campaign", "missionary strategy", "campus crusade", "occupying non-Christian areas", a "blitzkrieg" of missionaries, and sending "reinforcements" are used to get reinforcements and resources from foreign countries. They developed slogans such "India is waiting for Jesus," "save Hindus from hell," and we should reach "the unreached millions" in order to receive billions of dollars to convert India into a Christian nation.

BIBLE SANCTIONS DECEPTION

Apostle Paul openly admits that he used deception to convert people from other religion to Christianity. He lied and acted deceptively. He was like a chameleon changing colors to fit the occasion. That means if he meets a Jew, he would act like a Jew; and meets the poor, he would act poor only to convert others into Christianity. No morals, no ethics, no scruples and no principles are observed. Look at the third world countries. In fact, **Thomas Jefferson** was very critical of Christianity and its coercive and deceptive practices. *"Millions of innocent men, women, and children, since the introduction of Christianity, have been burnt, tortured, fined, imprisoned; yet we have not advanced one inch towards uniformity. What has been the effect of coercion? To make one half the world fools, and the other half hypocrites. To support roguery and error all over the earth."* In Christianity, none of reason, debate, dialogue, persuasion or discussion are encouraged. Puppets act according to the whims and fancies of the puppeteers. The missionaries are like puppets in the hands of the Church, or the Roman Catholic Church or Pope who control their thinking, their activities, their future salvation, and their tactics to convert other people. They have no independence or freedom to act.

Let us look at what Paul said about the deception he used to convert people. Since that time, he became a role model for **Mother Teresa** and many other similar evangelists. *"Though I am free and belong to no one, I have made myself a slave to everyone, to win as many as possible. To the Jews I became like a Jew, to win the Jews. To those under the law I became like one under the law (though I myself am not under the law), so as to win those under the law. To those not having the law I became like one not having the law (though I am not free from God's law but am under Christ's law), so as to win those not having the law. To the weak I became weak, to win the weak. I have become all things to all people so that by all possible means I might save some. I do it all for the sake of the gospel, that I may share with them in its blessings."* – 1 Corinthians 9:19-23.

WHAT THE BIBLE SAYS ABOUT SPREADING GOSPEL AND BAPTIZING.

"Go therefore and make disciples of all the nations, baptizing them in the name of the Father and the Son and the Holy Spirit, teaching

*them to observe all that I commanded you; and lo, I am with you always, even to the end of the age" (*Matthew 28:19-20*).*

Mathew 10: 16-18, *"Behold, I am sending you out as sheep in the midst of wolves, so be wise as serpents and innocent as doves. Beware of men, for they will deliver you over to courts and flog you in their synagogues, and you will be dragged before governors and kings for my sake, to bear witness before them and the Gentiles."*

Mark 16:15-18; King James Version (KJV)

15 - And he said unto them, Go ye into all the world, and preach the gospel to every creature.
16 - He that believeth and is baptized shall be saved; but he that believeth not shall be damned.
17 - And these signs shall follow them that believe; in my name shall they cast out devils; they shall speak with new tongues;
18 - They shall take up serpents; and if they drink any deadly thing, it shall not hurt them; they shall lay hands on the sick, and they shall recover.

CONVERSION IS VIOLENCE

In the name of humanitarian service, they would lie and cheat. They have no moral conscience, and no scruples, and with unlimited resources coming from European counties, with highly efficient planning and well organized administration, and with highly focused vision to destroy Hindu dharma, they have relentlessly converting Hindus to Christianity on a war footing. **Swami Dayananda Saraswati** equated the Southern Baptists' fanatical aggressiveness to the declaration of war, and war is synonymous with violence. He said that, **"conversion is an act of violence…aggressive religions have no God-given right to destroy ancient faiths and cultures… it is an act of violence because it hurts deeply, not only the other members of the family of the converted, but the entire community that comes to know of it. When the hurt becomes acute, it explodes into violence…humanity cannot afford to lose any more of its existing religious traditions."**

TWO FALLACIES

1) ALL RELIGIONS ARE SAME.

Only Hindus put signs of all religions to indicate that all religions are the same. Nothing is farther from the truth. If we look at all three major religions, Hinduism talks about ahimsa, tolerance, forgiveness, love, mutual respect, pluralism, freedom and independence. Other two religion speak about destruction, rape, killing, stoning to death, deception, allurement, breaking the idols, killing the nonbelievers and converting Hindus to their fold.

For the sake of the future of Hinduism, for the sake of our youth, and for the safety and security of humanity, let us explain the differences and why we are scientific, rational, independent and pluralistic? Let us make sure we will leave the legacy of freedom for our children to enjoy. Let us not deny them this freedom.

2) NOTHING WILL HAPPEN TO SANATANA DHARMA.

This is another argument many of our Hindus make by saying Sanatana dharma has survived for centuries. Nothing will happen to it. Nobody can destroy it. There is inherent strength in our dharma that will perpetuate and survive. But, what happened to the Hindu civilization that existed before the Abrahamic religion were born over two thousand years ago. It used to be practiced from Afghanistan and many Middle Eastern countries to Russia and all of the Eastern part of the globe until China. There is so much evidence surfacing over the years about relics of so many Temples and the images of Gods all over the world. How do you convince the hindu people in Bangladesh and Pakistan who might have thought in a similar manner thinking that nothing will happen to Sanatana Dharma? Now only handful of Hindus remain. Now Hindu space is shrinking day by day in states like West Bengal, Assam, Kashmir, Kerala and Telangana. Let us not be fooled into thinking that nothing will happen to Sanatana Dharma. Hindus cannot abandon the karma theory and stare at the sky.

We need to abandon these two fallacies and unzip our lips to have an open dialogue about the atrocities of other religions and also think of our fathers who were wiped out in our neighboring countries.

Never forget the past; "Those who do not learn history are doomed to repeat it."

GOA INQUISITION

The Christian historian, Dr. T. R. De Souza has written extensively about the atrocities Portuguese Christians inflicted on Hindus. According to him at least from 1540 onwards, 'Hindu idols disappeared because all the temples were destroyed, their sites and building materials were fully utilized to erect new Christian Churches and chapels. Various Church council decrees banished Hindu priests from Portuguese territories; banned public practices of Hindu rites including marriage rites; the State took upon itself the task of bringing up Hindu orphan children to raise them as Christian; and denied Hindus many types of employment opportunities, while converted Christians were preferred. They ensured that Hindus would not harass those who became Christians. Hindus were forced to assemble in Churches to listen to preaching and refute their religion.

THE BIG HOUSE WITH 200 CELLS

The Inquisition Laws filled 230 over pages. The place where the Inquisition was conducted was known as the **Big House** and the proceedings were always behind closed shutters and closed doors. The screams of agony of men, women, and children could be heard in the streets, in the stillness of the night, as they were brutally interrogated, flogged, and slowly dismembered in front of their relatives. Eyelids were sliced off and extremities were amputated so carefully that a person could remain conscious, even though the only thing that remained was his torso and a head.

HINDU KUSH MOUNTAINS

'Hindu Kush' mountain located in Eastern Afghanistan means 'Hindu Slaughter' or 'Hindu Killer'. According to the history, the Hindu culture flourished in that mountain range until about 1000AD. After Muslim leaders killed millions of Hindus on that mountain, it was deliberately named as 'Hindu Slaughter' by the Moslem conquerors, as a lesson to the future generations of Hindustan. Unfortunately,

Hindus are completely ignorant of the tragic genocide of their forefathers.

FAMOUS QUOTATIONS ON CHRISTIANITY

"Christianity has the rancor of the sick at its very core—the instinct against the healthy, against health. Everything that is well-constituted, proud, gallant and, above all, beautiful gives offence to its ears and eyes." **Friedrich Nietzsche**

"Of all the systems of religion that were ever invented, there is none more derogatory to the Almighty, more unedifying to man, more repugnant to reason, and more contradictory in itself, than this thing called Christianity. Too absurd for belief, too impossible to convince, and too inconsistent for practice, it renders the heart torpid, or produces only atheists and fanatics." **Thomas Paine**

"Christianity is the most ridiculous, the most absurd and bloody religion that has ever infected the world." **Francois Voltaire**

"The Bible is not my Book and Christianity is not my religion. I could never give assent to the long-complicated statements of Christian dogma." **Abraham Lincoln**

"Millions of innocent men, women and children, since the introduction of Christianity, have been burnt, tortured, fined, imprisoned; yet we have not advanced one inch towards humanity. What has been the effect of coercion? To make one half of the world fools, and the other half hypocrites. To support error and roguery all over the earth." **Thomas Jefferson**

"The bible is full of fairy tales and anyone who believes in the bible is unfit to be a parent or vote. ... (It) is a false book that must be burned and buried... Jehovah is no God, but a barbarous tribal idol." **George Bernard Shaw**

During the past few centuries the most belligerent, the most aggressive, the most rapacious, the most power-drunk section of humanity has been precisely, the Christian Western world. During these centuries western Christendom had invaded all other continents; its armies followed by priests and merchants have subjugated, robbed or pillaged most of the non-Christians. **Pitirim Sorokin**

BIBLE SAYS KILL THOSE WHO WORSHIP OR SERVE OTHER GODS

If anybody worships other Gods such Hindu Gods: "thou shalt surely kill him; thine hand shall be first upon him to put him to death, and afterwards the hand of all the people. 10And thou shalt stone him with stones, that he die; because he hath sought to thrust thee away from the LORD thy God," **Deuteronomy 13:6**

If anybody serves other Gods, Jesus commands: Thou shalt surely smite the inhabitants of that city with the edge of the sword, destroying it utterly, and all that is therein, and the cattle thereof, with the edge of the sword. **Deuteronomy 13: 13**

If anybody "hath gone and served other gods, and worshipped them, either the sun, or moon, or any of the host of heaven, which I have not commanded; ..... shalt thou bring forth that man or that woman, which have committed that wicked thing, unto thy gates, even that man or that woman, and shalt stone them with stones, till they die." **Deuteronomy 17:3**

BIBLE VERSES THAT ARE OFFENSIVE TO HINDUS

Friedrich Nietzsche (1844-1900), German philosopher, *"I call Christianity the one great curse, the one great intrinsic depravity, the one great instinct for revenge for which no expedient is sufficiently poisonous, secret, subterranean, petty-I call it the one mortal blemish of mankind. In Christianity neither morality nor religion comes into contact with reality at any point."*

Exodus 20:3-Thou shalt **have no other gods** before me.

Exodus 20:4-Thou shalt **not make unto thee any graven image,** or any likeness of anything that is in heaven above, or that is in the earth beneath, or that is in the water under the earth:

Exodus 20:5-Thou shalt not bow down thyself to them, nor serve them: for I the lord thy god **am a jealous god**, visiting the iniquity of the fathers upon the children unto the third and fourth generation of them that hate me;

Exodus 20:23-Ye shall **not make with me gods of silver**, neither shall ye make unto you gods of gold.

I John 5:21- Little children, **keep yourselves from idols**. Amen.

2 Kings 17:35-…The lord had made a covenant, and charged them, saying, ye shall not fear other gods, nor bow yourselves to them, nor serve them, nor sacrifice to them.

Deuteronomy7:25- The **graven images of their gods shall ye burn with fire**: thou shalt not desire the silver or gold that is on them, nor take it unto thee, lest thou be snared therein: for it is an abomination to the lord thy god.

Deuteronomy 4:24-For the lord thy god is a consuming fire, **even a jealous god.**

Deuteronomy 5:9 You **shall not bow down to them** or worship them; for I, the LORD your God, am a jealous God, punishing the children for the sin of the fathers to the third and fourth generation of those who hate me,

Deuteronomy 12:3 **Break down their altars, smash their sacred stones and burn their Asherah poles in the fire; cut down the idols of their gods and wipe out their names from those places.**

Jeremiah 25:6 **Do not follow other gods to serve and worship them**; do not provoke me to anger with what your hands have made. Then I will not harm you."

Exodus 23:13 "Be careful to do everything I have said to you. **Do not invoke the names of other gods**; do not let them be heard on your lips.

Exodus 23:24 Do not bow down before their gods or worship them or follow their practices. You must demolish them and break their sacred stones to pieces.

Exodus 34:13 **Break down their altars, smash their sacred stones** and cut down their Asherah poles.

Numbers 33:52 Drive out all the inhabitants of the land before you. **Destroy all their carved images and their cast idols, and demolish all their high places.**

Deuteronomy 7:5 This is what you are to do to them: **Break down their altars, smash their sacred stones**, cut down their Asherah poles and burn their idols in the fire.

Deuteronomy 7:25 The images of their gods you are to burn in the fire. Do not cover the silver and gold on them, and do not take it for yourselves, or you will be ensnared by it, for it is detestable to the LORD your God.

Deuteronomy 12:4 You must not worship the LORD your God in their way.

Judges 2:2 and you shall not make a covenant with the people of this land, but you **shall break down their altars**.' Yet you have disobeyed me. Why have you done this?

Zechariah 13:2 "On that day, **I will banish the names of the idols from the land**, and they will be remembered no more," declares the LORD Almighty. "I will remove both the prophets and the spirit of impurity from the land."

All Hindus must stand up for the TRUTH. Christians think that they have every right to convert Hindus into Christianity by any means possible but fail to give the same privilege to Hindus. Media has failed to investigate the conversion atrocities, allurement and deceptions. Media is the recipient of huge sums of money from Christian organizations. Consequently, they would not question the practices of Christianity or investigate the abuses of nuns by Church authorities, and sexual affairs of Bishops and Archbishops.

Hindus must wake up to the real Christianity and what it says about Hindus and their practices. If they remain silent, they may be wiped out. If they do not open their eyes and if they fail to understand what Bible says about them, their very survival is at stake. Think before you participate or celebrate Christmas. Pope and many Christian leaders have already commanded their sheep to put a cross on India in the third millennium. They want to see India as a Christian nation the way they were able to Christianize both Americas, Europe and Africa. They are at it feverishly, relentlessly, ruthlessly, brutally, and persistently with almost unlimited resources flowing from Western countries.

Let us remember the words of Swami Vivekananda delivered at the Parliament of Religions, **"Ye are the children of God, the sharers of immortal bliss, holy and perfect beings. Ye divinities on earth – sinners! It is a sin to call man so; it is a standing libel on human nature. Come up, lions! And shake off the delusion that you are sheep; you are souls immortal, spirits free, blest and eternal."**

RECOMMENDATIONS TO STOP CONVERSION AND START RECONVERSION

- ⚔ We should point out the difference between Hindu Dharma and other two Abrahamic religions. It would not be convincing if we only talk about the greatness and richness of our religion only. We should conduct courses on other religions the way other religions spend studying our religion for about two years.

- ⚔ We should adopt some of the methods and technics other religions are using to attract our Hindus, especially Dalits. If we do not visit their neighborhoods, identify with them and make them feel part of our Vasudaiva Kutumbam, we will continue to lose them day by day.

- ⚔ We have to train the people as Priests from different varnas/ castes to manage their temples. They can speak their language, they know how to behave, how to mingle and what to say appropriately.

- ⚔ All our Swamijis, Peethadhipathis and spiritual leaders should concentrate on conducting lectures in the Dalit or other minority communities and speak about all the stories that high light the stories of non-Brahmins who have contributed to the richness of culture. Talk about the Gods and Goddess, village Goddesses etc., to impress upon the fact that all the communities have been part of this big tent known as Hinduism.

- We all should try to see that all the illegal churches that are being built around all major Temples and also in villages creating havoc to the next-door neighbors. TTD and other religious and organizations should take legal action against these illegal structures.

- Conduct different festivals, Satyanarayana pujas, Srinivasa Kalyanam, Sitarama Kalyanam, etc. in these Dalit and other minority communities to make them feel that they are Hindus. Explain the meaning of these festivals and their impact on the pluralistic nature of our religion. One size does not fit everybody.

- Vigorous efforts must be made to reconvert Christians inti Hinduism with few incentives including special visit to TTD or any major Temple of their choice.

- All Temples should send blessings, bhajan CDs and Prasadam to the families who are engaged or conducting major Samskaras of our Hindu tradition – birth ceremony, namakarana, annaprasana, aksharabhyasam, seemantham, engagement, marriage, sashtipurthi, death ceremony, etc.

- Visit hospitals where any member of the village or the neighborhood may be hospitalized and take Prasadam and blessings from the Temple.

- All Hindu Temples and organizations must work to repeal all the conditions that allow the minority colleges to have special quotas. As we know many of the Christian colleges convert almost all their students who were admitted on special quota.

- We need to have Volunteers to monitor the employees of all Hindu Temples and find out how many of them are practicing Christianity through some sort surveillance.

- Develop a mechanism to monitor the employees of Hindu Temples who are attending Christian Churches. Need a team of people to expose their real faith and how they are abusing our Hindu Temples.

- Also have team who can assigned to find out how the Christians tap these innocent Hindus. Need some documentation and video proof.

⚔ Every temple should start Sunday school for children of different age groups. Provide them with incentives to attend and eventually feel proud of the richness of our culture. Meals, uniform, and may be yearly school supplies.

⚔ TIME LIMIT. Respond to any correspondence on a time basis. Approval or disapproval of any requests, release of funds and completion of the projects on a timely basis boosts the confidence and trust of Hindus in Hindu Temples and all other Hindu organizations. They should be role model for moral supremacy and ethical excellence.

⚔ We need to have a TV Channel Discussing these and other issues relevant to the survival of Hinduism. This is the channel that will present the proper perspective of Hinduism, monitor the distorted views expressed by other channels or other leaders, challenge them and invite them to this new channel and expose their biases and prejudices.

⚔ Licenses to shops doing business near or around Hindu Temples must be given only to Hindus.

⚔ Hindu Temples must hire only Hindu contractors to procure Prasadam material.

⚔ Similarly, Business contracts or building contracts should be given only to Hindus.

⚔ TTD should not contribute to any educational institutions that hire other religious people or that do not teach courses on Hinduism.

⚔ TTD must train a brigade of Hindu missionaries who can debate against Christian missionaries and expose their fraud and hypocrisy.

⚔ Hindu Temples' employees should be required to attend schools operated by Hindus or non-Christian schools.

⚔ All members attending this Sadassu and all employees of Endowment Act should work to repeal the Endowment Act allowing Hindus to manage their Temples without any interference from the government. Christians and Muslims have that freedom of managing their religious places. Why can't Hindus be given the same privilege and freedom to manage their own Hindu Temples?

⚔ Let us make sure these Sadassus are not cancelled anymore and all those who assemble here will have the courage to stand up and be counted to save the Temples from the secular government.

It is time to challenge the status quo and think "Hindu" and establish Hindu Nation. Jai Hind. Jai Bharat.

TWO-NATION THEORY: IMPLEMENTATION OR DECLARE BENIGN DICTATORSHIP

(NOTE: When I say "Muslims," I refer to the those who follow Quran scrupulously, believe in killing the kafirs, want to convert India into an Islamic Country, believe in breaking up India, accept the premise that only Allah's wishes will be implemented to rule the country, abhor democracy and secularism, want to enforce triple talaq, and deny the human rights as per the United Nations. There are many Muslims who believe in the ideals of democracy, who want to integrate into the Hindu society and who silently practice the ideals of Hindu nation. These are not included in the broad usage of "Muslims.")

"The only way to make Hindustan homogeneous is to arrange for exchange of population. Until that is done, it must be admitted that even with the creation of Pakistan, the problem of majority vs. minority will remain in Hindustan as before and will continue to produce disharmony in the body politic of Hindustan." **B R Ambedkar**

"There is no other way but to divide India. Give Muslims their homeland and give Hindus Hindustan." **Mohammad Ali Jinnah**

If Bharath has to protect its Hindu population, preserve it's territorial integrity, and stop the impending Hindu holocaust, India has to wake up fast. Hindus need to stand up and speak out first. Based on the two-nation theory, Muslims should be sent back to Pakistan or Bangladesh if we want to prevent Hindu holocaust at the hands of Muslims and if we want to keep India as Hindustan as was planned at the time of separation. Partition took place only on the basis of the vision of having one part as a Muslim Country and the other as a Hindu Nation. It is the ideology of Muslims to convert the whole world into Islamic countries through their sword that prompted us to revisit this theory. People in India would soon have to decide either to be killed or to be converted. We will soon witness a blood bath that might pale the genocide of Hindus during partition. Once this rampage starts there would be no place for Hindus either to hide or flee.

It is time for every Hindu to read the history of India over the last ten centuries, how the Muslims have ruled India and how they have tortured our forefathers, raped our sisters, ransacked our shops, ambushed the villages, maimed our bodies, slit our throats, and dumped the bodies in the gutters. More than 2000 Hindu Temples were destroyed and converted into mosques. Many of our revered Deities were broken into pieces only to be used as footsteps for their mosques.

Any indifference, negligence, silence on the part of Indian government and Hindus will be taken as sign of welcoming Muslims for more bloodshed and more destruction. Unimaginable misery and indescribable agony is awaiting Hindus. Hindus are the only ones scared of Muslims and unable to say it openly for fear of being attacked and killed. Hindu Politicians, for fear of losing their block of votes, would dare not talk about it.

How to Stop the Upcoming Hindu Genocide in India.

Continuation of appeasement of Muslims, our utter failure to name Islam as the enemy of humanity, our inability to quell the rising terrorism, our intentional overlooking of the verses in Quran which advocated the killing of nonbelievers, failure to recognize the Islamic intention of breaking India into three Muslim countries, incapability to enforce the law to stop the incessant atrocities committed against Hindus, and our powerlessness to enforce uniform civil code, are only few examples that will inspire Muslims to commit heinous crime on Hindu lives. If we want to stop the upcoming Hindu genocide, there are only two solutions:

   ⚔ Revisit and implement the Two-Nation Theory that was the basis for partition where all the Muslims were supposed to go to Pakistan while all Hindus and Sikhs remain in India. Inspite of all the arguments against implementation, the potential total decimation of Hindu population in India should convince the leadership to save the lives of Hindus. Once the carnage starts happening, nobody can stop it. Hindus have no nation to turn to escape from the bloodbath. Muslims have Pakistan and Bangladesh to go to as was originally planned during the Independence time. Further, Muslims have about 58 Islamic countries to seek shelter; or;

⚔ Benign DICTATORSHIP should be the second solution to avert the mass killings of Hindus in the future. A strong leader with courage and fearlessness, should make sure that all the citizens are given equal opportunities, all special privileges based on religion are removed, family planning is implemented uniformly, and uniform civil code is enforced, and territorial integrity is restored.

These solutions may seem preposterous, outrageous, abrasive, inhuman, notorious, despicable and intolerant to certain sections of the population. Similar opinions were expressed when two nation theory was being discussed. India was partitioned to make sure that all Muslims will live in Islamic country, Pakistan and all Hindus live in Hindustan, India. Since Independence, Hindu population in Pakistan dwindled to almost nil from about 18 percent in Pakistan and in Bangaldesh from 24 percent to about 6 percent. In a short period of time, Persia was changed to Iran by driving all the Zoroastrians, Afghanistan drove out all Buddhists to make it an Islamic Country, and once Christian dominated Lebanon was changed to Islamic country. In India, nearly 500,000 Kashmiri Pandits were thrown out mercilessly by Muslim majority, and in West Bengal Illegal infiltration and local Muslims are rampaging the villages and conducting numerous terrorist activities. At present, there are about 35 percent Muslims in Assam, 28 percent in Kerala, 20 percent in UP, 96 percent in Lakshadweep, and nearly 50 percent in Hyderabad alone. The more we wait, greater the chance of unimaginable multiplication of Muslim population.

Lessons from Partition: Hindus and Muslim Cannot Live Together

The whole premise for the partition of India into two countries is based on two arguments:

1) Hindus and Muslims cannot live together

2) Need a Separate Islamic Country to live according to the teachings of Quran

Number of years before the Independence, many Muslim leaders had argued that Hindus and Muslims cannot live together because of their differences in their religious beliefs. In his presidential address to the Muslim League at Lahore in 1940, Jinnah declared: "Islam and Hinduism are not religions in the strict sense of the word, but in fact different and distinct social orders, and it is only a dream that the Hindus and Muslims can ever evolve a common nationality.... To yoke together two such nations under a single state ... must lead to a growing discontent and final destruction of any fabric that may be so built up for the government of such a state." He argues that these two religions have different ethics, values, morals, worship methods, festivals, food habits, marriage systems, and allegiances to the God.

On March 22-23, 1940, Jinnah stated that, "The Hindus and Muslims belong to two different religious philosophies, social customs, literatures. They neither intermarry nor inter-dine together and, indeed, they belong to two different civilizations which are based mainly on conflicting ideas and conceptions. Their aspect on life and of life are different. It is quite clear that Hindus and Mussalmans derive their inspiration from diverse sources of history. They have different epics, different heroes, and different episodes. Very often the hero of one is a foe of the other and, likewise, their victories and defeats overlap. To yoke together two such nations under a single state, one as a numerical minority and the other as a majority, must lead to growing discontent and final **destruction of any fabric that may be so built for the government of such a state."**

The two religions are different as two belief systems and ideology. Islam is monotheistic, proselytizing, anti-idolatrous, fiercely doctrinal, aggressive, anti-secular, with strong ideas about heresy. Hinduism is pantheistic, pluralistic, non-violent, uninterested in converting other faiths, and rooted in the belief of Vigraha worship. They also believe in worship of multiple gods, expression of openness as seen in Khajuraho, different worship services, self-improvement, spirituality and yoga and meditation. Hinduism has never been interested in rooting out other religions, invading other countries because of their religious beliefs and submitting them to their way of life.

Hinduism does not believe that it has all the answers and does not call non-believers in Hinduism as kafirs or scums. Islam not only believes that those who do not accept Islam are 'kafirs', it also believes that it is Allah's wish that non-Islamic lands be treated as battlefields on which holy wars must be fought. Muslims believe that the entire world must be made Islamic, Darul Islam. To make it happen, Muslims carry out proselyting, terrorism, killings, don't allow Muslim girls to marry non-Muslims, produce more kids, declare jihad against non-Muslim countries, relying on Quran for justification. B R Ambedkar asserted that, "The brotherhood of Islam is not the universal brotherhood of man. It is brotherhood of Muslims for Muslims only. There is a fraternity but its benefits are confined to those within that corporation. For those who are outside the corporation, there is nothing but contempt and enmity" (Pakistan or Partition of India).

President Dr. Abdul Kalam said: "In 3000 years of our history, people from all over the world have come and invaded us, captured our lands conquered our minds. From Alexander onwards, the Greeks, the Portuguese, the Mughals, the British, the French, the Dutch, all of them came and looted us, took over what was ours. Yet we have not done this to any other nation. We have not conquered anyone. We have not grabbed their land, their culture, their history and tried to enforce our way of life on them. Why? Because we respect the freedom of others."

DEMAND FOR ISLAMIC STATE

In hindsight, anyone acquainted with the partition of India would agree that the struggle for separate Pakistan was solely based on religious terms. In August 1941, **Muhammad Al Jinnah** said while describing the distinctive feature of the Islamic state that "there is a special feature of the Islamic state which must not be overlooked. There, obedience is due to God and God alone, which takes practical shape in the observance of the Quranic principles and commands. In Islam, obedience is due neither to a king, nor to a parliament, nor to any other organization. It is the Quranic provisions which determine the limits of our freedom and restrictions in political and social spheres. In other words, the Islamic state is an agency for enforcement of the Quranic principles and injunctions".

He also stated, "There is no other way but to divide India. **Give Muslims their homeland and give Hindus Hindustan.**" Although the idea of creating a separate Pakistan was put forth by Sir Sayed Ahmed Khan, Mohamud Iqbal, Choudhary Rahmat Ali and others from 1930's, it was solidified by Muhammad Ali Jinnah who vehemently insisted on breaking India on religious lines.

Mohammud Iqbal explained to Jinnah his vision of a separate Muslim state in a letter sent on 21 June 1937: "A separate federation of Muslim Provinces, reformed on the lines I have suggested above, is the only course by which we can secure a peaceful India and save Muslims from the domination of Non-Muslims. Why should not the Muslims of North-West India and Bengal be considered as nations entitled to self-determination just as other nations in India and outside India are."

In 1939, a Hyderabad-born **Abul Ala Maududi** wrote in Jihad in the Way of Allah, that Islam wasn't a "hotchpotch of beliefs, prayers and rituals". Instead, it was "a revolutionary ideology which seeks to alter the social order of the entire world and rebuild it in conformity with its own (Islamic) tenets". **He concluded "if the Muslim Party commands enough resources, it will eliminate un-Islamic governments and establish the power of Islamic government in their place."**

The Indian wing of the **Jama'at-e-Islami asserts that all men "should refuse to acknowledge as valid all those allegiances which are not subservient to the allegiance of the One Allah and His Law"— presumably including the Indian state republic.**

In an interview with journalist **Beverley Nichols, Jinnah said, "In all these things, our outlook is not only fundamentally different but also opposed to Hindus. There is nothing in life that links us together. Our names, clothes, food, festivals, and rituals, all are different. Our economic life, our educational ideas, treatment of women, attitude towards animals, and humanitarian considerations, all are very different."**

Because of Jinnah's insistence and relentless argument for the separation of India into two nations, and his desire to be the Prime Minister, **Sardar Patel** realized there would be more tortures and more bloodshed flooding the Indian soil if separation is not granted. By early 1947, Patel started justifying the partition by saying, "In this way alone could we end the quarrel between Hindus and Muslims … if two brothers cannot stay together, they divide. After their separation, with their respective shares, they become friends. If, on the other hand, they are forced to stay together they tend to fight every day."

"Pakistan was founded because the Muslims of the subcontinent wanted to build up their lives in accordance with the teachings and traditions of Islam, because they wanted to demonstrate to the world that Islam provides a panacea to the many diseases which have crept into the life of humanity today.' Liaquat Ali Khan

Since there was a popular demand from all the religious leaders to change the Constitution to reflect the Islamization of Pakistan, the following Article 2A in inserted in the Constitution: "The Muslims shall be enable to order their lives in their individual and collective spheres in accordance with the teachings and requirements of Islam." The Constitution of Pakistan, part IX, article 227 says, **"All existing laws shall be brought in conformity with the Injunctions of Islam as laid down in the Quran and Sunnah**, in this Part referred to as the Injunctions of Islam, and no law shall be enacted which is repugnant to such Injunctions".

All across the globe, Muslims have been openly declaring death to the countries they live in and also announce that Islam will dominate, implement Sharia law, and kneel the other religious people to Allah. Few minutes of watching TV these days one cannot escape looking at the signs and banners by hundreds and thousands of Muslims such as "freedom can go to hell", "Islam will dominate the world", and "Shariah law - the true solution", "death to democracy", "Islam is coming to Denmark", "Islam is coming to America", "Behead those who insult Islam", as well as many other similar tag lines. They do not respect the majority views and take advantage of freedom of speech to over through the country that hosted them.

In Washington, DC, there is a group known as **As-Sabiqun**, and its leader is **Imam Abdul Alim Musa**. Its plans and goals are those of most Muslims across the globe. **Their goal is to see that the Islam will be able to control all human beings on Earth. Their mission is to make everybody submit to Islam, true to its real meaning. They passed some resolutions reflecting their commitment to dominate the world**:

> *"We resolve to shape the ideas, beliefs, and moral viewpoints of the people into an Islamic mold. Toward this end we will, insha'Allah, develop the comprehensive educational system that is necessary to inform, inspire, and direct the society toward Islamic revolution (or evolution)."*

> *"We resolve to utilize all the tools of Islam to develop an analysis and plan of action to totally and completely obliterate the hold of jahiliyyah and enable Islam to take complete control of our lives, and ultimately, the lives of all human beings on Earth."*

As late as January 31, 2016, Tamil Nadu Thowheed Jamath (TNTJ) vowed to end Idol worship and Hindu practices and all others which are not according to 'real Islam'. ISIS like organizations are sprouting across the country. Ant-Shirk Conference declared that it is sin to worship idols and they should be destroyed. All the speakers pledged to enforce Sharia law across India. They said they will use three weapons to destroy Hinduism: Shirk, Sharia and Jihad. Since the idol worship is against Islam, they said it should be banned.

They even posted many banners criticizing Idol worship near many Hindu Temples. Nobody was charged with creating disharmony in the community. Kamlesh Tiwari was arrested for saying Allah was homosexual. However, no action is taken against Muslim speakers who are criticizing Hindu practices of worship. Hindu days are numbered. It is a matter of a decade or less before Islam starts destroying the Temples, rampaging the Villages, raping the women, torturing Hindus and start forcing Hindus to convert to Islam or start killing Hindus.

The so-called intellectuals, artists, scientists, communists, secularists and cine artists have no comments and willfully hide from the scene to criticize this Anti Shirk Conference. Media will not talk about the growing threat to Bharath. All these are bought by Islamic Countries who may have paid them to shut their mouths.

In Islam, shirk (Arabic term) is the sin of practicing idolatry or polytheism, i.e. the deification or worship of anyone or anything other than the singular God i.e. Allah. Literally, it means ascribing or the establishment of "partners" placed beside God. It is the vice that is opposed to the virtue of Tawhid (monotheism).

SHARIA OR ISLAMIC LAW

Sharia, Islamic sharia or Islamic law is the basic Islamic legal system which derived its authority from the Islamic teachings of the Quran and the Hadith. The term sharia is an Arabic term to mean a body of moral and religious laws consistent with Islamic scriptures that may be opposed to human rights. **Sharia law is antithetical to the prevailing legal system and against the individual rights. If the Muslims are able to institute Sharia in India, the modern secular democracy we have known for years will be vanished from Bharath.** Every aspect of life is molded, guided, and dictated as per Islamic law that was adopted in Pakistan.

Sharia deals with many topics, including crime, politics, marriage contracts, clothing, religious prescriptions, sports, amusements and banking, as well as personal matters such as sexual intercourse, hygiene, diet, prayer, everyday etiquette and fasting. Adherence to Sharia has served as one of the distinguishing characteristics of the Muslim faith historically. In its strictest definition, Sharia is considered in Islam as the infallible law of Allah and it cannot be questioned.

Sharia is considered the law of Allah meaning that it is the best to be followed across the globe. Consequently, Muslims who believe firmly, fanatically and devoutly, are in constant struggle(jihad) with the people of the country and in continuous battle with their ruling government to establish Islamic Sharia. Islamic law has certainly aimed at "controlling the religious, social and political life of mankind in all its aspects, the life of its followers without qualification, and the life of those who follow tolerated religions to a degree that prevents their activities from hampering Islam in any way." 345

The all-embracing nature of Islamic law can be seen from the fact that it does not distinguish among ritual, law (in the European sense of the word), ethics, and good manners. In principle, this legislation controls the entire life of the believer and the Islamic community. It intrudes into every nook and corner, everything—to give a random sample—from the pilgrim tax, agricultural contracts, boarding and lodging of slaves, the invitation to a wedding, the use of toothpicks, the ritual fashion in which one's natural needs are to be accomplished, the prohibition for men to wear gold or silver rings, to the proper treatment of animals is covered."

Ibn Warraq (Why I am Not a Muslim)" described the unworthy principles as thus: intolerance of pagans, the call to violence and murder, the lack of equality for women and non-Muslims, the acceptance of slavery, barbaric punishments, and the contempt for human reason.

According to The Week, in Saudi Arabia (ironically, the head of the United Nations Human Rights Council), women cannot go anywhere without a chaperone, drive a car, "wear clothes or make-up that show off their beauty," interact with men they're not related to and many other oddities.

Crimes that are punishable by death in Saudi Arabia (often by public beheading or stoning), according to *Vocativ*, include adultery, "consensual gay sex with an adult," robbery, drug distribution and possession, apostasy, consumption of intoxicants, sorcery and witchcraft. One can also be executed for being gay and being an atheist.

According to a poll done by Pew Research Center in 2013, which asked Muslims of various countries (such as Albania, Russia, Bosnia, Kyrgyzstan, Turkey, Malaysia, Indonesia, Pakistan, Afghanistan, Palestine, Egypt, Jordan and others) about the penalty for apostasy, many of them supported the death penalty. In Egypt, 86 percent supported killing apostates.

Some examples of Sharia LAW:

Once Muslims have the power and make laws based on Quran and Hadiths, All Hindus will have to follow these rules, failing which can result in severe punishments and deaths. More than that, all Hindus would lose their freedom to express because that would be incompatible with Islamic Jurisprudence. It would have drastic effect on Bharath as a country for generations to come.

- Theft is punishable by amputation of the right hand
- Criticizing or denying any part of the Quran is punishable by death.
- Criticizing or denying Muhammad is a prophet is punishable by death.
- A Muslim who becomes a non-Muslim is punishable by death.
- A non-Muslim who leads a Muslim away from Islam is punishable by death.
- A non-Muslim man who marries a Muslim woman is punishable by death.
- A man can marry an infant girl and consummate the marriage when she is 9 years old.
- Girls' clitoris should be cut (per Muhammad's words in Book 41, Kitab Al-Adab, Hadith 5251).
- A woman can have 1 husband, but a man can have up to 4 wives; Muhammad can have more.
- A man can unilaterally divorce his wife but a woman needs her husband's consent to divorce.

⅄ A man can beat his wife for insubordination.

⅄ Testimonies of four male witnesses are required
to prove rape against a woman.

⅄ A woman who has been raped cannot
testify in court against her rapist(s).

⅄ A woman's testimony in court, allowed only in
property cases, carries half the weight of a man's.

⅄ A woman inherits half of what a male heir inherits.

⅄ A woman cannot drive a car, as it leads to fitnah (upheaval).

⅄ A woman cannot speak alone to a man
who is not her husband or relative.

⅄ Meat to be eaten must come from animals that
have been sacrificed to Allah - i.e., be Halal.

⅄ Muslims should engage in Taqiyya and lie
to non-Muslims to advance Islam.

⅄ A Muslim will not get the death penalty
if he kills a non-Muslim

⅄ A Muslim woman must cover every inch of her body,
which is considered "Awrah," a sexual organ.

⅄ All the Hindu Temples could be demolished
since they are against "idolaters."

⅄ Taharush is the Arab word that denotes the encircling
of girls and women by group of Muslim men for
sexual harassment, including assaults, groping and
even rapes. The seizure of Infidel females and their
use as sex slaves is sanctioned in the Koran.

Once the Muslims dominate the political structure in India, they
can pass the Sharia law and all Hindus can be subjected to the above
commands of Islam.

JIHAD

A number cases across India are reported about the extent of **Love
Jihad, Sex Jihad, Snake Jihad** and simple Jihad itself targeting Hindu
girls. Balbir Punj's investigative report revealed that there are "Several
instances of young Muslim boys enticing Hindu and Christian girls

in Kerala, Karnataka, Andhra and several other parts of the country with the show of wealth and promises of marriage and then, ferrying them to Kashmir and other places, converting them and recruiting them forcibly into Islamist Jihad came to light. Concerns at this Love Jihad were raised." Many of the Muslim boys change their identity and assume the Hindu names to trap the innocent girls, marry the, and sell them to other Arb countries. Even the Muslim girls conceal their identity as non-Muslims trapping gullible men into Islamic ideology and recruit them for ISIS.

Sex Jihad is being operated at two levels. Based on the stories we heard from reliable sources that the Muslim boys will be watching few families to find out some kind of discord in the young families and approach the young wives to help them emotionally and financially. The Muslim boys are urged to be tactful and clever in enticing these young married women, offer any amount of money, exploit them sexually and blackmail them with pictures taken hideously. At another level, several girls from different counties offer themselves to Islamists fighting in Syria. ISIS maintains sex jihad cells in the area where the women cannot escape and each girl served as many as 30-40 soldiers a day. These soldiers conduct sex jihad spree wherever they go and rape as many women as they want in their houses.

Hindus should recognize that the Hadith Al Bukahri stated that Muslims have the right to kill non-Muslims if they do not submit to Allah. They have the right to take over or destroy the property, siege the towns, massacre men, rape women, and enslave children. "Allah's Apostle said, "I have been ordered to fight the people till they say: 'None has the right to be worshipped but Allah'. And if they say so, pray like our prayers, face our Qibla and slaughter as we slaughter, then their blood and property will be sacred to us and we will not interfere with them except legally." (Bukhari 8.387)

Jihad is broadly defined to mean an offensive war waged against the non-Muslims to convert them to Islam or kill them if they fail to embrace Islam, mainly to establish Islamic Nation. Sayyid Abu Ala Maududi', in his book Al Jihad fil-lslam ("Jihad in Islam"), says that Muslims believe in Jihad because "Islam is all-encompassing,

the Islamic state was for all the world and should not be limited to just the homeland of Islam".

In no uncertain terms, Islam has been planning to destroy all states and governments anywhere on the face of the earth which are opposed to the ideology and programme of Islam. The goal of Islam is to set up a State which will be run by the Quranic principles and it should obey the injunctions of Allah. **No individual freedom of judgement is allowed in an Islamic State. Jihad should be used to press into action all forces at their disposal to eliminate and non-Islamic nations and establish Islamic State.**

Maududi taught that the destruction of the lives and property of others was lamentable (part of the great sacrifice of jihad), but that Muslims must follow the Islamic principle that it is better to "suffer a lesser loss to save ourselves from a greater loss". Though in jihad "thousands" of lives may be lost, this cannot compare "to the calamity that may befall mankind as a result of the victory of evil over good and of aggressive atheism over the religion of God."

Jihad is the major tool that Muslims use to dominate the world through terror, torture and death. It is the religious duty of all Muslims who are commanded to wage a holy war against infidels. Some of the Muslim leaders claim that Jihad is mainly a spiritual struggle to mislead the people, an examination of the commandments of Koran give a horrendous picture. Sura 9:29 commands the Muslims to "Fight those who do not believe in Allah or in the Last Day and who do not consider unlawful what Allah and His Messenger have made unlawful and who do not adopt the religion of truth from those who were given the Scripture - [fight] until they give the jizyah willingly while they are humbled."

Since 9/11 there have been an estimated 27, 704 deadly Muslim terrorist attacks across the globe. In India alone there are more than 40 terrorist attacks killing and injuring many Hindus. The objective of these Jihadi philosophy is not only to convert Hindus into Islam but most importantly to control the political sphere of India and try to enforce sharia law. With the help of media and the so called Hindu liberals, intellectuals and secularists abetting the process to establish more and more terrorist cells and ISIS operations. Tufail Ahmad observed that they routinely advise the government in foreign policies. "Many journalists based in Delhi are also on the payroll of the Pakistani Military's Inter-Services Intelligence (ISI), which creates and nurtures terrorist groups." Their loyalties are mortgaged with the enemy of the country where they make a living.

FATWA

All Hindus should be aware of the number of Fatwas being rendered by Ulemas (Islamic scholars) that leave punitive effect on the lives of Muslims. Once they reach a certain percentage in a given state or India, they can also force all Hindus to abide by these fatwas which have serious consequences for their lives and the freedom they are enjoying at present. Overwhelming decimation of Hindus may not be an exaggeration.

Fatwa is defined as a legal opinion or a decree issued by Islamic Scholars on a specific topic. Any Muslim can seek an opinion from Ulemas from an Islamic point view on any given topic and get directive for them to follow. The range of fatwas issued include death sentence to food, medicine, dress code, marital issues, divorce, entertainment, music, and host of other topics. Some of these fatwas are serious which may lead to killing of the individuals while others may not be enforceable.

Let us look at some of the fatwas issued that may have lasting impact on Muslims as well as Hindus. Fatwas are rendered against Solomon Rushdie's life for penning The Satanic verses considered insulting to Islam; Taslima Nasreen's life for writing a book Lajja considered un-Islamic; Surya Namaskar since it is against Islam to worship other than Allah; Vandemataram as some of the verses are considered against the tenets of Islam; noodles and ketchup for allegedly containing pig fat; actress Veena Malik for objectionable photos; firecrackers for misuse of money; Madhubala book by Harivansh Rai Bachchan for hurting Muslim sentiments; birthday celebrations because they are of western culture; professional models for being un-Islamic custom; Aroopa Alam the female journalist for going alone to interview ex-Chief Minister without being accompanied by a male relative; grown up girls for riding bicycles as it is bound to result in undue exposure; Shah Rukh Khan who was expelled from Islam for insulting his faith; A. R. Rahman for providing music to the movie on Muhammad: Messenger of God; and many other similar topics.

The primary motive for one-third of Muslim population to stay back in India is establish Islamic State either by waging war against Hindu infidels, threatening the political leaders or demanding special privileged to dominate the political structure to establish Islamic rule in India. On July 13, 2011, a group known as Darul Ulloom Deobad issued Fatwa in Nagpur on Hindus living in Muslim-majority areas demanding that they should either accept Islam or pay 10 percent of their income as 'Jizya.' **If they do not obey the Fatwa, Hindus should be prepared to fight. It is further stated that,** *"This country does not belong to Hindus now and it never belonged to Hindus. This country was ruled by Muslims for so many years ... that the areas where Muslims are in majority, the governance should be by Muslims as per 'Shariat' law."* **Hindus are in a precarious situation and they are ignoring it as if nothing is happening. They are becoming immune to the atrocities, fatwas and slow implementation of Sharia law in Bharath.**

REPEAT OF ISLAMIC ONSLAUGHT ON HINDUS
DO HINDUS EVER LEARN?

"Those who do not learn from history are doomed to repeat it"
George Santayana

It is the need of the hour for all Hindus to go back to the Islamic atrocious memory lane spanning close to ten centuries. What is it that the Hindus must learn from the history to avoid the same mistake our forefathers made? Was it so cruel that Hindus need to heed and take necessary steps to implement the two-nation theory where by all Muslims will go to either Pakistan or Bangladesh as was originally planned. Or are we going to ignore the past and negate the atrocious conquest of India by Muslims?

Throughout human history, Islam has been championing the philosophy of exclusivity to the extent of annihilations of entire human race. Muslims want to dominate the world by the SWORD. All non-Muslims are kefirs and infidel who can be dispensed with death to establish Dar-ul-Islam. Terror and Jihad are the means to achieve the goal of establishing Islamic nations across the globe. The have established 57 Islamic nations with the sword.

Hindus must learn from the history of Muslim dominance and mass killings of Hindus. Hindus should not negate, ignore or slight the past. History of Islamic barbarism should guide the Hindus and learn from the past to make sure the history is not repeated. Following are some of the detailed descriptions of persecution, torture, terrorism and barbarism. Learn from the history before it is too late.

Mohammud and Masood Ghazni (1000 – 1040 AD): *"The blood of the infidels flowed so copiously [at Thanesar] that the stream was discolored, notwithstanding its purity, and people were unable to drink it. The Sultan returned with plunder, which is impossible to count. Praise he to Allah for the honor he bestows on Islam and Muslims."*

"The Sultan gave orders that all the temples (in Mathura) should be burnt with naphtha and fire, and leveled with the ground." The pillage of the city continued for 20 days.

Shamsuddin Iltutmish destroyed an ancient temple at Vidisha (1240 AD). Badauni reports in his 'Muntakhab-ut-Tawarikh': *"Having destroyed the idol temple of Ujjain which had been built six hundred years previously, and was called Mahakal, he leveled it to its foundations, and threw down the image of Rai Vikramajit from whom the Hindus reckon their era, and brought certain images of cast molten brass and placed them on the ground in front of the doors of mosques of old Delhi, and ordered the people to trample them under foot."*

Amir Timur (1399) in his Tuzk-i-Timuri described the atrocities as follows:
"In a short space of time all the people in the fort were put to the sword, and in the course of one hour the heads of 10,000 infidels were cut off. The sword of Islam was washed in the blood of the infidels … They set fire to the houses and reduced them to ashes, and they razed the buildings and the fort to the ground."

At Sarsuti, the next city to be sacked, *"All these infidel Hindus were slain, their wives and children were made prisoners and their property and* *goods became the spoil of the victors... plundered every village, killed the men, and carried number of Hindu prisoners, both male and female".*

Firoz Shah Tughlaq described his terror on Hindus in the 'Sirat-i-FirozShahi" he himself wrote or dictated: *"he ordered the image of Jagannath to be perforated, and disgraced by casting it down on the ground. They dug out other idols which were ... laid in front of the mosques along the path of the Sunnis and the way of the 'musallis' (Muslim congregation for namaz) and stretched them in front of the portals of every mosque, so that the body and sides of the images might be trampled at the time of ascent and descent, entrance and exit, by the shoes of the feet of Muslims."* **Sirat-i-Firuz Shahs records: "Women with babies and pregnant ladies were haltered, manacled, fettered and enchained, and pressed as slaves into service in the house of every soldier."**

HINDU TEMPLES – WHAT HAPPENED TO THEM?

It is a two-volume book written by Sita Ram Goel, Arun Shourie, Harsh Narain, Jay Dubashi and Ram Swarup. The first volume, which was published in spring 1990, includes a list of 2000 mosques that were built on Hindu temples. Also included are the names of the original Hindu Temple and the Mosque – district-by-district and state-by-state. This list is based primarily on the books authored by Muslim historians of that period, the inscriptions of the mosques or personal investigation.

Let us look at few Temples that are so sacred to Hindus and how they have insulted, demeaned and destroyed these places of Hindu Worship to eliminate the Kafirs and make India an Islamic country.

Tajmahal is Tejo Mahal (Shiva Temple): Tajmahal is not an Islamic mausoleum but an ancient Shiva Temple known as Tejo Mahalaya, which the 5th generation Moghul emperor Shajahan grabbed from the then Maharaja of Jaipur. A visitor can find such symbols such as ruined defensive walls, hillocks, moats, cascades, fountains, majestic garden, hundreds of rooms, arcaded verandahs, terraces, multi stored towers, secret sealed chambers, guest rooms, stables, the trident (Trishul) pinnacle on the dome and the sacred, esoteric Hindu letter

"OM" carved on the exterior of the wall of the sanctum sanctorum now occupied by the cenotaphs. For detailed proof of this breathtaking discovery, you may read the well-known historian Shri. P. N. Oak's celebrated book titled "Tajmahal: The True Story ".

Sri Rama Temple at Ayodhya: On the site of the birth of Lord Rama, a magnificent temple devoted to Him was erected. However, Babur, fifteenth Mogul invader, brutalized India, destroyed Rama Temple, and raised a structure in its place, which he called Babri Masjid. The temple complex comprised of the Janmasthan of Sri Rama at Kot Ram Chander, the private apartments (mahal sarai) of King Dashrath and Sri Rama, and a temple and a kitchen popularly known as Sita Ki Rasoi, where tradition held that Sita (wife of Sri Rama) lived. All three were demolished and a mosque constructed upon it in 1528 A.D. For centuries Hindus tried to recover this auspicious site. In 2010, somewhat confusing verdict was issued by Allahabad High court accepting Ayodhya as a birth of Rama.

Krishna Janmasthala in Mathura: The Keshava Rai Temple at Mathura was built by Bir Singh Deo Bundela during Jahangir's time at a cost of thirty-three lakhs of rupees. The Dehra of Keshava Rai was one of the most magnificent temples ever built in India and enjoyed veneration of the Hindus throughout the land. **Alberuni observed that this temple was approximately 20 times larger than the largest mosque he ever saw in his life.**

Viswanath Temple in Benares was the target of Islamic Terror: Kashi Viswanath Temple is dedicated to Lord Shiva. It is popularly known as the 'Golden Temple' due to the gold plating done on its 15.5-meter high spire. One ton of gold donated by Maharaja Ranjit Singh has been used in the gold plating of the spire. The temple was destroyed by various invaders and was rebuilt in 1776 by Rani Ahilyabai of Indore. **The Mughal Emperor Aurangzeb who built the Gaynvapi Mosque in its place destroyed the Viswanath temple. Even today the western wall of the mosque shows the remnants of a temple, which had very intricate and fine artwork on it.**

The cruelty, brutality, barbarism, torture, destruction and blood bath inflicted on Hindus during Islamic Period in India by

Muslims should never be forgotten. Every Hindu should be taught and it should be mandatory by all educational institutions to transmit this horrific tale to the next generation. Regarding the Muslim conquest of India, let us remember the words of the following writers:

Will Durant: *"The Islamic conquest of India is probably the bloodiest story in history. It is a discouraging tale, for it is evident moral that civilization is a precious good/commodity, whose delicate complex of order and freedom, culture and peace, can at any moment be overthrown by barbarians invading from without or multiplying within."*

Koenraad Elst: *"The Muslim conquests, down to the 16th century, were for the Hindus a pure struggle of life and death. Entire cities were burnt down and the populations massacred, with hundreds of thousands killed in every campaign, and similar numbers deported as slaves. Every new invader made (often literally) hills of Hindus skulls. Thus, the conquest of Afghanistan in the year 1000 was followed by the annihilation of the Hindu population;* **the region is still called the Hindu Kush, i.e. Hindu slaughter. The Bahmani sultans (1347-1480) in central India made it a rule to kill 100,000 captives in a single day,** *and many more on other occasions. The conquest of the Vijayanagar empire in 1564 left the capital and large areas of Karnataka depopulated. And so on."*

Alain Danielou: *"From the time Muslims started arriving, around 632 AD, the history of India becomes a long, monotonous series of murders, massacres, spoliations, destructions.* **It is, as usual, in the name of 'a holy war' of their faith, of their sole God, that the barbarians have destroyed civilizations, wiped out entire races.***"*

ISLAMIZATION OF INDIA CONTINUES UNABATED TO DECIMATE HINDUS

Muslims are enjoying a vast number of privileges, freedom and special rights in India. No other Muslim country offers similar privileges. Hindus have been denied of these privileges in their own country. Uniform civil code does not apply them. Successive governments provided infinite array of minority appeasement in the fields of education, government positions, and religious practices which were denied to Hindus. India has tampered with the meritocracy and replaced it with mediocracy. They can issue fatwa demanding killing a certain person, assemble unlawfully on the streets by lakhs of people, drive Hindus from the villages by setting fire to their houses, threaten to kill all Hindus once they become majority, and question the guts of Hindus with no recourse from the government. They can break any law on the books while the government looks the other way encouraging them to commit even more crimes. **Tufail Ahmad rightly assessed high status that Muslims are enjoying in India:** *"Muslims in India enjoy complete political and religious liberty, a free legislative environment to undertake economic and educational initiatives, a vibrant television media and cinema that teach liberal coexistence, and access to a vast number of universities and institutes of modern education. There is absolutely no Muslim country that offers such a vast array of freedoms to its people."*

The government funds Madrassas who have become the centers of terrorism, or institutions of mediocre educational schools to train them in fundamental Islam instead of training them in the modern educational system to compete in the society. Government will send Muslim pilgrims to Hajj annually spending crores of rupees using mainly Hindu generated money, build Hajj Houses with the modern facilities in every State, construct Hajj terminals, and allot crores of rupees to celebrate Islamic festivals. Where do you see Hindu Houses and Hindu terminals for Hindus to visit their Hindu Temples such as Kasi Viswanath Temple, Balaji Temple, Amarnath Temple, and other pilgrimage centers. Government allows Hindus to sleep on the streets like beasts when they trek to their sacred temples.

Millatu Ibrahim of Perth Australia declared his hatred toward non-believers on his Facebook: 'We hate the Kuffar and everything that they worship. We hate their constitutions, we reject their way of life, we reject their political systems, we reject their parliaments, we reject their democracy, capitalism, liberalism, socialism, communism and every other filthy disbelieving 'ism' that has come to act as a hindrance from Islam, the pure religion of Allah to rule from the east to the west.'"

Let us summarize the perks the Muslims receive and how they are using them to perpetuate more terror, root out Hindu kaffirs and establish Caliphate. **Following are some examples where the Muslims influenced the government to provide more incentives or where they were not charged for breaking the law and order:**

- No action is taken against Muslims who refused to sing Vandemataram and Jana Gana Mana.
- Fatwas issued against Yoga and Suryanamaskaras
- U.P. government sanctioned 556 crores for promotion of Arabic and Persian languages and defund Sanskrit courses.
- Madrassas that are known for training terrorists are funded by the government.
- Unable to implement Article 370 to equal rights to Hindus in Kashmir
- Unable to enforce Uniform Civil Code for citizens of India
- No action is taken against the Muslims who block National Highways to conduct prayers
- Unable to curtail Bangladesh infiltration
- All Mosques urge Allah to destroy all non-believers in Islam.
- Mullahs receive salaries from State government, but not Hindu priests.
- Appeasement of Muslims continues with reservations in educational institutions and government jobs
- Force Hindu Temples either to be close or stop the Arthi during Muslim festivals
- Muslim lobby was able to revoke Narendra Modi's US Visa
- Muslims continue to increase their population day by day
- Nearly 500,000 Kashmiri Pundits were thrown out of their state by Muslims making the state as a Muslim State.
- Fails to act against Mullahs and other Muslim leaders who have been openly threatening Hindus, Hindu Temples and Murthy worship

- Incapable of monitoring the noise level of doing namaz by Mosques five times a day disturbing the sleep and peace of the neighborhoods
- No action is taken against people who hoist Pakistan flag and more recently ISIS flag.
- Failed to act against Muslim leaders who passed resolutions to ban Idol worship and Hindu rituals

GOVERNMENTS ARE FEEDING THE POISONOUS SNAKES

It is unfortunate that the successive governments since Independence have been bending their backs to please Muslims giving all sorts of perks making them to demand even more insatiable privileges while ignoring their open threats to break up India and making it an Islamic country. Hindus are losing their freedom of expression, being arrested for making certain statements. **Similar and even more insulting and bitter statements from Muslims receive no attention from the government. Selective, preferential treatment of Muslims blind the government's eyes and plug their ears.**

For example, Kamalesh Tiwari of Hindu Mahasabha, was arrested for reacting to the outrageous statement by Azam Khan, the UP minister for urban development, who was quoted as saying, "many RSS leaders are unmarried because they are homosexuals." No action was taken against the Azam Khan branding all RSS people as homosexuals. In a different case, Police arrested Hindu Sena chief Vishnu Gupta in connection with ransacking of a Pakistan International Airlines (PIA) office in New Delhi, Times of India reported.

Gupta, who heads the Hindu Sena – a group of right-wing Hindu hardliners – claimed responsibility for the vandalism at PIA's office and vented anger at Pakistan, holding it responsible for the siege at the Pathankot air base as well as at the attack on the Indian consulate in the Afghan city of Mazar-i-Sharif recently.

"Gupta has been arrested under Sections 120B (being party to a criminal conspiracy), 147 (rioting), 149 (being the member of unlawful assembly guilty of offence committed in prosecution of common object), 427 (mischief causing damage to property) and 452 (house-trespass after preparation for hurt, assault or wrongful restraint) of IPC," the police was quoted as saying.

No such arrests would be forthcoming for Muslims who freely commit various crimes, insult Hindu Gods, destroy Hindu deities, and openly challenge Hindu guts. They explicitly made several statements challenging the government to take an action. Indifference to these Muslim taunts and government inaction encouraging the Muslim leaders and terrorist organizations to plan even bigger schemes to make the government to kneel to its feet.

ISLAMIC TERROR CAUSING HAVOC ALL ACROSS INDIA

On September 3, 2014 **Ayman al-Zawahiri, head of Al Qaeda**, formed an Indian branch known as Qaedat al-Jihad. This group, "is the fruit of a blessed effort of more than two years to gather the mujahedeen in the Indian subcontinent into a single entity." **This group would fight for an Islamic state and impose Sharia laws across the Asian region including India, which they consider "was part of the Muslims' territories before it was occupied by the infidel enemy.** Their mission is to "raise the flag of jihad and the return of the Islamic rule in the subcontinent, which one day used to be part of the land of the Muslims until the infidel enemy took it over and divided it."

Another deadly group known as **Islamic State, popularly known as ISIS**, has been planning to take over large parts of the world, including almost the entire Indian subcontinent, within the next five years. **Andrew Hosken** showed an alarming map in a new book entitled **"Empire of Fear: Inside the Islamic State ISIS"** about this most dreaded terror group. According to the map, the Indian subcontinent which would be known as '**Khurasan**' would be taken over within the next five years. They have written a 268-page manual describing the methods of extreme brutality and inhuman violence to achieve a vast Islamic State as envisioned by Isis leader Abu Bakr al-Baghdadi: "Rush O Muslims to your state! Yes, it is your state. Rush, because Syria is not for the Syrians, and Iraq is not for the Iraqis. The earth is

Allah's." He further goes on to say that "Islam never was for a day the religion of peace …[but] of war. Your Prophet …was ordered with war till Allah is worshipped alone." The author concludes that "Every atrocity, torture, assassination and they are simply a means to one overpowering obsession – to destroy nation states, seize territory and build a caliphate from the ashes."

On July 28, 2015, USA Today newspaper which has the document entitled "**A Brief History of the Islamic State Caliphate (ISC), The Caliphate According to the Prophet,**" found this sentence: 'Accept the fact that this caliphate will survive and prosper until it takes over the entire world and beheads every last person that rebels against Allah … This is the bitter truth, swallow it." The document also warned that preparations are underway for an attack in India and predicts that it might provoke an apocalyptic confrontation with USA. **Bruce Riedel**, a senior fellow with the Brookings Institution who served more than 30 years in the CIA said striking in India would magnify the Islamic State's stature and threaten the stability of the region, and "Attacking in India is the Holy Grail of South Asian jihadists."

The **ISIS** is preparing to "to trigger a war in India" to provoke an Armageddon-like 'end of the world," according to a document found in Pakistan. ISIS has been working tirelessly to unite dozens of factions of the Pakistani and Afghan Taliban into a single army of terror, the daily said. "It includes a never-before-seen history of the Islamic State, details chilling future battle plans, urges al-Qaeda to join the group and says the Islamic State's leader should be recognized as the sole ruler of the world's 1 billion Muslims under a religious empire called a 'caliphate'." The ISIS document explicitly mentioned about the Dadri lynching of 50-year-old Muslim by Hindus over suspicion of eating beef accusing Modi as a "right-wing Hindu nationalist who worships weapons and wants a movement to kill cow eaters." Now ISIS is planning to use this incident and create chaos by staging some protests and also killing cows and eating beef. ISIS is planning to protect those Muslims who allegedly were being beaten by Hindus for eating beef and carry on the movement against Hindus who may have killed Muslims who ate beef. They are going to orchestrate the whole scene to create this beef controversy and take the law into their own hands by rampaging on Hindus. They are hatching a number of schemes to create mayhem forcing the two religions to engage in a war like situation.

In November 2015, **Madhav Nalapat,** based on a number of sources, wrote that India was "very much within the target list of ISIS because of the informal and clandestine connections between that terror constellation and ultra-Wahhabist mid-level officers in the ISIS", who are eager to ensure a major strike in India "so as to do further damage to the social and economic fabric of the country". His sources stated that, "it may become necessary for Prime Minister Narendra Modi to take personal charge of the defenses against ISIS by having security services and the military "work out swift responses to a possible mass terror attack" by ISIS.

MODI'S LIFE THREATENED

On January 19 2016, Goa Police received an anonymous letter purportedly signed by ISIS threatening to kill Prime Minister Narendra Modi and Defense Minister Manohar Parrikar. There is growing activities in the internet and across India conducted by ISIS who is being taken seriously by the governments at all levels. **"ISIS threat is real. As per our input, the days leading to the Republic Day is crucial. We have instructed everyone to be alert against the possibility of 'lone wolf attack' anywhere in the country," a senior government official said.**

Preparations for an attack on India are under way as the threats to strike at the Republic day are mounting. As of January 23 National Intelligence Agency (NIA) and other intelligence agencies arrested 14 people belonging to 'Janood-ul-Khalifa-e-Hind' (Army of Caliph of India), who were allegedly planning to attack ahead of Republic day function. Intelligence agencies appear to have credible information about ISIS which engaged in radicalizing Indian youth by inspiring and encouraging them to join the terrorist organization. NIA claimed that the accused were regularly in touch with active members of ISIS in Syria through Internet chatting via 'Skype', 'Signal' and 'Trillion' and were also using the social networking sites to motivate young men to join the feared terror outfit which has captured vast swathes in Syria and Iraq.

The intention of ISIS and all other Islamic Terrorist organizations is to establish caliphate in India by Killing non-Muslims, sabotaging temples, looting our temples, raping Hindu women, ransacking villages, creating acts that instigate Hindus to react, destroying huge buildings, and creating fear among Hindus. Before the 2016 Republic Day functions letters were send threatening the lives of Prime Minister **Narendra Modi,** Ex-Defence Minister **Manohar Parrikar,** and Ex-France President **François Hollande** who was attending Republic Day function. Earlier similar threats were issued against the lives of Sri Sri Ravi Shankar, and Swami Baba Ramdev.

"The Islamic State was reportedly planning to attack malls and shopping complexes, including Select Citywalk, DLF Promenade and the Great India Place. Para-military forces were deployed across the city, security blockades are set up on many roads to screen vehicles, high-rise buildings near Lutyens' Delhi were shut down and sniffer dogs were on the prowl in metro stations."

Why ISIS is so violent in killing non-Muslims, eliminating apostates, destroying villages, and planning to establish caliphates across the globe. Where do these people get the idea of establishing Islamic supremacy by converting all nations into Islamic countries? **It is Quran that is the source and inspiration for ISIS to wage war against the mankind. It is foolhardy to think that they are extremists and terrorist and they do not represent Islam. They, in fact, interpret the Quranic commands literally and follow the barbaric leadership as followed by the prophet Mohammad.**

BHARAT WILL SOON BE LIKE MALDA

Muslims can get away with any number of insulting statements against Hindus. By blocking the roads to enter the Hindu Temples, banning Hindu worship services, killing Hindus, threatening the lives of Hindus and Hindu traditions by issuing fatwas, raising Pakistan flags on the Indian soil, ransacking Hindu houses, molesting and raping Hindu girls, forcing Hindu girls to convert to Islam, making statements provoking Hindus to react, without any recourse from the government. Some of the state governments for their selfish interest to get elected, give special privileges to the Muslims, allow them to break law with no recourses. They even order police to ignore any complaints from Hindus and ban certain politicians to enter the state to speak at the meetings.

That is what happened in the case of Malda. No government was able to stop it. Police became a mere spectator. Muslims know that no government has guts to arrest them, put them in prison and allow the legal system to take its course. Knowing that their activities will not be challenged or curtailed, with reinforced confidence and power, they galvanize their troupes to repeat the terror and violence on the lives of Hindus. Muslims were protesting against the statement made by **Kamalesh Tiwari** who was reacting to the Muslims statement that all RRS people were homosexuals. When Tiwari reacted to that statement by saying that Mohammad was the first homosexual, the hell broke loose. Muslims across the country expressed outrage over his statement and demanded that Tiwari be hanged. About 150,000 Muslims gathered in Kaliachak's Chowringhee area. **Ipsika Chakravarty**, tne things turned ugly. Protesters blocked the highway and got into an altercation with a Border Security Force vehicle. Shots were fired in the air .... By all accounts, an angry mob broke away from the rally and headed toward the police station, where they set fire to about two dozen vehicles and ransacked the thana (district). The mob swept on to Baliadanga, a quiet locality behind the police station, inhabited mostly by Hindu families. A few shops were burnt and some houses stoned. Nineteen-year-old Tanmoy Tiwari, returning home from the market, took a bullet in a leg. Another Baliadanga resident claimed his 13-year-old daughter was punched when she tried to stop the mob from burning a motorcycle parked in their portico. Suddenly, a religious protest seemed to take on an ugly communal hue." (Scroll. in; January 12, 2016). The protesters had set on fire about two dozen vehicles and attacked the Kaliachak police station, setting it on fire.

Mamata government is determined to make West Bengal a Muslim State. The British Newspaper "The Sunday Guardian" says that Mamata Banerjee is allowing Bangladeshi Muslims to enter freely

into India and create fear among Hindus by allowing Muslims to rampage the villages and driving people to be replaced by **Bangladesh Muslims.** Counterfeit currency is all over the state bribing the politicians and compromising on the security of the state and India itself. Even the Congress leaders were concerned about this influx. Mamata is arresting the activists while allowing these terrorists roam freely across the country. Will Hindus be ever safe and secure with these Muslin terrorists?

VIOLENT VERSES FROM QURAN

Many Political Leaders across the world and Muslim leaders claim that the atrocities committed by ISIS do not represent Islam. Every time there is a terror attack in such places as Jakarta, Istanbul, San Bernardino, Paris, Pathankot (India) by ISIS, it is redundantly repeated by the apologists that these attacks do not represent Islam, the religion of peace. U.S. President Barack Obama says ISIS "is recognized by no government, nor the people it subjugates. ISIL is a terrorist organization, pure and simple. And it has no vision other than the slaughter of all who stand in its way." Fadel Boula, Iraqi journalist, contradicted Obama and said that ISIS and other terror organizations "are motivated by an extremist Salafi (Muslim) ideology and claim that their atrocities represent Allah's will and directives."

"The terror that is shaking the world today is not a natural disaster like a tornado, a thunderstorm or an earthquake, and it is not perpetrated by savage tribes," Boula wrote. "It is perpetrated by people who enlist [because they are] inspired by a religious ideology. [These people] advocate enforcing and spreading [this ideology as a set of] dogmatic principles that must be imposed by the force of the sword, and which [mandate] killing, expulsion and destruction wherever they go."

There are over one hundred verses in the Quran that call for war, many of which are directed specifically at nonbelievers. According to Quran, it is abundantly clear that Allah, with no uncertain terms calls for the mutilation and slaughter of all those who oppose Islam. **Some of these verses describe the violent nature of Islam in a very graphic manner as follows:**

"The punishment of those who wage war against Allah and His messenger and strive to make mischief in the land is only this, that they should be murdered or crucified or their hands and their feet should be cut off on opposite sides or they should be imprisoned; this shall be as a disgrace for them in this world, and in the hereafter they shall have a grievous chastisement." (5:33)

"I will cast terror into the hearts of those who disbelieve. Therefore, strike off their heads and strike off every fingertip of them." (8:12)

"As for the unbelievers for them garments of fire shall be cut and there shall be poured over their heads boiling water whereby whatever is in their bowels and skins shall be dissolved and they will be punished with hooked iron-rods." (22:9)

"When you meet the unbelievers, strike off their heads; then when you have made wide slaughter among them, carefully tie up the remaining captives." (47:4)

"Slay them wherever you find them. Drive them out of the places from which they drove you. Idolatry is worse than carnage." (2:191)

"When the sacred months are over, slay the idolaters wherever you find them. Arrest them, besiege them, and lie in ambush everywhere for them." (9:5)

"Prophet, make war on the unbelievers and the hypocrites and deal rigorously with them. Hell shall be their home: an evil fate." (9:73)

"Believers, make war on the infidels who dwell around you. Deal firmly with them. Know that God is with the righteous." (9:123)

"And KILL them (the unbelievers) wherever you find them, and drive them out from whence they drove you out, and persecution is severer than slaughter, and do not fight with them at the Sacred Mosque until they fight with you in it, but if they do fight you, then slay them; such is the recompense of the unbelievers." (Sura 2, verse 191).

"Let not the believers take the unbelievers for friends rather than believers; and whoever does this, he shall have nothing of (the guardianship of) Allah, but you should guard yourselves against them,

guarding carefully; and Allah makes you cautious of (retribution from) Himself; and to Allah is the eventual coming." (Sura 3, verse 28).

"And whoever does not believe in Allah and His Apostle, then surely We have prepared burning fire for the unbelievers." (Sura 48, verse 13).

These and many other verses in Quran, Hadiths and many Mullahs have been providing incentive and inspiration for ISIS to declare war on India. With so many intellectuals, liberals, secularists, communists and media harping on the intolerance of Hindus, the terrorist organizations are receiving even more stimulus to create fear and rampage the country. **It is time to discuss about the implementation of two nation theory or announce the benign dictatorship to preserve the rich cultural heritage of Hinduism. Longer we wait, more blood will flow on the streets. We should learn from the history of long Muslim conquest of India. With Al Quaid, ISIS and other terrorist organizations' explicit plan to make India a Caliphate; Quran's open declaration of killing all the non-believers; and disunity among Hindus; India has no future unless sudden and speedy action is taken to protect the country from Muslims.**

ISLAM IS INCOMPATIBLE WITH DEMOCRACY

Islamic law based on Quran, Hadiths and Sunnah is totally incompatible with democracy. Allah is the head of the theocratic order of governance. People have no choice except to obey, surrender and submit to Allah. Democracy will be thrown out and replaced with Caliphate. Once these democracies are overthrown, strict Islamization of the country will be imposed through Sharia law denying all the rights to non-Muslims. **Ann Elizabeth Mayer** observed that Islamization "did much to eliminate due process, to erode the independence of the judiciary, to place legal proceedings under the control of political leaders, and to convert courts into instruments of repression and intimidation. Thus, in all three countries Islamization became associated with a decline in the quality of the administration of justice."

American scholar **Jamal Badawi** states that it is the duty of Muslims to bring about Islamic rule: *"The Qur'an is full of direct and indirect, implicit and many times explicit indications that show that the establishment of the Islamic order is a requirement on Muslims whenever possible."* He also scoffs at secularism: *"If a Muslim believes that there is any human being who has the right to make laws other than Allah then obviously this is total divergence from the path of Islam. Or any person who believes that secularism is superior to the law of Allah, he's violating the basic Quranic tenets."*

Islamic scholar **Sayyid Abul Ala Maududi** writes that *"Islam wishes to destroy all States and Governments anywhere on the face of the earth which are opposed to the ideology and programme of Islam regardless of the country or the Nation that rules it. Islam requires the earth – not just a portion – but the whole planet."*

Sahih Muslim Book 019, Hadith Number 4294, clearly directs the Muslims to fight with nonbelievers. *"When you meet your enemies who are polytheists, invite them to three courses of action. If they respond to any one of these, you also accept it and withhold yourself from doing them any harm. Invite them to (accept) Islam; if they respond to you, accept it from them and desist from fighting against them ... If they refuse to accept Islam, demand from them the Jizya. If they agree to pay, accept it from them and hold off your hands. If they refuse to pay the tax, seek Allah's help and fight them."* **Non-Muslims are intended to be surrendered to Islam.**

Most of the Muslim countries declared themselves as theocratic governments with Allah alone as their head. Allah's law is interpreted by a ruling body of clerics. The governments are totally governed by Islamic sharia law. There is no room for a secular political system in which all people are treated as equals. In Muslim societies, with a few exceptions, modernization has been synonymous with dictatorship, repression, and corruption—in short, social injustice.

Many Western experts assert that the two are incompatible and a truly democratic system will never succeed in a Muslim country. It is certainly true that most Islamic regimes are authoritarian and have not been democratically elected. In places like Sudan, Iran under Khomeini, and Taliban-controlled Afghanistan, Islam has been used in ways that have led to repression, violence, and injustice. Now, ISIS using Islam as the source of inspiration to wage war against all non-Muslim countries as well as Muslim countries considered moderate claimed to have defied Allah.

Church and state are one in Islam. Islam of course knows of no such separation. There is no sacred-secular distinction in the Muslim world. Everything is religious and everything is political. As Rodney Stark wrote, "Muhammad was not only the Prophet, he was head of state. Consequently, Islam has always idealized the fusion of religion and political rule, and sultans have usually also held the title of caliph" (The Victory of Reason).

ISLAM IS INCOMPATIBLE WITH SECULARISM?

Secularism is incompatible with Islam. In secularism you do not give any preference to any particular religion. It is up to the individual to practice whatever faith he chooses. **Ernest Gellner** commented: **"To say that secularization prevails in Islam is not contentious. It is simply false. Islam is as strong now as it was a century ago. In some ways, it is probably much stronger." He goes on to elaborate on this point by saying that Islam "totally and effectively defies the secularization thesis ... [and] there is no indication that it will succumb to secularization in the future either."**

Muslims oppose secularism because of their firm belief that there is no God but Allah. Unlike Hinduism, Muslims believe that Islam came into being to replace the previous manifestations of other faiths and govern them, control them and wipe them out. That was the command of Allah. They believe that Islam affects all aspects of their life such as marital affairs, role of women, business, eating habits, manner of sleeping, dress code, work ethics, prayer, and other aspects of life. Islam should also have complete control on the political system of the nation. Government should operate as per the Sharia law and everybody should obey and surrender to Allah.

Let us start with the **Indian Constitution**. During the dark days of Emergency in 1976 'Sovereign Democratic Republic' was changed to '**Sovereign Socialist Secular Democratic Republic**'.

Sovereign means self-governing, our governments have replaced it with selfish governing; socialist means collective, now it is replaced by corruption; secular means irreligious while our government uses it as anti-Hindu. These three deadly S's are destroying the country and chipping away the fundamental freedom of Hindus. Their life is in persistent danger and their future is in perennial gloom.

SECULARISM – WHAT DOES IT MEAN?

According to **Thomas Jefferson** "Erecting the 'wall of separation between church and state,' therefore, is absolutely essential in a free society."

Dr. S. Radhakrishnan, former President of India, observed: "When India is said to be a secular state, it does not mean that we reject the reality of the unseen spirit or the relevance of religion to life or that we exalt irreligion. It does not mean that secularism itself becomes a positive religion or that State assumes divine prerogatives. We hold that not one religion should be given preferential status."

Donald E. Smith, Professor of Political Science in Pennsylvania University provided what he regarded as a working definition of a secular state. This was in his book, "India as a Secular State." "The secular State is one which guarantees individual and corporate freedom of religion, deals with the individual as a citizen irrespective of his religion, is not constitutionally connected to a particular religion, nor does it seek to promote or interfere with religion."

REJECTION OF SECULARISM:

Muslims do not see secularism as a method of governing the nation where every individual is allowed to practice their faith. Many Islamic countries rejected the secular concept of government as can be witnessed by some of the statements by political leaders.

In winter of 1970, Ayatollah Khomeini observed: "This slogan of the separation of religion and politics and the demand that Islamic scholars not intervene in social and political affairs has been formulated and propagated by the imperialists; it is only the irreligious who repeat them. Were religion and politics separate in the time of the Prophet.... Did there exist, on one side, a group of clerics, and opposite it, a group of politicians and leaders? ... These slogans and claims have been advanced by the imperialists and their political agents in order to prevent religion from ordering the affairs of this world and shaping Muslim society, and at the same time to create a rift between the scholars of Islam, on the one hand, and the masses and those struggling for freedom and independence, on the other. They have thus been able to gain dominance over our people and plunder our resources, for such has always been their ultimate goal."

Similarly, in the summer of 2007, the deputy prime minister of Malaysia, **Najib Razak**, emphatically declared that Malaysia was not a secular state but an Islamic one. "Islam is the official religion and we are an Islamic state. But as an Islamic state, it does not mean that we don't respect non-Muslims," he told reporters after officiating at the International Conference on the Role of Islamic States in a Globalized World in Kuala Lumpur. **When asked by one reporter whether Malaysia was not seemingly moving toward being a secular state, Razak fired back: "I have to correct you. We have never, never been secular because being secular by the Western definition means separation of the Islamic principles in the way we govern a country**. We have never been affiliated with that position. We have always been driven by our adherence to the fundamentals of Islam. So, your premise is wrong." Mushir-ul-Haq also stated that Indian Muslims are not secular and in fact anti-Hindu; in fact, Islam is incompatible with Hinduism.

Yusuf Al-Qaradawi says that "For Muslim societies, the acceptance of secularism means something totally different; i.e. as Islam is a comprehensive system of worship (ibadah) and legislation (Shariah), the acceptance of secularism means abandonment of Shariah, a denial of the divine guidance and a rejection of Allah's injunctions; It is indeed a false claim that Shariah is not proper to the requirements of the present age. The acceptance of a legislation formulated by humans means a preference of the humans' limited knowledge and experiences to the divine guidance: "Say! Do you know better than Allah?" (2:140).

Secularism is at odds with Islamic political theory because the state and religion has to be intertwined. Whatever the religion teaches to be prohibited, the state must also prohibit. Secularism and western democracy allows elected individuals to formulate laws in parliament. In Islam, the caliphate recognizes Allah's role as the supreme legislator meaning that his law is the supreme law. No law can supersede or overrule his law. The reason why most Islamic countries are not secular is due to the stiff opposition to secularism. Most Muslims see secularism as an innovation and a western invention. **In fact, secularism can be interpreted as shirk which considers worship of any God other than Allah as sin, which the Lord will never forgive. Thus, secularism hasn't achieved mainstream support in the Islamic world.**

One of the foremost Islamic scholars, **Yusuf Qaradawi**, says Allah knows better than anybody. According to him: "Islam is a comprehensive system of worship (ibadah) and legislation (Shariah), the acceptance of secularism means abandonment of Shariah, a denial of the divine guidance and a rejection of Allah's injunctions; It is indeed a false claim that Shariah is not proper to the requirements of the present age. The acceptance of a legislation formulated by humans means a preference of the humans' limited knowledge and experiences to the divine guidance: "Say! Do you know better than Allah?" (2:140). For this reason, the call for secularism among Muslims is atheism and a rejection of Islam. Its acceptance as a basis for rule in place of Shariah is downright riddah. The silence of the masses in the Muslim world about this deviation has been a major transgression and a clear-cut instance of disobedience which produces a sense of guilt, remorse, and inward resentment, all of which have generated discontent, insecurity, and hatred among committed Muslims because such deviation lacks legality."

ISLAM ABHORS HUMAN RIGHTS

Islam would not recognize the Universal Declaration of Human Rights (UDHR) and it is incompatible with the human rights, dignity and respect. Unless these rights are couched in Islamic

doctrine, they are unacceptable. In fact, Muslims have no rights; Quran emphasizes only the obligations to his Allah.

Cairo Declaration on Human Rights in Islam (CDHRI) was developed by 45 Muslim countries especially for the adherents of Islam in response to UDHR which emphasizes the universal rights for all human beings irrespective of religion, race or sex. Article 24 of the declaration states: "All the rights and freedoms stipulated in this Declaration are subject to the Islamic Sharia." Article 19 also says: "There shall be no crime or punishment except as provided for in the Sharia." Article 10 of the Declaration states: "Islam is the religion of unspoiled nature. It is prohibited to exercise any form of compulsion on man or to exploit his poverty or ignorance in order to convert him to another religion or to atheism."

UN Iran's Representative, Said Rajaie-Khorassani argued that these human rights cannot be used to judge Islam's human rights. He stated that, "It recognized no authority . . . apart from Islamic law . . . conventions, declarations and resolutions or decisions of international organizations, which were contrary to Islam, had no validity in the Islamic Republic of Iran. . . . The Universal Declaration of Human Rights, which represented secular understanding of the Judeo-Christian tradition, could not be implemented by Muslims and did not accord with the system of values recognized by the Islamic Republic of Iran; his country would therefore not hesitate to violate its provision.

Iranian Constitution provided sweeping constitutional justifications for infringing on rights and denying freedom. Article 4 of the Iranian Constitution, quoted here, illustrates what Islamization meant for Iran's rights' guarantees:

"All civil, penal, financial, economic, administrative, cultural, military, political laws and regulations, as well as any other laws or regulations, should be based on Islamic principles. This principle will in general prevail over all of the principles of the constitution, and other laws and regulations as well. Any judgment in regard to this will be made by the clerical members of the Council of Guardians."

President Zia of Pakistan stated in 1983 insisted on his commitment to pursue Islamization as the justification of his presidential powers and abolition of constitutional rights.

"One basic point that emerges from a study of the Quranic verses and the Prophet's sayings . . . is that as long as the Amir or the head of State . . . abides by the injunctions of Allah and his Prophet (PBUH) ["peace and blessings upon him"] his obedience becomes mandatory for his subjects or the people, irrespective of the personal dislike that someone may harbor for the Amir or any of his actions. . .. Not only in my opinion but also in the opinion of legal experts and scholars, my Government, too, is a constitutional Government, which has been acting upon the tenets of Islam . We are . . . devout Muslims. I concede, and I am proud of it."

A K Brohi, former Minister of Law and Religious Affairs in Pakistan said that, "The individual, if necessary has to be sacrificed in order that the life of the organism be saved. Collectivity has a special sanctity attached to it in Islam."

"The Western liberal emphasis upon freedom from restraint is alien to Islam . . .. Personal freedom [in Islam] lies in surrendering to the Divine Will."

Failure to surrender their personal freedom to Allah they may face severe consequences. Recently the ISIS jihadist group has reportedly beheaded a teenager listening to the pop music and shot dead two others for missing the Friday prayers in Mosul. The case of this boy listening to Western music was referred to Sharia court which issued a decision to execute. One eye witness reported that the boy's parents were forced to witness the beheading of their son.

HUMAN RIGHTS OF ISLAMIC WOMEN

Women are allowed limited and conditional freedom confined only to household matters. They are denied many rights that are allowed under international law. They are given subordinate and inferior role denying equal rights. A wife must always obey her husband, should not go against his wishes, should not leave the house without husband's permission, take care of husband's needs, invite quests only with husband's agreement, forbidden from participating in sports, uphold family honor, and stay secluded.

Women are inferior under Islamic law as their testimony is worth only half of that of a man. They cannot marry whom they want. They are commanded to marry only Muslims. The rights of divorce for women are not the same as for men and they are not entitled to maintenance. Women are prevented from acquiring education, are not allowed to choose their work in Islam, and forbidden to work outside their home. They may be beaten by their husbands as per Islam. They are subjected to gruesome mutilation of genitals.

Sultan Hussein Tabandeha asserted that "Women are therefore ordered not to do what would titillate men's feelings of lust. She must therefore **cover her body**, and not show her adornments of beauty or of jewelry or make-up to the outside world or to strangers. She must not frequent, more than absolutely essential, public gatherings attended by men. She must spend much time at home." It is based on Quranic verse 4:34; "Men are in control of women, because Allah hath made them one of them to excel the other, and because they [the men] spend their property [for the support of women]." ...And reveal not their adornment save such as is outward; and let them cast their veils over their bosoms (Qur'an 24:31).

Riffat Hassan: The Quranic description of man and woman in marriage: "They are your garment/And you are their garments" (Surah 2: Al-Baqarah: 187) implies closeness, mutuality, and equality. However, Muslim culture has reduced many, if not most, women to the position of puppets on a string, to slave-like creatures whose only purpose in life is to cater to the needs and pleasures of men. Not only this, it has also had the audacity and the arrogance to deny women direct access to God. It is one of Islam's cardinal beliefs that each person -man or woman- is responsible and accountable for his or her individual actions. How, then, can the husband become the wife's gateway to heaven or hell?

At only a 10% population in Philippines, Muslims do what they do everywhere: ethnic cleansing, invasion, terrorism, rape, murders and beheadings in efforts to convert people and try to take over the country and create a separate Islamic state.

ISLAM VS HINDUISM / MONOTHEISM VS POLYTHEISM

"Islamic rule in India as a "colonial experiment" was "extremely violent", and "the Muslims could not rule the country except by systematic terror. Cruelty was the norm - burnings, summary executions, crucifixions or impalements, inventive tortures. Hindu temples were destroyed to make way for mosques. On occasion, there were forced conversions. If ever there were an uprising, it was instantly and savagely repressed: houses were burned, the countryside was laid waste, men were slaughtered and women were taken as slaves." **(Fernand Braudel: A History of Civilization)**

Hindus believe in and practice polytheism, worship of variety of Gods and Goddesses. Islam embraces monotheism believing in only God, that is Allah. Polytheism is inherently pluralistic, humanistic, tolerant, accommodative, peaceful and equalitarian. In contract, monotheism is innately intolerant, violent, exclusive, dictatorial and non-accommodative. From the inception of Islam, it's main mission is to get rid of polytheism from the Arab world. This monotheistic arrogance spread the hatred across the globe.

There are no compelling arguments in favor of monotheism, as opposed to polytheism, neither philosophically nor scientifically. Indeed, as **David Hume** showed, there is nothing inherently absurd in polytheism. And as to the Koranic hint at the argument from design, Hume showed that all hypotheses regarding the origins of the universe were equally absurd. **David Hume argued that unlike monotheism, polytheism is pluralistic in nature, unbound by doctrine, and therefore far more tolerant than monotheism, which tends to force people to believe in one faith." He believes that polytheism is more conducive in maintaining peace and virtue in society. It's tolerant diversity of ideas and practices and readily accessible to chosen gods, encourages "activity, spirit, courage, magnanimity, love of liberty, and all the virtues which aggrandize a people."** David Hume has argued that monotheism is less pluralistic and thus less tolerant than polytheism because the former stipulates that people pigeonhole their beliefs into one. In the same vein, Auguste

Comte argues, **"Monotheism is irreconcilable with the existence in our nature of the instincts of benevolence" because it compels followers to devote themselves to a single Creator.**

Monotheism is not only inherently intolerant but it promotes violence and terror. We know from the Koran itself the hatred preached at all kinds of belief labeled "idolatry" or "polytheism." Dictionary of Islam acknowledges that Muslim writers are "unanimous in asserting that no religious toleration was extended to the idolaters of Arabia in the time of the Prophet. The only choice given them was death or the reception of Islam." Implicit in all kinds of monotheism is the dogmatic certainty that it alone has access to the true God, it alone has access to truth. Everyone else is not only woefully misguided but doomed to perdition and everlasting hellfire.

Arthur Schopenhauer asks us to reflect on the "cruelties to which religions, especially the Christian and Mohammedan, have given rise" and "the misery they have brought on the world." Also, think of "the bloody and terrible conquests of the Mohammedans in three continents.... In particular, let us not forget India ... where first Mohammedans and then Christians furiously and most cruelly attacked the followers of mankind's sacred and original faith. **The everdeplorable, wanton, and ruthless destruction and disfigurement of ancient temples and images reveal to us even to this day traces of the monotheistic fury [my emphasis] of the Mohammedans which was pursued from Mahmud of Ghazni of accursed memory down to Aurangzeb the fratricide."**

Schopenhauer contrasts the peaceful historical record of the Hindus and the Buddhists with the wickedness and cruelty of the monotheists, and then concludes:

"Indeed, intolerance is essential only to monotheism; only one God is by nature a jealous God who will not allow another to live. On the other hand, polytheistic gods are naturally tolerant; they live and let live. In the first place, they gladly tolerate their colleagues, the gods of the same religion, and this tolerance is afterwards extended even to foreign gods who are accordingly, hospitably received and later admitted, in some cases, even to an equality of rights... Thus it is only the monotheistic religions that furnish us with the spectacle of religious wars, religious persecutions, courts for trying heretics, and also with that of iconoclasm, the destruction of the images of foreign gods, the demolition of Indian temples and Egyptian colossi that had looked at the sun for three thousand years; all this because their jealous God had said: "Thou shalt make no graven image" and so on."

W A Palgrave vividly described the Koranic God as thus: **"He is ever more prone to punish than to reward, to inflict pain than to bestow pleasure, to ruin than to build. It is His singular satisfaction to let created beings continually feel that they are nothing else than His slaves, His tools—and contemptible tools too—that they may thus better acknowledge His superiority, and know His power to be above their power, His cunning above their cunning, His will above their will, His pride above their pride; or rather, that there is no power, cunning, will, or pride, save His own."**

In the ancient times, monotheism was blamed as the instigator of violence in its early days as it inspired the Israelites to wage war upon the Canaanites who believed in multiple gods. **Sarvepalli Radhakrishnan, former President of India, regarded monotheism to be one reason of violence, said:**

"The intolerance of narrow monotheism is written in letters of blood across the history of man from the time when first the tribes of Israel burst into the land of Canaan. The worshippers of the one jealous God are egged on to aggressive wars against people of alien cults. They invoke divine sanction for the cruelties inflicted on the conquered. The spirit of old Israel is inherited by Christianity and Islam, and it might not be unreasonable to suggest that it would have been better for Western civilization if Greece had molded it on this question rather than Palestine." As compared to Abrahamic religions, religions of the east (Hinduism, Buddhism, Jainism,) have always believed in *'Sarva Dharma Samabhava'* which literally means that all Dharmas are equal to or harmonious with each other.

Muslim theologians are unanimous in declaring that no religious toleration was extended to the idolaters in the past and will not be in the future. The only choice given them was death or the acceptance of Islam. Osama Bin Laden said that "what is false is false -- even if a billion individuals agree to it; and truth is truth -- even if only one who has submitted [a Muslim] holds on to it," and also said that "Battle, animosity, and hatred -- directed from the Muslim to the infidel -- is the foundation of our religion. And we consider this a justice and kindness to them" (The Al Qaeda Reader, pgs. 42-43).

TIME TO IMPLEMENT TWO NATION THEORY OR DECLARE BENIGN DICTATORSHIP

It is time to discuss, debate and dialogue the consequences of appeasement policies toward Muslims, not adopting family planning, failure to stop the Bangladesh infiltration, not implementing the uniform civil code, inability to stop the relentless terror, ever increasing rampage of the Hindu villages, never ending insulting remarks against Hindus, and determination to convert India into a Muslim Country. Hindus being silent, indifferent, tend to postpone the discussion and they are unable to publicly name the Muslims as the enemies of democracy, as terrorists, and as the traitors of India. After visiting India **Tarek Fatah** rightly observed, *"As a Muslim, I found it fascinating that this is the only place in the world where Muslims exert influence without fear. Muslims are better equipped in India than in Pakistan and Bangladesh."* By avoiding an open discussion about the impending take-over of India by Muslims in less than a decade, Hindu politicians, Hindu organizations and the government are going to fulfill the long-cherished dreams of Muslims to convert Hindu country into an Islamic State. It would not be too long to see the carnage of Hindus since they have no place to go. They will be shackled, cornered, tortured and killed. The only option left for Hindus would be convert to Islam to save their lives.

If we don't act and take necessary steps to curtail the inflow of Bangladeshi Muslims into India, control the intentional breeding of the Muslims to outnumber the locals, and root out terrorist cells and their atrocities, Hindu lives will be in perennial danger. If Hindus fail to scrap all the appeasement policies toward Muslims, if they continue to ignore the statements of annihilating Hindus, if they do not take appropriate action against the Muslim leaders who openly pronounce the hateful speeches calling Hindus as weaklings, dummies, boneless, gutless, spineless, etc.; and if the government and Hindus abrogate their responsibility to protect the Hindus from being bullied, bruised, humiliated, raped, tortured, maimed, and killed, Hindu genocide is around the corner. There would not be any place for Hindus either to hide or run from the ruthless Islamic sword.

We Hindus must recognize that Islam and Hinduism are incompatible in their ideologies, values, practices, human rights, inclusiveness, women's rights, tolerance toward each other, marriage customs, and democratic principles. Hindus must realize the gravity of the precarious situation that majority of them are facing in the hands of Muslim minorities who are using every means to create fear among Hindus and drive them out from their villages. It needs be pointed out that in the very near future the Hindus are going to be corned similar to the one during Independence time, not too far in sight. It is a matter of years not decades. **Muslims stayed back only to recapture India through violent means. Their loyalty is not to India but for global dominance and supremacy over all religions.** They are in India not to integrate, accommodate, adjust and assimilate in the main stream of India but to dominate, subjugate, subdue, control and suppress Hindus through Islamic Justice which allows them to dispose of all Hindus at their will, reminiscent of Islamic brutal, barbaric and ruthless dominance of Hindu India for eight centuries. **Islamization using the Sharia law is already taking place that undermines the human dignity and denies the human rights for non-Muslims.**

Let us remember the resolution passed by the Council of the **All-India Muslim League** on June 6, 1946 to protect the lives of Muslims by breaking up India to create Pakistan. It says, "…the attainment of the goal of complete sovereign Pakistan still remains an unalterable objective of the Musalmans in India, for the achievement of which they would, if necessary, employ every means in their power and consider no sacrifice or suffering too great."

Similarly, Jinnah insisted that the Muslims of India are a nation with a "distinctive culture and civilization, language and literature, art and architecture, law and moral codes, customs and calendar, history and traditions."

Ambedkar foresaw a bleak and brutal future for India as long as Muslims remain in India. **He unequivocally advocated the population exchange in case of partition. He wanted Hindus and Sikhs from Pakistan to come to India and all the Muslims from India to go to Pakistan. "That the transfer of minorities is the only lasting remedy for communal peace is beyond doubt...there is no reason to suppose that what they did cannot be accomplished by Indians.** After all, the population involved is irreconcilable and because some obstacles require to be removed, it would be the height of folly to give up so sure a way to communal peace... **The only way to make Hindustan homogeneous is to arrange for exchange of population. Until that is done, it must be admitted that even with the creation of Pakistan, the problem of majority vs. minority will remain in Hindustan as before and will continue to produce disharmony in the body politic of Hindustan."**

"The brotherhood of Islam is not the universal brotherhood of man. It is brotherhood of Muslims for Muslims only. There is a fraternity but its benefit are confined to those within that corporation. For those who are outside the corporation, there is nothing but contempt and enmity. ... In other words, Islam can never allow a true Muslim to adopt India as his motherland and regard a Hindu as his kith and kin," said Ambedkar.

Rabindranath Tagore said that Muslims and Hindus can coexist as long as they accept the principle of ahimsa and the ideology of live and let live. Knowing the irreconcilable differences between these two religions, and the Muslims' intention to dominate the world through the sword, he predicted in 1911, **"The world-wide problem today is not how to unite by wiping out all differences, but how to unite with all the differences intact; a difficult task, for it permits of no trickery and calls for mutual give-and-take...** *The Muslims in our country are striving for advancement as a separate community. However disagreeable and disadvantage that may be for us for the time being, it is only right way to achieve genuine unity some day in the future."*

Annie Besant says, "The world has gone beyond such so-called theocracies, in which God's commands are given through a man. The claim now put forward by Musalman leaders that they must obey the laws of their particular prophet above the laws of the State in which they live, is subversive of civic order and the stability of the State ... Malabar has taught us what Islamic rule still means, and we do not want to see another specimen of the 'Khilafat 5 Raj' in India ... there is no place in a civilized land for people who believe that their religion teaches them to murder, rob, rape, burn, or drive out of the country those who refuse to apostatize from their ancestral faiths ... Such 'Laws of God' cannot be allowed to override the laws of a civilized country ... In fact, Muslim sects are not safe in a country ruled by orthodox Muslims."

Hindus should wake up to the fact that their lives are in grave danger. Muslims have been committing countless atrocities across the countries and waging war on Hindu "infidels" in India. Hindu leaders, politicians, liberals, intellectuals and media are not even recognizing the gravity of the potential threat to the country although the terrorist organizations and many Muslim leaders openly advocating the hostile takeover of India by Muslims. They have been openly declaring to make India a Muslim country. They are not hiding their intentions. Hindus are totally failing in their responsibility to recognize the potential holocaust and denying the most obvious threat for their survival. ISIS has already moved to India, flexing its forces by recruiting young men and bringing terrorists from Pakistan to create panic by blowing up few buildings and killing several people on the way to establish Caliphate. Longer the Hindus wait, more agony they must endure. **Only choices are left for Hindus to avoid their holocaust:**

⅄ **Implement the original two-nation theory developed during the time of Independence allowing all Muslims to go to Pakistan to create an Islamic country and all Hindus to India to establish Hindustan**. Theoretically it may make more sense to protect the lives of Hindus, it is almost impractical to implement at present considering the number of Muslims living in India and increasing day by day.

ᚼ **Second option is to establish a benign dictatorship for a period of ten years** with a mission to enforce uniform civil code, remove all the minority privileges, dismantle all minority departments, eliminate all quota systems, stop illegal infiltration from Bangladesh, prosecute those who demean the country, pass anti-conversion laws, declare cow as the animal of the country, introduce Sanskrit as national language, assure equal rights to Hindus to manage their Hindu Temples, and revise the school curriculum to teach the morals and ethics that have sustained the greatness of Sanatana Dharma for millennia.

ᚼ **Revise the Indian Constitution by removing all the privileges accorded to any given religion.**

India must be made Hindustan as was planned during the Independence and as was envisioned by **Jinnah** who said, "*Hindu and Muslim cultures constitute two distinct, and frequently antagonistic, ways of life, and that therefore they cannot coexist in one nation.*" Let very body remember what was discussed at the time of Independence and implement, although it is late by 68 years. "*At the time of partition some of the two-nation theory protagonists proposed that the entire Hindu population should migrate to India and all Muslims should move over to Pakistan, leaving no Hindus in Pakistan and no Muslims in India ...*"(**S. Harmon**).

There is no question that Muslims want India to be converted into Islamic Country. It is their "**unfinished business.**" **Indian Muslims are dreaming and planning break up India into three Islamic countries - Mughalistan, Dravidistan and Dalitisthan. Asaduddin Owasi** has publicly announced that he would not call India as Bharat Mata. He said he would wipe out all Hindus in fifteen minutes if police force is withdrawn. **Gulab Nabi Azad** equated RSS with ISIS. He refused to apologize for saying. ISIS has already announced that it will take over India and make it an Islamic Country. The writing is on the wall. **Hindus have not read the writings on the wall, have not recognized the threat, have not challenged the Muslims for their anti-Hindu statements and are refusing the acknowledge the potential threat. Hindu holocaust is around the corner.** Hindus must face it otherwise they will be finished.

Hindus have experienced the Islamic atrocities for nearly ten centuries. If they have not learned from the history of Islamic invasions, and brutality inflicted on our forefathers, we are likely to experience the same fate as our ancestors. It is the dharma of every Hindu to preserve and protect the Hindu lives for the sake of our future generations, for the sake of the freedom we have been enjoying, and for the sake of humanity. Let us not allow this freedom slip away from our fingers.

Across the globe, scholars and philosophers have been writing about the barbarism, bloodthirstiness, savagery, and viciousness of Islam. As far back as 1921, **Andre Servier** elaborated the nature of Islam: "Islam was not a torch, as has been claimed, but an extinguisher. Conceived in a barbarous brain for the use of barbarous people, it was—and it remains—incapable of adapting itself to civilization. Wherever it has dominated, it has broken the impulse towards progress and checked the evolution of society." (P; 153)

Sri Aurobindo predicated way back in 1909 that, "Every action for instance which may be objectionable to a number of Mahomedans is now liable to be forbidden because it is likely to lead to a breach of the peace, and one is dimly beginning to' wonder whether the day may not come when worship in Hindu temples may be forbidden on that valid ground." Indeed, Sri Aurobindo's predictive statement needs to be heeded as soon as possible. Many Hindu Temples across India are not allowed to do worship services, sing bhajans, chant mantras, ring bells, install pendals, but they are forced to endure the loud speakers announcing the greatness of Allah.

Let us remember the words of **Anne Besant** and inspire every Hindu to champion the cause of Hindutva. **"After a study of some forty years and more of the great religions of the world, I find none so perfect, none so scientific, none so philosophic, and none so spiritual as the great religion known by the name of Hinduism**. The more you know it, the more you will love it; the more you try to understand it, the more deeply you will value it. **Make no mistake; without Hinduism, India has no future. Hinduism is the soil into which India's roots are struck**, and torn of that she will inevitably wither, as a tree torn out from its place... **And if Hindus do not maintain**

Hinduism, who shall save it? If India's own children do not cling to her faith, who shall guard it? India alone can save India, and India and Hinduism are one."

Jai Hind

www.ingramcontent.com/pod-product-compliance
Lightning Source LLC
LaVergne TN
LVHW051726080426
835511LV00018B/2909